D1526978

Oil, Illiberalism, and War

Oil, Illiberalism, and War

An Analysis of Energy and US Foreign Policy

Andrew T. Price-Smith

The MIT Press
Cambridge, Massachusetts
London, England

MIT Press books may be purchased at special quantity discounts for business or sales promotional use. For information, email special_sales@mitpress.mit.edu.

Set in Stone by the MIT Press. Printed and bound in the United States of America.

Library of Congress Cataloging-in-Publication Data are available.
ISBN: 978-0-262-02906-3

10 9 8 7 6 5 4 3 2 1

Contents

Acknowledgments

This volume marks a significant intellectual departure from my earlier work on the political economy of global health, and so I owe a significant debt to the many colleagues, family members and friends who provided comments, inspiration, and support during the writing.

First, I would like to thank my wonderful colleagues in the Department of Political Science at Colorado College, in particular David Hendrickson and John Gould for our frequent debates regarding the nexus between energy and international affairs. I would also like to thank G. John Ikenberry, who encouraged me in my efforts to develop a pessimistic reformulation of Liberal Institutionalism, and to whom I am indebted intellectually for his pathbreaking work in IR theory. I would also like to thank the three anonymous reviewers for the MIT Press, who astutely recommended that I shorten the manuscript considerably and refrain from expansive theoretical debates. I would also like to thank my Master's thesis advisor, Professor Salim Mansur, who oversaw my original work on the Gulf War and who provided consistent encouragement.

Further, I am grateful to everyone at the MIT Press, particularly Clay Morgan, Beth Clevenger, Paul Bethge, and Miranda Martin, for their patience and assistance. Additionally, I would like to thank my research assistants at Colorado College who contributed to this volume, particularly Jackson Porreca, Mallory Lee-Wong, Bryce Rafferty, and Allyson Siegel. I would also like to thank the many other students who contributed to the Energy, Environment and Security Project at Colorado College over the years.

Generous financial support during the writing of this work was provided by the Government of Canada, the Social Sciences Executive Committee and Deans Office of Colorado College, and the US National Intelligence Council. Moreover, I was fortunate to be Associate Advisor to the National

Intelligence Council from 2008 to 2014. For this I am particularly thankful to Stephen S. Morse and the late Chris Decker, who introduced me to those circles. Research for this work was conducted in the Widener Memorial Library at Harvard University, and I am grateful for the kind assistance of the librarians at that institution. And I thank Judicial Watch for permission to reproduce the figures in chapter 4.

I owe the greatest debt to my stepfather, Jack McLeod, for being an enduring inspiration to me, in academe and in life. He always taught me to seek truth and to reveal injustice. This critique of US foreign policy, and of theory, is part of his courageous legacy. He has been a powerful and incredibly positive influence on my life.

Furthermore, I wish to thank my father, Richard Price-Smith, who introduced me to the world of energy at an early age. His work to develop solar cells to provide affordable power to the people of the least developed countries was truly inspirational.

Finally, I want to thank my dear wife, Janell, who has endured years of my academic ramblings, and been a constant source of wisdom and assistance. I also want to thank my mother, Cynthia, my sister Adrienne, and my in-laws Gerry and Maria Harvey, who have all provided so much help over the years.

This book is dedicated to my wonderful and inquisitive children, Will and Tori.

Introduction

Policy makers increasingly confront novel and diffuse threats to the interests of the state, and to the body politic; challenges in the form of global economic destabilization, the degradation of the biosphere,[1] cyber insecurity,[2] the proliferation of diseases,[3] and terrorism.[4] Energy (and crude oil in particular) has risen once again to the realm of "high politics," in that it acts as a powerful influence on the conduct of US foreign policy, and affects international security in a manner hitherto unexamined. The argument here is that the United States' addiction to crude oil has distorted its conduct of foreign policy in profound and malign ways, guiding the US into unnecessary conflicts, promoting highly illiberal behavior by a supposedly liberal hegemonic power, and creating a spectrum of malign externalities that undermine both US national security and international security.

The aspiration of international relations, as a discipline of inquiry, is the construction of models that assist in averting both the loss of life and economic destabilization. Though there are many popular works that examine the linkages between oil and US foreign policy, many of them lack a substantive theoretical component. In the realm of academic discourse, realist conceptualizations of energy security typically ignore positive outcomes resulting from the interactivity of international institutions, regimes, and markets that collectively facilitate global governance in the domain of energy. Conversely, liberal international relations theorists examine the influence of energy on international politics through a theoretical lens that includes a range of actors, but often minimizes the importance of hard power and the potential for conflict, leading them to assume a sanguine world of global energy governance that is increasingly illusory.

I argue herein that it is time to consider a reformulation of liberal internationalism that is intrinsically more pessimistic, one that pays attention to the dynamics of power, and to cooperation and conflict over *material* resources. Contrary to the optimistic assumptions of the archetypal vision of liberal internationalism,[5] this darker vision of liberal theory holds that *complex interdependence* is *not* an intrinsically benign phenomenon; that it may generate malign externalities such as terrorism and global economic upheaval that challenge the interests of the state. Although archetypal liberal theories of international relations remain largely correct in their conceptualization of agency, and in their argument that the quality of anarchy may be cooperative,[6] they also require some conceptual revision to explain a significant degree of *illiberal* conduct in the domain of US foreign policy as it pertains to energy.[7] I call this pessimistic theoretical reformulation *shadow liberalism*.[8]

The Gift

For a century, civilization's addiction to fossil fuels has proved to be both boon and bane. In many ways oil (and its distillates) are a Faustian gift—one that enabled the rise of modern industry, the development of international trade and commerce, the global movement of peoples, spurred economic development on a global scale, and profoundly shaped the contours of contemporary society. Thus, the production and refinement of oil is inextricably linked to the rise of industrial civilization, and to the power of the modern industrial state.[9]

The "discovery" and mass production of oil in North America (and its subsequent refinement into distillates such as gasoline) had additional positive outcomes for humanity. The advent of petroleum powered the combustion engine, enhanced domestic trade and mobility, and prompted rapid economic growth in the United States. Widespread use of petroleum also resulted in dramatic increases in global food production through increased availability of cheap fertilizers, and resulted in a plethora of new consumer products, notably plastics. In the military domain, the discovery and production of oil in North America (and subsequently the Persian Gulf) provided a substantial strategic edge to the Allies during their campaigns against the Central Powers in World War I, and against the Axis powers during World War II. Thus, the discovery of oil in North America, and the profound technological transformations that resulted from it, were dynamics that made a powerful contribution to the rise of US economic and military power throughout much of the twentieth century.

Unfortunately, the increasing empirical scarcity of conventional (i.e., cheap) oil, and the heightened global *perceptions* of the scarcity of crude oil at the turn of the century resulted in higher prices for petroleum, which in turn generated externalities such as economic and social fragility in consumer nations (and in some producer nations). In recent decades the United States' profound addiction to oil has resulted in diminishing returns to prosperity and stability, spurred widespread and numerous interventions by the US into the domestic affairs of other countries, locked the US into patterns of excessive militarism, drove policy makers in Washington to undertake largely unnecessary conflicts (for example, in Iraq and Libya), and undermined the security of the republic in the twenty-first century.

The Argument

The discovery and production of oil in the United States bequeathed enormous economic and military power to the country in its infancy, providing a material basis for the rise of the US to hegemonic status. Subsequently, the US directed that economic and military power toward the achievement of global hegemony during the Cold War. Even as oil conferred enormous power capabilities upon the US, mechanisms of path dependence, as reinforced by domestic factions (e.g., the oil lobby), ensured that the US would remain engaged in a perennial and externalized quest for ever more energy. This pursuit of energy resources became manifest in a symbiotic relationship between state and industry (the oil industry) wherein the state (and its power resources) were used to open up new frontiers for energy extraction via the international oil corporations. Thus, the American flag has truly followed the dollar, at least in the domain of energy. Over time these dynamics have contributed to the construction of a de-territorialized American empire, in the form of a web of bases that encircle the globe and enable the projection of US military power.[10]

This enduring addiction to oil, and the symbiosis between the state and the energy industry, has led the United States to engage in a pattern of highly illiberal conduct over the past century, despite the cloaking of this behavior beneath a facade of liberal internationalism. Specifically, a hunger for oil has contributed to the United States' involvement in various foreign interventions that were (at the very least) counterproductive and (at the worst) completely antithetical to the national interest. These persistent deviations from a rational foreign energy policy have primarily resulted from this synergetic relationship between the state and the international oil companies (IOCs), wherein the permeable apparatus of a weak state has been systematically penetrated by corporate energy interests.

Admittedly, the United States often exhibits liberal behavior consistent with its role as a benign hegemon,[11] particularly in its relations with European countries since 1945. Undeniably, the US served as a benign hegemon in its promotion of security guarantees to Western European countries (and to Japan) during the Cold War era, and sought to generate global public goods in the form of international institutions that would moderate the global economy and diminish the probability of war in the international system. However, I argue that this liberal hegemonic behavior is primarily regionally specific, and tied to the transatlantic relationship between the US and European countries.

However, the United States often exhibits modes of behavior that could be seen as illiberal or quasi-imperial, particularly in its relations with non-European countries.[12] Beneath the facade of liberalism and altruism that the US presents to the world, a malign element lies at the core of US foreign policy in the domain of energy. This shadowy core of US foreign energy policy is predicated upon the historical exploitation of other peoples (largely in the developing world) in order to ensure the continual flow of crude oil to the Organisation for Economic Cooperation and Development countries. Given that such energy flows support the international economy, I argue that there is a fundamentally illiberal core to the modern liberal international energy order.[13]

Nonetheless, the broader liberal institutionalist theoretical argument remains intact. Many of the tenets of the liberal school of international relations theory are basically correct, but facets of the argument are in need of greater refinement to illustrate the double-edged nature of certain postulates, such as complex interdependence. Thus, the re-conceptualization of certain aspects of archetypal liberal international relations theory, to include this illiberal core, and to grasp the negative manifestations of complex interdependence is in order. I call this variant of archetypal liberal internationalism *shadow liberalism*.

In his extensive body of work, Michael Klare frequently argues that an increasing scarcity of crude oil may impel the great powers to make war upon one another.[14] Similarly, the economist Dambisa Moyo has argued that a growing competition over scarce material resources, most importantly oil, may drive China and the United States to war in the foreseeable future.[15] Conversely, I argue that these popular arguments of a looming war between the great powers as a result of *empirical* energy scarcity are fundamentally illogical, and that they may constitute "threat inflation." The balance of evidence presented below indicates that the dominant patterns of international conflict associated with oil are in fact highly asymmetrical, wherein stronger countries often lash out at weaker ones. This finding of a pattern of asymmetrical aggression, over the control (or transport of) oil resources and flows, diverges from the quasi-realist literature in the field of energy and international security that holds that increased scarcity of oil will induce war between the great powers.[16] Furthermore, the finding of a pattern of asymmetrical conflict also differs from the archetypal liberal institutional literature, which argues that oil plays little or no role in provoking conflict between sovereign states.[17]

I argue that the probability of war between the great powers over a static (to marginally increasing) oil supply[18] is rather low (at least in the near term), although the possibility of accidental conflict remains. Simply put, conflict between the great powers is extremely unlikely because of the existence of nuclear weapons that make the costs of war unacceptable. Additionally, the prosecution of wars by the great powers would consume a vast amount of energy resources. Paradoxically, then, a bellicose state suffering from energy deprivation might deplete its marginal energy reserves in the very effort to acquire more. Thus, the probability of war between great powers over the *perceived* scarcity of energy resources is very low, but owing to the possibility of misperception and miscalculation[19] it is not zero.

There is a far greater probability of great powers making war against lesser powers, in order to (A) make increased oil flows available to international markets, which may then reduce energy costs to the great powers and their allies, (B) control the transit of lucrative energy flows, or (C) exert direct and sovereign control over such energy reserves. The United States' frequent interventions in the Persian Gulf since the declaration of the Carter Doctrine in 1979 have primarily been in order to satisfy conditions A and B, and thus to maintain an element of hegemony over international energy flows. The involvement of the US in Iraq since 2003 fits this pattern. Increasingly bellicose behavior by China and Russia in the domain of energy and international politics, largely to satisfy conditions B and C, is consistent with a pattern of asymmetrical violence by great powers versus weaker states (discussed in detail below).

Consequently, hegemonic powers or hegemonic aspirants often seek to lock up energy supplies deemed to be within their "sphere of influence," either through invasion, through bilateral (neo-mercantilist) mechanisms, or through the hardening and/or reinforcement of existing energy infrastructure. Doubtless, this effect will accelerate as demand starts to match and/or exceed supply due to the plateauing rates of global oil production. There is also a significant probability that oil will continue to foment internal instability, violence, and even intra-state war within oil-producing countries (e.g., Nigeria), although I argue that the effects of these conflicts on US energy security will actually be indirect and quite marginal. Moreover, oil generates globalized architectures of insecurity that manifest in the form of malign externalities, namely interstate conflict, terrorism, intra-state violence, and ecological destruction. Such externalities may threaten the vitality of the body politic, the security of the sovereign state (particularly the US), and undermine effective global governance.

The concept of "peak oil" is rather problematic, and frequently associated with misunderstanding and polemics that often serve to obscure any sensible debate on the matter. The dire predictions of the neo-Malthusian camp,[20] that argued that there were no more giant oil fields to be found, have turned out to be wanting. The increasing price of oil (and its distillates) in the early years of the twenty-first century has resulted in increased incentive structures for the generation of novel technologies that have made the extraction of oil from unconventional sources (oceanic, tight oil) economically viable. As such, declines in conventional oil production from existing fields will be mitigated to a considerable extent by these recent technological advances (e.g., computer visualization, fracking, horizontal drilling) that have resulted in both significant deep-sea discoveries, and by the enhanced extraction of oil from unconventional terrestrial sources.

Nonetheless, the depletion of massive reservoirs, as seen in the North Sea, Cantarell, and Ghawar fields,[21] suggests that increasing global production of crude oil beyond a certain plateau may be increasingly difficult. As such, technologically induced advances in production capacity are locked in a perpetual race with inexorably increasing demand resulting from increasing global population and the rise of the global middle class. Technologically induced increases in oil supply may simply be absorbed by the surging demand of the emerging industrial economies of the developing world. Thus, Daniel Yergin's conceptualization of a global production plateau, instead of a peak—is probably the correct model to employ for some time.[22] Higher oil prices will, in turn, incentivize the production of more efficient vehicles, and contribute to the discovery and development of *unconventional* oil reserves (at least for the next several decades).

In the domain of political economy I argue that the financialization of oil (manifest in "paper barrels"—oil sold and traded on the open market but not actually shipped), and consequently rampant speculation, has contributed to the augmented volatility of oil prices, and to the increased global price of oil in the years 2000–2014. Early in the twenty-first century, elevated energy prices imposed considerable costs on the populations of consumer states (particularly the less developed countries) and contributed to the fragility of the global economy. Energy deprivation[23] (and consequently increasing energy costs) erodes firm productivity, imposes direct and indirect costs upon families, firms, and the state, depletes savings, and may compromise society's ability to generate social and technical ingenuity. At the macro level, energy deprivation generates a significant contraction in the production possibilities of a given economy, perhaps even generating economic dislocation and decline. Such economic contraction may also impose constraints upon the revenues that the state may extract from the populace through taxation, further limiting state capacity. Conversely, energy abundance[24] will generate a range of positive effects by keeping the costs of production lower, limiting inflationary pressures in the economy, and presumably limiting outflows of capital from importing states. While infrequent, oil price shocks destabilize markets, undercut international trade and commerce, and may result in the massive transfer of capital flows from the US and other consumer states to other producer states.

The availability of energy directly contributes to the vitality of the body politic, and therefore to the stability and *puissance* of the country. A shortage of affordable energy then represents a direct threat to the population (as food costs soar and nutrition declines), erodes national economic productivity, and may generate capital outflows from consumer to producer states, that deplete the coffers of the former. As the economic capacity of government declines it then compromises the ability of the state to provide public goods, which may in turn compromise popular perceptions of governmental legitimacy, and consequently exacerbate intra-class tensions within the state. Thus, a significant shortage of energy could fundamentally threaten the material and ideational interests, and the political stability of an affected polity.

Furthermore, I argue that existing international institutions and regimes in the domain of energy are exceedingly weak. Specifically, those international institutions that have been crafted to mitigate global oil shocks, stabilize global oil markets, and facilitate global energy security, are now increasingly ineffective and archaic, as they exclude such rising powers as China, Brazil, and India. Moreover, OPEC is increasingly riven with discord between "price hawks" and "price doves," and Saudi power to moderate international oil prices has declined somewhat. In sum, international institutions in the domain of energy appear increasingly sclerotic and dysfunctional.

The dynamics of energy depletion and discovery suggest a long-term shift in economic and political power away from countries with depleted conventional oil reservoirs (e.g., Philippines, Mexico) toward countries with increasing endowments of unconventional resources (e.g., Canada and Brazil). Thus, one should expect to see longer-term changes in relative power between the United States and Mexico, to the advantage of the former. Countries that experience declining revenues from oil extraction may observe declining state capacity and consequently increasing domestic political instability. Technological advances in the discovery and extraction of oil, and the resulting increases in domestic production will bolster the United States' economic vitality and augment US power. Increasing domestic oil production should also temper some of the United States' bellicose behavior, at least in the realm of foreign energy policy, and diminish the probability of US interventions against weaker states.

The State of Knowledge on Energy Security

In the literature on international relations energy resources have historically oscillated between "low" and "high politics," occupying a place of academic prominence when oil prices soared, only to retreat to the academic shadows as prices descended. Thus, the perennial volatility in global oil prices has been reflected in the oscillation of the energy sector's status in the realm of international relations, the economic boom and bust cycle of commodities replicated in academe.

Petroleum's elevation to the realm of high politics resulted from the multiple energy shocks of the 1970s and the significant economic dislocation that they produced in the OECD countries. In the years that followed the energy crises of the 1970s, the political scientists Stephen Krasner,[25] Joseph Nye,[26] Raymond Vernon,[27] G. John Ikenberry,[28] Ethan Kapstein,[29] and Daniel Deudney[30] argued that oil (among other strategic resources) was worthy of consideration as an issue of high politics. Henry Kissinger, one of the leading students of *realpolitik*, once argued that "aside from military defense, there is no project of more central importance to national security and indeed independence as a sovereign nation than energy security."[31] The Nixon administration was the first to openly recognize the United States' increasing dependence on imported oil. However, the declaration and subsequent implementation of the Carter Doctrine in the Persian Gulf resulted in the increased recognition of oil as vital to US national security. Tacit extensions of the Carter Doctrine by the Reagan administration, the George H. W. Bush administration, the George W. Bush administration, and the Obama administration have resulted in the recurrent deployment of American hard power to reinforce the global energy infrastructure.

As the price of oil fell in the late 1980s, interest in the field of energy as an issue of high politics diminished temporarily. However, in the early years of the twenty-first century the analysis of oil's effects on international politics has returned to the fore, particularly given the sharp increases in the price of oil in the years 2000–2014 and continuing sensitivity to volatility in oil prices by major consumers (including the United States, China, and Japan). In the realm of high politics, oil is now recognized as a mechanism of political leverage, as a potential trigger of inter-state conflict, as a political source of conflict within oil-producing countries, and as a vital resource for US national security.[32]

Promising recent works by Steve Yetiv[33] and by Doug Stokes and Sam Raphael[34] approach questions of energy diplomacy and international security through the lens of the broader literature on international relations.[35] For example, Yetiv analyzes the effects of oil dependence on national and international security primarily through the lens of archetypal liberal institutionalism. He emerges with an optimistic view of the global energy framework wherein international institutions and markets work together with individual countries in a spirit of cooperation.[36] Stokes and Raphael employ a much darker (quasi-realist) lens of analysis, arguing that oil has driven the United States to adopt a draconian foreign policy and to engage in multiple conflicts. I argue that elements of both analyses ring true to a certain extent, but I shall argue in this volume that both the realist perspective and the liberal perspective are in need of some fundamental revision, at least in their application to the domain of energy.

Optimistic and archetypal liberal theories of international politics provide us with a valuable lens through which to perceive and analyze the political universe. Archetypal liberal theory acknowledges the interplay of multiple types of actors, from sovereign states and international organizations, to multinational corporations and networks. This emphasis on non-state actors is absolutely essential to understanding political outcomes at the nexus of energy and international political economy. However, I argue that archetypal liberal institutionalist théory is often overly optimistic in some of its assumptions about the quality of influence of various agents. Archetypal liberalism tends to exaggerate the power of international institutions, and embellishes the efficacy of cooperation between countries, particularly in the case of energy.

Unfortunately, the dominant archetypal variant of liberal theory, with its emphasis on rationality and cooperation, often ignores certain illiberal actions taken by the pillars of the Western "liberal" order, including the United States and Britain. The literature of archetypal liberalism tends to willfully ignore the illiberal core of the modern liberal international energy order. For example, archetypal liberals often turn a blind eye to the historical use of covert action and/or hard power in illiberal fashion by various Western powers, particularly by the US in its pursuit of its energy foreign policy goals.

The success stories of liberal institutionalism tend to focus on the enduring Atlantic concord between the United States and Europe, celebrating American benign hegemony in its contribution to the defeat of Nazi Germany and the containment of the Soviet Union. As such, archetypal liberal approaches correctly recognize and laud American efforts to reconstruct European economies in the post-1945 era through the Marshall Plan, the United States' subsequent efforts to stabilize Western Europe, and its support for the development of the European Union as manifestations of benign hegemony.[37] Despite the viability of such archetypal liberal analysis in the context of the United States' postwar relations with the European powers and Japan, this archetypal liberal perspective tends to discount those illiberal actions taken by the US in other "developing" regions of the world, notably in the Persian Gulf and Latin America.

The realist project is also problematic in its analysis of international energy politics. Structural realism is particularly awkward as a tool of analysis of political outcomes in the domain of energy, primarily because of its exclusive focus on sovereign states (particularly the great powers) as the only actors that really count in generating international political outcomes.[38] Moreover, the distribution of relative power in the context of a competitive and anarchical international environment doesn't tell us much about the United States' political behavior in the realm of energy, beyond the rather obvious conclusion that a great power would seek to maintain its hegemony through the domination of global energy supplies.

Yet certain elements of realist thought remain valuable in our quest to analyze US behavior in the domain of energy; Realist perspectives acknowledge that great powers (including the US) often act in illiberal fashion in order to attain their material and ideational interests.[39] In the pages below I present a theoretical reformulation of archetypal liberalism that includes certain insights from the realist project.[40] This reformulation acknowledges the illiberal heart of the liberal international system, a theoretical variant of liberal institutionalism that I call *shadow liberalism*.

A Darker Liberalism

In this volume I argue for a reconceptualization of archetypal liberal international relations theory[41] to take account of fundamentally illiberal oil-induced distortions in the foreign policy behavior of states.[42] For example, even as the US projects the mythology that its international energy policies are uniformly liberal and benign, there is a darker and fundamentally illiberal core to these "liberal" policies; a core that is based upon the exploitation of other countries, manifest in a history of manipulation and both covert and *overt* interventionism. This darker core to US foreign energy policy motives should not be surprising to students of US history. After all the early expansion of the US was predicated upon military power. This coercive element was clearly visible in the United States' seizures of territory through military force from the Native Americans, the Mexicans, and the British. Thus, it should come as no great surprise that US foreign energy policy contains such elements of coercion and manipulation, as it simply extends patterns that have persisted for hundreds of years.[43] However, such actions do contradict the mythology of the US as a perennially benign liberal hegemon that is only interested in generating global public goods. I propose that the conduct of US foreign policy oscillates between the poles of illiberal and liberal conduct, particularly in the domain of energy, largely as a function of the historical symbiosis between corporations and the state. Indeed, empirical studies by Lawrence Jacobs and Benjamin Page indicate that the greatest single influence upon the United States' foreign policy is in fact international business interests,[44] as represented through their lobbyists in Washington.

A consequence of the United States' addiction to petroleum is that US military forces now span the globe, protecting the global oil infrastructure from attacks by terrorist networks and from foreign militaries. The protection of global energy assets and infrastructure involves the inexorably increasing projection of US "hard" power, and the exorbitant costs to the republic that are associated with maintaining such a global reach. These costs impose an enormous financial burden on the republic in the form of massive budget outlays for the Department of Defense and the various intelligence services. In addition to those expenditures incurred by the hardening of global energy infrastructure, the US has now been involved in two costly major wars in the Persian Gulf region, the Gulf War (1990–91) and the Iraq War (2003–2011), primarily in order to protect the supply of oil from that region to global energy markets. Thus, considerable "blood and treasure" has been sacrificed in order to satisfy the global addiction to petroleum, to sustain American hegemony over the oil resources of the Persian Gulf region, and to maintain the global public good of energy flows that support the global economy.[45] Ultimately, I argue, the production and consumption of oil may generate global architectures of insecurity in the form of profound externalities (such as inter-state conflict and terrorism) that erode the well-being and security of the body politic.

The Scope of the Problem

Before venturing deeper into the historical and theoretical terrain, I will examine the modern empirical context of the nexus between oil and foreign policy and analyze current trajectories in the disparate domains of demography, oil production, and oil consumption. I will then provide a brief analysis of the "peak oil" argument.

Demography

Population growth operates as a significant influence upon global energy consumption.[46] As the global population surges there will be more people on the planet driving automobiles, requiring electricity, and generally consuming material resources. Increasing energy demand can be mitigated to a degree by increasing efficiency, but such increases in efficiency must keep up with demographic growth rates in order to keep aggregate oil consumption levels in check. As we shall see below, increases in efficiency have not kept pace with global population growth, and thus we have seen steadily increasing global demand for energy resources.

As of June 2014, the US Census Bureau estimated the global population to be approximately 7.173 billion,[47] and according to its projections it will surpass 9 billion by 2042. Similarly, projections by the United Nations (2011) hold that the global population will hit 9.3 billion as early as 2050 and surpass 10.1 billion in 2100. This surprising increase is largely a function of surging growth rates in South and East Asia, and in Africa, as the population of that latter continent is projected to grow from about 1 billion in 2011 to 3.6 billion by the end of the century.[48] This picture of global population growth is largely a function of demographic momentum and unexpectedly shallow declines in fertility in poor countries, and surprising increases in fertility in certain OECD countries (e.g., the United States, the United Kingdom, and Denmark).[49] One obvious caveat to such projections is that many of these countries (particularly the least developed countries) may not be able to sustain such massive populations over the longer term due to chronic shortages of food and fresh water and debilitating shocks such as war and disease.

Furthermore, the UN forecasts that the population of the United States, with its attendant high energy consumption rates, will increase from 310 million in 2011 to 478 million in 2100.[50] The US Census Bureau, though slightly more conservative, largely confirms these forecasts of US population growth, projecting the population of the US to increase from 317.36 million in 2014 to 439.01 million in 2050.[51] Even the conservative estimate indicates a significant projected increase of 38.77 percent in the US population alone over forty years Despite anticipated increases in fuel efficiency, these projected increases in the US and global populations are sobering. Collectively, such demographic trends suggest that the global demand for

Table I.1
Thousand of barrels of crude oil produced by US fields, 1980–2012.

1980	3,146,365	1991	2,707,039	2002	2,096,588
1981	3,128,624	1992	2,624,632	2003	2,060,085
1982	3,156,715	1993	2,499,033	2004	1,989,263
1983	3,170,999	1994	2,431,476	2005	1,892,796
1984	3,249,696	1995	2,394,268	2006	1,857,322
1985	3,274,553	1996	2,366,017	2007	1,853,086
1986	3,168,252	1997	2,354,831	2008	1,830,136
1987	3,047,378	1998	2,281,919	2009	1,953,800
1988	2,979,123	1999	2,146,732	2010	1,999,731
1989	2,778,773	2000	2,130,707	2011	2,062,934
1990	2,684,687	2001	2,117,511	2012	2,377,434

Source: US Energy Information Administration (www.eia.gov/dnav/pet/hist/Leaf Handler.ashx?n=PET&s=MCRFPUS1&f=A)

energy (and oil in particular) remains on a trajectory of acceleration that may prove unsustainable.

In this portion of the chapter, I consider the trajectory of both domestic (US) and international oil production. Recent increases in the price of oil, in conjunction with the emergence of novel exploration and drilling technologies to increase the availability of oil from unconventional sources, suggest increasing US domestic oil production.[52] In North America, substantial unconventional sources of oil become economically viable at $90 a barrel, such as the Bakken formation of North Dakota (which was producing 867,000 barrels per day in September of 2013),[53] the Eagle Ford area of Texas, the oil shale of the Rocky Mountain region, or the vast oil sands of Alberta.

The data above indicate that US domestic production of crude oil declined from 3.146 million barrels per day in 1980 to a nadir of 1.812 million barrels per day in 2008. However, since that point, technological advances (including the ability to get at tight oil in rock formations, and deep-sea drilling) have enabled a surge in US domestic oil production to 2.071 million barrels per day, an increase of 14.29 percent.

As table I.2 shows, cumulative global production of crude oil has increased from 63.987 million barrels in 1980 to 89.362 million barrels in 2012, an increase of 39.67 percent over a roughly 30 year period. Modern productive capacity for distillates (e.g., gasoline) is constrained by the limited number of refineries, both globally, and particularly in the United States. The country's refinery capacity has increased only marginally over the decades, from

Table I.2
Global oil production (thousands of barrels per day), 1980–2012.

1980	63,987	1991	66,339	2002	77,071
1981	60,602	1992	66,552	2003	79,510
1982	58,098	1993	67,101	2004	83,035
1983	57,928	1994	68,637	2005	84,520
1984	59,563	1995	70,305	2006	84,502
1985	59,156	1996	71,986	2007	84,347
1986	61,534	1997	74,220	2008	85,476
1987	62,099	1998	75,681	2009	84,580
1988	64,394	1999	74,838	2010	87,076
1989	65,519	2000	77,721	2011	87,333
1990	66,435	2001	77,657	2012	89,154

15,659 thousand barrels per day (bpd) in 1985 to 17,819 thousand bpd in 2013,[54] an increase of only 13.8 percent over almost 30 years. Conversely, the average retail price of gasoline in the United States increased over the decades from $1.175 per gallon in November of 1994 to peak at $3.59 per gallon on March 28, 2011, an increase of 305.53 percent in the post–Cold War era alone. In one sense the increased price of gasoline acts as a significant constraint upon the US economy as it drives up the costs of production and transportation of goods. On the other hand the increased price also facilitates the development of new and increasingly efficient technologies, and increasing fuel costs may help to slow the loading of the atmosphere with carbon emissions. Moreover, the United States' penchant for oil consumption is unparalleled by any other modern polity. As of 2011 there were 253.2 million vehicles on the road in the US,[55] almost a vehicle per person, and the vast majority of these vehicles, with gasoline or diesel engines, were running on petroleum distillates.

As the above data indicate, the United States consumed roughly 17 million barrels of crude oil per day in 1980. Consumption peaked at 20.8 million barrels per day in 2005, then declined to 19.2 million bpd in 2011. Despite moderate advances in technology (e.g., improvements in engine efficiency), in conjunction with economic fragility since 2008, US consumption of crude oil has declined only marginally. Why should this be the case? First, demographic growth in the US has led to more vehicles on the road over the past few decades, and many of those means of transport are trucks and so-called sport-utility vehicles that exhibit limited fuel efficiency. Recent declines in consumption may be the result of said improvements in efficiency, but they

Table I.3
US oil consumption (thousands of barrels per day), 1980–2011.

	Consumption	Change
1980	17,056.00	—
1981	16,058.00	–5.85%
1982	15,296.00	–4.75%
1983	15,231.00	–0.42%
1984	15,725.61	3.25%
1985	15,726.42	0.01%
1986	16,280.63	3.52%
1987	16,665.04	2.36%
1988	17,283.31	3.71%
1989	17,325.15	0.24%
1990	16,988.50	–1.94%
1991	16,713.84	–1.62%
1992	17,032.86	1.91%
1993	17,236.73	1.20%
1994	17,718.16	2.79%
1995	17,724.59	0.04%
1996	18,308.90	3.30%
1997	18,620.30	1.70%
1998	18,917.14	1.59%
1999	19,519.34	3.18%
2000	19,701.08	0.93%
2001	19,648.71	–0.27%
2002	19,761.30	0.57%
2003	20,033.51	1.38%
2004	20,731.15	3.48%
2005	20,802.16	0.34%
2006	20,687.42	–0.55%
2007	20,680.38	–0.03%
2008	19,497.96	–5.72%
2009	18,771.40	–3.73%
2010	19,180.13	2.18%
2011	18,949.43	–1.20%

Source: Index Mundi (http://www.indexmundi.com/energy.aspx?country=us&product=oil&graph=consumption)

are also a function of the persistent weakness of the US economy since the global economic collapse of 2008, combined with elevated prices for gasoline.

Since the United States consumes now about 18.4 million barrels per day out of a total global consumption of roughly 85 million bpd, it accounts for about 21.6 percent of total global oil consumption on any given day.[56] Recent increases in US domestic production due to the enhanced extraction of oil from unconventional sources suggest that domestic production will soon exceed oil imports for the first time since 1995.[57] Thus, in the US the short-term trajectory is away from a pronounced dependence on foreign oil. Over the longer term (more than 30 years), however, the depletion of *economically viable* domestic sources of oil is probable. Despite the surge in domestic production the US will continue to import large quantities of foreign oil for some time, and consequently the US probably will continue to exhibit both short-term sensitivity and longer-term vulnerability to shortfalls in global oil production, and volatility in the price of oil.

Edward Morse and other technological optimists have argued that scientific advances will generate increasingly efficient engines, allowing the global consumption of crude oil to plateau or even decline.[58] However, the data above clearly indicate that the global consumption of crude oil has continued to steadily *increase* over time, from 59.93 billion barrels a year in 1980 to 87.36 billion barrels a year in 2012. This represents an aggregate increase of 45.08 percent in the global consumption of oil over the past 30 years, which refutes the arguments of the techno-optimists, as modest improvements in efficiency have failed to limit the global surge in demand for oil. Thus, it appears that global demographic growth, in conjunction with the rise of the middle class in developing countries, has effectively nullified minor increases in energy efficiency, leading to aggregate increases in global oil consumption. Global energy consumption is projected to rise by over 50 percent during the next two decades, to approximately 700 quadrillion British Thermal Units by 2030.[59] Although a portion of this increase will originate in the OECD countries, the greatest increases in consumption are projected to result from surging demand in the economies of East and South Asia.[60]

The role of the developing countries in increasing demand for crude oil cannot be overstated. Consumption by the OECD countries has increased by a mere 0.3 percent per year since 1980. However, over the same period

Table I.4
Global cumulative oil consumption (thousands of barrels), 1980–2011.

	Consumption	Change
1980	59,928.84	—
1981	58,013.31	–3.20%
1982	56,722.96	–2.22%
1983	56,002.25	–1.27%
1984	57,075.78	1.92%
1985	57,377.88	0.53%
1986	58,979.14	2.79%
1987	60,363.82	2.35%
1988	62,249.45	3.12%
1989	63,478.19	1.97%
1990	63,849.71	0.59%
1991	66,955.40	4.86%
1992	67,137.59	0.27%
1993	67,569.16	0.64%
1994	68,890.91	1.96%
1995	70,096.50	1.75%
1996	71,686.80	2.27%
1997	73,447.96	2.46%
1998	74,102.60	0.89%
1999	75,865.10	2.38%
2000	76,779.14	1.20%
2001	77,468.54	0.90%
2002	78,163.60	0.90%
2003	79,708.27	1.98%
2004	82,564.87	3.58%
2005	84,067.14	1.82%
2006	85,132.05	1.27%
2007	85,901.96	0.90%
2008	85,463.22	–1.67%
2009	84,756.56	0.35%
2010	87,371.34	3.09%
2011	87,356.29	–0.02%

Sources: Index Mundi and US Energy Information Administration

of time oil consumption by the developing world has surged at the rate of 2.0 percent per year, with China's consumption surging at 5.5 percent annualized growth rate since 1980.[61] Even as certain polities in Europe have increased their fuel efficiency, and consequently reduced their per capita energy consumption, global demand for oil has not been offset by technological advances so much as by economic weakness. Rather than fostering greater collaboration and global interdependence, increasing *perceptions* of energy scarcity and consequently soaring prices may instead have fostered increasingly bellicose behavior from those great powers in the throes of oil addiction. Such illiberal behavior will often be deliberately framed by said powers in the more palatable language of liberation and freedom.

Despite the pessimism of some quasi-Malthusian scholars,[62] the past decade has witnessed some fascinating discoveries of significant oil reservoirs. The Tupi Field (now called Lula), discovered in 2007 off the coast of Rio de Janeiro under several thousand feet of water, is one example of an enormous new field. Other huge pre-salt-layer fields have been discovered close to the Tupi (Lula) Field in the Santos Basin off the Brazilian coast—notably the Libra Field, which may be the largest discovery in the Americas since 1976.[63] Another large oceanic pre-salt-layer field, named Sea Lion, was discovered in 2010; it straddles the border between Argentina and the Falklands (or Malvinas). Although the Sea Lion Field promises to bring considerable wealth to the people of the Falklands, it has also fostered tensions with Argentina, which is pressing claims of sovereign jurisdiction over the field.[64] Furthermore, if the price of Brent Crude continues to hover around $80 a barrel, the non-conventional oil sands of Alberta remain economically viable, and other deposits of heavy crude oil, such as those of the Orinoco Belt in Venezuela, become viable at $100. This all leads us to the inescapable conclusion that the days of cheap oil (<$30/barrel) are now past. In all probability, the price of oil will continue to rise with increasing global demand, and new discoveries and increased production through fracking and sub-sea drilling will ameliorate the depletion of our conventional reservoirs, but only for a limited time.

Peak Oil: An Assessment

Increasing oil prices and technological advances may not overcome the inescapable and absolute limits that geology imposes upon the availability of crude oil within the crust of the planet. The natural production of oil is subject to the constraints of time and geology—taking place in what geologists call the "oil window": a certain combination of heat, depth, geological formations, and time. Crude oil and natural gas form as a result of the pressure and heating of ancient fossilized organic materials (primarily zooplankton and algae) over millions of years. If temperatures are not high enough this precursor organic material remains in a pre-oil state known as kerogen, but if temperatures are excessive then the kerogen simply transforms into natural gas. The oil that is formed must then be trapped in a sealed geological reservoir structure, with an impermeable cap rock formation above the oil to seal it in and prevent its leakage to the surface. This is the process of oil formation for many "conventional" reservoirs.[65]

Those who subscribe to the "peak oil" hypothesis are typically heir to those intellectual traditions broadly influenced by the work of Thomas Malthus.[66] Historically, the energy Malthusians have been influenced by William Jevons, who argued that the inevitable exhaustion of Britain's coal would result in the decline of Britain's power over its empire.[67] Malthus, a British clergyman, argued that Britain's population growth would exceed its capacity to produce food, as the trajectory of the former (population) was exponential whereas increases in food production were held to be linear. Thus, at some point, population growth would cross a threshold beyond which the demands of the population for sustenance would exceed food production, and as scarcity grew it would translate into the disintegration of social order, and ultimately even violent conflict.

Broadly put, the Malthusian tradition holds that humanity exists in a finite world, and that human population pressures will combine with increased consumption of key resources (e.g., food, water, and oil) to generate scarcity. As such material goods become increasingly scarce, Malthusian thought holds that we will witness increasing poverty, the inequitable distribution of said goods, social strife, and possible even political violence between those competing for scarce resources. Thus, Malthusian thought is laced with a degree of pessimistic political realism, and enjoys a considerable degree of support among biologists, chemists, and certain scholars in the social sciences.

After Malthus, other scholars examined the dynamics of scarcity and carrying capacity in what the biologist Garret Hardin termed the Tragedy of the Commons. In this case, individually rational maximization would result in the degradation and depletion of the commons over time. In this manner individually rational decisions can lead to collectively irrational (and destructive) outcomes for the community in the aggregate. The biologist Paul Ehrlich predicted that population growth and consumption would degrade ecological systems and exceed the planet's carrying capacity, leading to strife and the breakdown of civilization.[68] In each of these cases, the authors were correct in estimating that human population would strain the carrying capacity of complex ecosystems through mechanisms of increasing consumption and pollution, but they were incorrect in discounting human ingenuity and assuming that carrying capacity was finite. Ultimately, the Malthusian case has been weakened by the fact that human ingenuity has proved capable of increasing yields from crops, the recycling of materials, increasing fuel efficiency, and extracting progressively greater amounts of energy from the biosphere.[69]

In contrast, the Cornucopian school argues that there are no empirical (or theoretical) limits to human population growth, or to the human consumption of natural resources. With theoretical assumptions derived from classical economics and dominated by figures such as Julian Simon, Cornucopians hold that human ingenuity has always triumphed over scarcity, largely through the mechanism of the market. Thus, as a good becomes overly scarce, its price will increase according to the dynamics of demand and supply. According to this logic, when the price of a good reaches a certain threshold the "substitution effect" will kick in, and firms will employ technical ingenuity to create substitutes for the scarce good.[70] Though the market and ingenuity may often combine to create effective substitutes, there are also grounds for reasonable skepticism regarding the theory. For example, it is very difficult to "substitute" for depleted fresh water resources in the semi-arid regions of the planet. In land-locked places such as Colorado, Utah, and New Mexico, aquifers are now rapidly being pumped dry, and there is little realistic probability of desalinated ocean water being pumped over thousands of miles to the region. Moreover, neither ingenuity nor capital are equitably distributed across the planet, such that "substitution" for scarce goods is extraordinarily difficult in the least developed countries (e.g., Haiti, Ghana). Thus, while optimists speak of "substituting" for oil, it is important to realize that these distributional constraints represent serious obstacles to the global poor.

The reality of the situation lies in the nuanced gray area between the Cornucopian and Malthusian extremes. We have already witnessed the peak production and subsequent decline of several major oil fields in recent years. As the economist James Hamilton notes, several mature oil fields "are now in significant decline, including the North Sea (which had accounted for 8 percent of the world's production in 2001) and Mexico's Cantarell Field (formerly the world's second most productive field). Production declines caused former OPEC member Indonesia to become an oil importer, and the nation dropped out of OPEC in 2008."[71] Furthermore, China, which until 1992 had historically been self-sufficient in energy, became the world's largest importer of crude oil in 2014, largely because of the depletion of its domestic oil fields and its inexorably increasing demand. The political scientist Shane Mulligan notes that "peaks to date have occurred in up to 54 of the world's 65 largest oil producing states."[72]

The analytical firm Energy Intelligence "estimates that the world's surplus oil-production capacity peaked at around 12 million barrels per day in 1985, was eliminated soon after Iraq invaded Kuwait in 1990 and the United Nations embargoed oil from Iraq, and climbed back to over five million barrels a day in mid-2002."[73] However, in 2002 and 2003 the world's excess oil-production capacity vanished unexpectedly and rapidly. One factor was the waning of Saudi Arabia's "swing" capacity (the ability to increase production in order to moderate prices) from 2003 to 2009. This rapid reduction in global production "slack" seems to have exacerbated market speculation in oil futures, and oil-producing countries subsequently chastised the OECD countries for failing to curb such rampant speculation.[74] Excess capacity wasn't to return until the global recession of 2008–09 as substantial declines in global demand for crude oil once again allowed for slack, in the form of OPEC's excess productive capacity. Of course, declines in production are not just produced by geological constraints, but may also result from political constraints such as political tensions and violent conflicts with or within oil-producing states.

The story of "peak oil" is admittedly complex. Even as several major former producers have now passed their peak productive capacity, global oil production continues to increase as other newer fields have been brought on line to offset the above declines. Thus, even as certain national peaks in production have been empirically verified, global production levels have continued to increase. Daniel Yergin argues that this produces an effect of rolling peaks that collectively produce a production plateau effect, and thereby attenuate any peak in global production in the near future.[75] This plateau effect will be reinforced by technical advances that allow for the extraction of tight oil and deep-sea oil.

Thus, the complex question of "peak oil" hinges upon technology, price, geology, and time horizons. Technical advances will push the peak of global oil production into the future. Nevertheless, the geological quantity of oil in the planet's crust is basically finite, at least at prices that would allow modern economies to remain intact. Humanity is still rapidly depleting the planet's essentially finite oil resources. Moreover, despite the high probability that we will continue to witness the plateau effect for some time, humanity is likely to experience infrastructural bottlenecks in the form of a shortage of drilling equipment, including rigs and drilling ships. The US Joint Forces Command offers the following assessment: "The central problem for the coming decade will not be a lack of petroleum reserves, but rather a shortage of drilling platforms, engineers and refining capacity. Even were a concerted effort begun today to repair that shortage, it would be ten years before production could catch up with expected demand."[76]

The world will not be "running out of oil" in the next few decades then—but it is running out of cheap oil, and extraction of the remaining oil will be increasingly costly, often fraught with political risk, and ecologically destructive. As certain polities pass peak conventional oil production they may become increasingly vulnerable to imports, rapidly shifting capital out of depleted countries to these new oil-producing countries. What we are observing, then, is a continual "power shift," with economic power increasingly shifting from older producers to newer ones—particularly as the older producers develop and reinforce malign path dependences that constrain their capacity to adapt. Political power may also shift from consumer states to these new producers of oil from unconventional sources, as determined by the energy intensiveness of the economies of the consumer states.

According to the US Energy Information Administration, as of August 2012 the world rankings in proven oil reserves were as follows, in billions of barrels[77]:

1. Saudi Arabia (267)
2. Venezuela (211.2)

3. Canada (173.6)

4. Iran (151.2)

5. Iraq (143.1)

6. Kuwait (104.0)

7. United Arab Emirates (97.8)

8. Russia (60.0)

9. Libya (47.1)

10. Nigeria (37.2)

11. Kazakhstan (30.0)

12. United States (26.5)

In this volume I take issue with many archetypal liberal arguments, including assumptions of benign hegemony, assumptions of liberal energy markets, and the supposedly robust nature of the global energy regime. I argue that facets of archetypal liberal institutionalism remain useful tools of analysis, but that certain Panglossian assumptions must be re-conceptualized. First, this volume is primarily a historical and theoretical work wherein cases and process tracing are used to develop the outlines of a theoretical construct (e.g., shadow liberalism) that will enable future scholarship in the realm of international affairs and its intersections with the domains of energy and security. Just as importantly, this book is decidedly not an empiricist and/or econometric analysis. Other scholars (notably Michael Ross) are already working in that empirical arena of specialization,[78] and I shall leave the large-N multivariate regressions to them. Furthermore, this volume doesn't contain an analysis of the ecological externalities generated by oil, and the threat they pose to the vitality of the body politic, and to the integrity of the global commons.[79]

In chapter 1, I present a historical analysis of the United States' conduct in the realm of foreign energy policy, particularly in the domain of oil. I argue that the US has often displayed both liberal and strikingly *illiberal* behavior, coupled with a disturbing tendency toward bellicose interventionism. This historical analysis demonstrates that US foreign energy policy is actually quite *illiberal*, which contrasts with the portrait of the US as a benign hegemon that archetypal liberals seek to paint.

In chapter 2, I analyze of the political economy of oil, arguing that many of the suppositions underlying the "liberal" market-based model are in fact increasingly archaic, and/or inaccurate, with serious consequences for US foreign energy policy. First, I argue that the supposed liberal free market in international oil is more mythology than substance, largely as a result of the rise of energy statism in the form of national oil companies (NOCs). The NOCs present a substantive challenge to the United States' free-market system which is based on the assumed dominance of the IOCs. Consequently, the US finds itself locked in a race for oil against an array of increasingly mercantilist energy competitors, notably China. Thus, the global energy economy also exhibits properties of illiberalism, manifest in statist mercantilism.

In chapter 3, I provide some evidence to support the archetypal liberal hypothesis, in that the United States has been a critical proponent of international institutions that support the sharing of data and fuel, and promote collaboration among countries, in times of energy crisis. However, I argue that the existing global energy regime is extremely weak, and moreover that it deliberately excludes rising consumer powers (e.g., China and India) and oil producers (e.g., Brazil) from participation. Thus, even in the domain where evidence to support archetypal liberal theory should be strongest, the evidence for the archetypal variant is rather weak.

In chapter 4, I argue that oil has in fact operated as a major agent of destabilization in the Persian Gulf, specifically through its capacity to exacerbate the security dilemma that permeates that region. Indeed, I argue that in the absence of oil, the regional security dilemma that permeates the Gulf would exist in only the weakest form. Oil functions in a complex fashion as a target of aggression, and the production of oil provides revenue flows that facilitate militarization and inter-state aggression.

In chapter 5, I argue that the United States' grand energy strategy, particularly in the Persian Gulf region, contains a strong core of illiberalism. Such illiberal conduct is particularly vivid in the United States' actions toward Iran during Operation Ajax, in the Twin Pillars strategy, and during Desert Storm and the Iraq War. I conclude that the United States' desire to augment Iraq's oil production, and to release that oil to international markets, combined with other motives to play a major role in the George W. Bush administration's decision to invade Iraq in 2003. Thus, the paradox wherein the United States' desire to provide global public goods (e.g., enhanced global energy flows) has resulted in the adoption of a highly illiberal strategy that focuses on power projection and in periodic bouts of military conflict. I conclude that the United States' grand energy strategy is not explained by the archetypal variant of liberal theory. Rather, the intermittent phases of institution building and the provision of public goods by the US contrast with periods of fundamentally illiberal behavior. Collectively, this mercurial comportment supports the darker variant of liberal theory, *shadow liberalism*, proposed herein.

Editor's note

The author updated portions of the text in proofs to acknowledge developments that had occurred between the time of writing and the middle of December 2014.

1   The History of Oil and International Affairs

Civilization has progressed through various modes of energy, from our ancient ancestors who used fire, to the use of livestock and agricultural energy during the Roman era, to the harnessing of wind and water, and then to the use of coal that led to the invention of the steam engine and the advent of industrialization.[1] In the modern era we have seen humans develop and utilize electricity, utilize oil as a major source of energy, exploit nuclear power, and develop new renewable energy technologies. Each of these energy transitions has had momentous consequences for the development of a given society; and the advent of oil resulted in increased economic productivity, enhanced physical mobility of goods and peoples, and augmented military strength for those countries that adopted oil-based military systems before their competitors.

In this chapter, I analyze the historical influence of oil on the conduct of US foreign affairs. I argue that the United States' symbiotic relations with the corporate sphere, in its quest to obtain foreign oil (for itself and for the other OECD countries), has contributed to its frequently illiberal behavior in the conduct of foreign policy. Thus, the United States' drive to maintain its hegemony over international energy flows (particularly oil) has revealed the illiberal core of the modern liberal international order. Moreover, I argue that this symbiotic association between the state and oil corporations has generated path dependences that limit adaptation and has fostered much of the illiberal behavior that we frequently observe in US foreign energy policy.

Energy, History, and Society

Aristotle was the first philosopher to recognize the importance of energy for civilization, conceptualizing such forces or energies as "prime movers."[2]

Saint Thomas Aquinas used the term "prime mover" to refer to any machine that transmuted natural energy into work.[3] In 1909, the German chemist Wilhelm Ostwald was the first to recognize the link between energy and levels of civilization, arguing that transitions from one lower state of energy use to another higher state (e.g., from wood to coal) propelled civilizations to ever higher states of complexity.[4] The anthropologist Leslie White argued that this association between energy and the pace of civilizational complexity was the principal law of societal development. "The civilizations or cultures of mankind," White argued,

may be regarded as a form or organization of energy. Culture is an organization of phenomena—material objects, bodily acts, ideas, and sentiments—which consists of or is dependent upon the use of symbols. Culture is a kind of behavior. And behavior, whether of man, mule, plant, comet or molecule, may be treated as a manifestation of energy.

White continued:

And one of the ways of making culture a more powerful instrument is to harness and to put to work within it more energy per capita per year. Thus, wind, and water and fire are harnessed; animals are domesticated, plants cultivated; steam engines are built. The other way of improving culture as an instrument of adjustment and control is to invent new and better tools and improve old ones. Thus energy for culture-living and culture-building is augmented in quantity, is expended more efficiently, and culture advances.[5]

The historical progression of energy regimes over millennia began with the solar agricultural regime and progressed through a range of pre-industrial prime movers (such as wind and hydropower) through the age of coal and steam into the modern age of electricity, petroleum and nuclear energy.[6] Those societies that made the conversion from one fuel regime to another before their competitors did gained specific advantages; in providing greater food for their populations, in increasing economic productivity, and in their capacity to project augmented political and military power both at home and abroad.

The anthropologist Joseph Tainter wasn't quite as deterministic as Ostwald and White, holding that it was the specific dynamic between energy and social organization that provided for societal evolution to higher states of complexity. Tainter argued as follows:

Human societies and political organizations, like all living systems, are maintained by a continuous flow of energy. ... The institutions and patterned interactions that comprise a human society are dependent on energy. At the same time, the mechanisms by which human groups acquire and distribute basic resources are conditioned by, and integrated within, sociopolitical institutions. Energy flow and sociopolitical organization are opposite sides of an equation. Neither can exist, in a human group, without the other … . Energy flow and sociopolitical organization must evolve in harmony.[7]

Tainter's model is more compelling than the models proffered by Ostwald and White because it alludes to co-evolutionary principles, to the perennial interactivity of *physis* (e.g., energy) and *nomos* (e.g., society) in the development of civilizations. The historian William McNeill echoed this sentiment: "I see two paramount themes in the history of the past century: the growth of human control over inanimate forms of energy; and an increasing readiness to tinker with social institutions and customs in the hope of attaining desired goals."[8] If energy functions as the life force of a polity, enhancing the vitality of the body politic and the capacity of the state, then the denial of energy resources would have dire, perhaps even catastrophic consequences.

The Transition to Fossil Fuels

For millennia the dominant fuel sources for societies were animal labor and biomass (wood), in what the historian Alfred Crosby has called the "culture of fire."[9] Waterwheels then emerged in ancient Mesopotamia, along the Tigris River, and windmills first appeared in Persia in the first century AD.[10] Various civilizations had been aware of hydrocarbon resources for thousands of years, typically in the form of tar pits, seeps, and gas flares. However, the earliest known use of fossil fuels was undertaken by the Chinese people during the Han dynasty (200 BC). The Chinese were the first to develop percussion drilling,[11] using it to tap deposits of natural gas at Xinhai.[12]

The transition to coal began with the first recorded mining of coal, in Belgium in 1113. Intercontinental trade in energy then ensued. As a result of acute shortages of firewood and an abundance of coal, Britain was the first country to complete the transition to a coal-based economy, between 1540 and 1640.[13] The coal regime was then subsequently adopted in Russia, the United States, Canada, and Japan. This transition to coal prompted the development of the steam engine in Britain by Thomas Newcomen in

1712, primarily in order to drain the coal mines of water. This development of the steam engine, and its later refinement by James Watt, contributed to the emergence of the Industrial Revolution in Britain.[14]

Historically crude oil was used for protective coatings or for building materials, but only rarely did ancient societies use it for the purpose of combustion, one example being the heating of Constantinople's *thermae* during the era of Byzantine Rome.[15] In 1778, the British explorer Alexander Mackenzie discovered the "bituminous fountains" of northern Alberta, in the area that would eventually come to be known as the Canadian oil sands.[16] Societal conversions from coal to petroleum began in the latter years of the nineteenth century, primarily spurred by a desire for illumination. During the 1700s, whale oil was used to provide light, but it had the odious side effect of destroying the whales, which in turn resulted in soaring market prices for the oil.[17] This problem was eventually solved by the Canadian chemist Abraham Gesner, who first distilled petroleum into kerosene in 1853.[18] The replacement of whale oil with kerosene provided the impetus for the development of the rock oil industry. The first free-flowing crude-oil well was discovered by James Williams in Oil Springs, Ontario, Canada in 1858, which then set off a wave of drilling for oil across North America.[19] The next major oil well was developed by the American Edwin Drake, who in August of 1859 used steam engine technology to facilitate percussion drilling at Oil Creek, Pennsylvania.[20] Soon afterward, the nascent petroleum industry was tapping oil fields from Ploesti to Baku, Sumatra, Iran, Mexico, and Venezuela.

With a higher energy density than coal, and existing in a liquid form that made transportation simple, oil rapidly replaced coal and gas lamps. By 1900 global production of petroleum had reached about 150 million barrels, but by 2000 the world was producing 26 billion barrels per year.[21] After Thomas Edison's "invention" of the electric light in 1879, kerosene would soon be replaced as a source of illumination by electricity.[22]

The development of the first internal combustion engine by the German engineer Nicholas Otto (from 1863 to 1876), set the stage for the advances in engine technology achieved by Gottlieb Daimler, Karl Benz, and Wilhelm Maybach. The rise of the engine, and hence the automobile, generated major markets for petroleum in the twentieth century. Thus, it is the interface between certain material and technological variables, notably drilling and refining processes, and the advent of engine technologies, which permit the emergence of oil as a driver of the modern industrial era. In all these developments, crude oil and the technology to use it were of paramount importance to the rise of modern political economy, and to the rise of the engines of war.

The US oil industry emerged in a way that didn't require explicit state intervention (at least at the outset) and it led to the rise of powerful domestic influences (or factions) in the US energy industry that would in time come to exercise powerful influence over the state. This penetration of the weak and divided state by powerful energy interests would often render the US government beholden to the interests of the petroleum industry.[23] Thus, the symbiosis of the oil industry and the state resulted in a process of co-evolution over time, a complex process that reinforced path dependence and that has limited the country's capacity to free itself from the grip of oil interests.

The Shadow of the Past

Each [nation] is the prisoner of its own history ... .
Raymond Vernon[24]

One cannot derive patterns of political and societal conduct without being cognizant of the variable of time, as revealed through historical processes. As the economist Douglass North warned, "without a deep understanding of time, you will be lousy political scientists, because time is the dimension in which ideas and institutions and beliefs evolve."[25] All too often, modern political science resorts to taking "snapshots" of the relations between a constellation of variables, when in fact we should be looking at the evolution of patterns over time—what the political scientist Paul Pierson aptly describes as "moving pictures.'[26] Only through examining the patterns of human behavior over time do we gain the capacity to analyze those patterns and then develop theoretical constructs in the realm of the political.

Many influential social scientists, including Tocqueville, Marx, Weber, Ikenberry, and Deudney, have adopted historical approaches to their analysis. However, it is not enough to simply say "History matters." Being cognizant of patterns of change over time provides a vantage point that allows one to perceive phenomena that may remain invisible to the observer from just one limited point in time. Thus, Pierson's concept of moving pictures allows us to capture the *flow of processes over time*, as opposed to the temporal constraints evident in a snapshot of political phenomena at one moment in time. "Attentiveness to issues of temporality," Pierson argues, "highlights aspects of social life that are essentially invisible from an ahistorical vantage point."[27]

If one were to examine US foreign energy policy through the truncated temporal lens of a decade; one would have little understanding of the historical chain of events that led the United States to become highly dependent on foreign oil supplies. Similarly, a snapshot of time would not allow any substantive understanding of the United States' decades-long involvement in the Persian Gulf. One would then have no understanding of the course of events that led to Operation Desert Storm in 1991, and then to the subsequent US invasion of Iraq in 2003, and hence the United States' aggressive and hegemonic presence in the Gulf region. Only a deep understanding of these historical processes permits substantive analysis of US foreign energy policy.

One of the more widely used mechanisms to understand the influence of the "shadow of the past'[28] upon the present is *path dependence,* which (despite its growing use) is often a poorly defined concept. Margaret Levi provides a concise definition: "Path dependence has to mean ... that once a country or region has started down a track, the costs of reversal are very high. There will be other choice points, but the entrenchments of certain institutional arrangements obstruct an easy reversal of the initial choice."[29] The political scientist Jacob Hacker echoes this point, arguing that "path dependence refers to developmental trajectories that are inherently difficult to reverse."[30]

Pierson argues that any conceptualization of the concept of path dependence must focus on "the dynamics of self-reinforcing or positive feedback processes in a political system." He continues:

There are strong grounds for believing that self-reinforcing processes will be prevalent in political life ... . Once established, patterns of political mobilization, the institutional "rules of the game," and even citizens basic ways of thinking about the political world will often generate self-reinforcing dynamics. Once actors have ventured far down a particular path, they may find it very difficult to reverse course. Exploring the sources and consequences of path dependence helps us to understand the powerful inertia of "stickiness" that characterizes many aspects of political development.[31]

Exploring the evolution of processes and institutions through the lens of path dependence is valuable because the temporal order of events is critical in determining the outcome. To pose it in a counterfactual manner, if events are placed out of their proper temporal order, the outcomes would probably look very different than what has actually transpired. Social scientists typically invoke the concept of path dependence to claim that "specific patterns of timing and sequence matter," and that "large consequences may result from relatively 'small' or contingent events; particular courses of action, once introduced, can be virtually impossible to reverse; and consequently, political development is often punctuated by critical moments or junctures that shape the basic contours of social life."[32]

The other advantage of looking at political evolution through the lens of historical analysis is that it allows us to examine the power of incremental processes that are attenuated over time, from decades to centuries. Again, imagine the prospect of explaining current US foreign energy policy if (counterfactually) the initially vast conventional petroleum reserves of the United States had not been largely squandered over the past century. A historical "snapshot" approach would likely render conclusions that were quite divorced from the historical evolution of US dependence on foreign oil, particularly in the Persian Gulf region. For the purposes of this inquiry, a historical investigation of path-dependent processes is certainly called for, although we are bound by the fact that the era of oil and foreign policy is only about a hundred years old. While that necessarily limits us to roughly a century of data, it also means that much of the historical record is quite good.

Path dependence implies that the trajectory of downstream policy decisions is often determined by the tyranny of initial conditions in a given system. In the case of the United States, these initial conditions were an astonishing abundance of natural resources, particularly in the case of hydrocarbons like oil. The historian William Appleman Williams once wrote of an America in which "abundance was freedom and freedom was abundance."[33] "The US system of governance and the country's ideological preferences," Raymond Vernon notes, "were conceived and developed over several centuries during which the United States was plentifully supplied with its critical raw materials, was relatively isolated in economic terms, and was relatively safe in military terms. ... The US response to its raw material problems is likely to be constrained by these historical factors."[34] Thus, material abundance was a critical factor in the development of the American psyche, and helped to determine the form of domestic political institutions.

Early in the twentieth century this perception of perpetual material abundance became entrenched within the policy-making community as well as in academe. Henry Kissinger recalled this mindset: "In 1969, when I came to Washington, I remember a study on the energy problem that proceeded from the assumption that there would always be an energy surplus. It wasn't conceivable that there would be a shortage of energy."[35]

Path dependence can be readily observed in the deep canyons of the American Southwest. Just as a river carves a channel ever deeper into the bedrock over centuries and millennia, the initial conditions of a system help to create a trajectory that is very difficult to alter at some later point. In a similar manner the abundance of cheap oil in the fledgling United States led to the rise of the automobile culture, vast networks of highways that link the nation together, the rise of the suburbs (and now the exurbs), and a conspicuous lack of energy-efficient public transportation options across much of the country. Thus, one could argue that the modern American appetite for cheap oil, in conjunction with weak to non-existent institutions and regulations, reflected the polity's enormous sensitivity to initial conditions.[36]

Scott Page argues that path dependence can manifest through several mechanisms, including "increasing returns, self-reinforcement, positive feedbacks, and lock-in." "Increasing returns," he writes, "means that the more a choice is made or an action is taken, the greater its benefits. Self-reinforcement means that making a choice or taking an action puts in place a set of forces or complementary institutions that encourage that choice to be sustained. With positive feedbacks, an action or choice creates positive externalities when that same choice is made by other people. Finally, lock-in means that one choice or action becomes better than any other one because a sufficient number of people have already made that choice."[37]

The principle of increasing returns is illustrated by American behavior in the early years of the twentieth century. Millions of Americans began to use automobiles and gasoline, improving mobility of goods and persons; economies of scale then improved for gasoline and cars. Consequently, the prices of both declined, making such goods increasingly affordable to the average citizen. In a deregulated market environment wherein powerful energy lobbies infiltrate weak state and federal governments, the structure of path dependence is primarily the result of self-reinforcement. In the case of self-reinforcement the interests of the oil and automobile industries became intertwined with that of state and federal governments. Governments chose to support the creation of infrastructure that would support and augment such industries, and in the meantime such institutions ignored the need to create and support effective public transit systems. Finally, lock-in has occurred as the oil and auto industries have come to exert a dominant influence over governments at the state and federal level in the US.

Insofar as the American people have been psychologically conditioned by historical abundance, this mindset, and ubiquitous infrastructural rigidities, may limit the United States' ability to adapt to future conditions of increasing scarcity of resources (in general) and oil in particular. The path dependencies set up by cheap oil have conditioned us not only economically and psychologically but also institutionally. To this day the dominant institutions of energy governance within the US are the Department of Energy and Department of Interior, which were apt to act as support mechanisms for the international oil companies (many of which originated in the US and remain based here). One may recall the public opprobrium visited upon the Department of the Interior after the Deepwater Horizon blowout of 2010, in which millions of gallons of oil spilled from a damaged BP wellhead into the Gulf of Mexico, damaging the livelihood of local peoples and harming the ecology of the region.[38] A subsequent investigation into these events found that the Department of the Interior's Minerals Management Service was deeply corrupt, as its modus operandi was simply to placate the oil companies, issuing seabed drilling permits without any serious analysis of corporate plans, routinely failing to inspect rigs, or enforce federal regulations.[39] In the case of the US, it is striking how existing institutions of governance in the domain of energy have served primarily as the vassals of industry, and have done relatively little to protect the interests of the body politic, the American people.

Prelude to World War I

The history of oil is the history of imperialism, in one guise or another.
Anthony Giddens[40]

To paraphrase Giddens, the history of oil is the history of *power*—economic, political, and military power. Countries that historically

possessed oil benefitted from their oil-derived wealth, and were often vic-
torious over energy-poor countries in war. Nations that didn't possess significant oil reserves initially often sought to seize those resources through
coercion and imperial expansion (notably Germany and Japan). Thus, oil
provided a mechanism to permit the projection of power and also served as
a target during wartime.

The first recognition of the strategic advantages conveyed by oil begins
with the British Royal Navy, which began the conversion of their smaller
vessels to oil in 1902. In 1904 the US Navy's Fuel Oil Board argued for the
wholesale conversion of the US fleet from coal to oil, although the US fleet
didn't begin wholesale conversion until 1913.[41] The association between
oil and national security intensified with Admiral Winston Churchill's fateful decision, in July of 1913, to convert the entire British Royal Navy from
coal to oil. One primary advantage of ships that ran on oil was that they
could be refueled at sea. Because ships that consumed coal had to be refueled at a terrestrial base, about 30 percent of a coal-powered fleet would
be unavailable for active duty at any particular time.[42] "As a coal ship uses
up her coal," Churchill argued, "increasingly large numbers of men had to
be taken, if necessary from the guns, to shovel the coal … thus weakening
the fighting efficiency of the ship at the most critical moment in the battle
… . The use of oil made it possible in every type of vessel to have more
gun-power and more speed for less size or cost."[43] In 1914, Churchill advo-
cated the creation of a British crown corporation to obtain oil from Persian
fields, and in a subsequent vote of 254 to 18 the British Parliament voted to
become a part owner of the Anglo-Persian Oil Company.[44] In this manner
the entry of the great powers into the Persian Gulf had begun, and from
the outset Western involvement in that region was based on the dictates of
national energy security concerns.

Clearly, the exigencies of war demanded technological advances, many
of which were directly facilitated by the conversion to oil. Oil based engines
facilitated the rise of tanks, airplane, trucks, automobiles, and motorcycles,
technologies that greatly enhanced the destructive capacity of war in the
early years of the twentieth century. During World War I, the Central Powers found themselves increasingly limited by the shortage of crude oil in
their territories, which ultimately drove the Germans to seize the oil fields
at Ploesti in Romania.[45] Conversely, the extraordinary abundance of oil
enjoyed by the Allies—some of it from the vast fields in the United States,

some from the Persian Gulf—proved decisive in the Allied victory. After the Armistice, Lord Curzon of Britain recognized the profound significance of petroleum to the Allied war effort, proclaiming that "the Allies floated to victory on a wave of oil."[46] This recognition of the new strategic importance of oil was echoed by the French. Henri Berenger, France's Commissioner-General for Fuel, astutely advised Clemenceau that "who has oil has Empire."[47]

In 1919, the US Petroleum Committee for War (which had developed oil strategy during World War I) metamorphosed into the American Petroleum Institute. Thus, during World War I an energy-based military-industrial complex began to emerge. International oil companies became allied with US military institutions to ensure the security of the nation. According to Stephen Krasner, fears of petroleum shortages grew to dominate the mindset of US policy makers during the twentieth century: "During and after the war ... policy-makers feared that reserves within the United States would be exhausted and the most promising overseas fields would fall under the control of foreign powers ... . They felt this posed a threat to the functioning of the economy in general and naval capabilities in particular."[48] As an illustration of Krasner's point, in 1939 Congress passed the National Stockpiling Act, which permitted the government to purchase those materials deemed crucial to the national defense and the stockpiling of oil began in earnest.[49] As early as 1939, President Franklin D. Roosevelt was cognizant of the United States' wasteful behavior in the domain of energy, and of its growing dependence on foreign imports: "Our energy resources are not inexhaustible, yet we are permitting waste in their use and production. ... Future generations will be forced to carry the burden of unnecessarily high costs and to substitute inferior fuels for particular purposes."[50] Until the early 1940s, the US government's foreign energy policy was nebulous at best. The historian Michael Stoff argues that the US began its quest to articulate a long-range policy on foreign oil in 1941. "Until then," he writes, "foreign oil policy, as a discretely defined set of precepts, remained indistinct from the general commercial policy of the United States government."[51]

World War II

After World War I, energy systems were deliberately targeted during interstate conflicts. During World War II, both Allied and Axis powers sought to disrupt or destroy the adversaries' stocks of petroleum and gasoline, and the infrastructure for producing such energy resources. "Nazi U-boats came close to severing the flow of oil from the Western Hemisphere to Britain and Allied forces in Europe," the oil historian Daniel Yergin notes. "Later in the war, both the Nazi-controlled Romanian oil fields at Ploesti and Germany's synthetic fuel plants were main targets of Allied bombing."[52]

By 1941 both the US Navy and the US Army had established their own oil divisions or hired industry consultants, and in the latter half of that year President Roosevelt ordered the creation of the Foreign Petroleum Policy Committee under the auspices of the Board of Economic Warfare.[53] At this point, Walter Ferris of the Department of State presciently observed that the depletion of domestic resources to fight the Axis powers would force the US to pursue a "more and more aggressive foreign oil policy aimed at assuring access to petroleum overseas."[54]

After World War II, Albert Speer, who had been the Third Reich's Minister of Armaments and War Production, admitted that oil had been a major factor in Adolf Hitler's fateful decision, in 1941, to embark upon Operation Barbarossa, the invasion of the Soviet Union.[55] A lack of oil had long been one of Germany's greatest vulnerabilities, and it threatened to bring the Axis war machine to a grinding halt. Thus, Hitler reasoned that the survival of the Third Reich was contingent upon the acquisition of the vast oil-production center of Baku in the Caucasus.[56] The Nazis launched their offensive against the Soviet Union on June 22, 1941. Despite substantive initial gains, it would ultimately prove a disastrous decision for the Nazi regime as the furious Soviet counterattack in the East facilitated the opening of a second front in the West.[57]

In 1942 President Roosevelt ordered the consolidation of the Board for Economic Warfare and the distinct military oil divisions of the Navy and Army into the US Petroleum Administration for War.[58] Such was the importance of petroleum to the Allied side during the war against the Axis powers that US Secretary of State Cordell Hull created the Committee on International Petroleum Policy in January of 1943.[59] That year also saw the first formal recognition of Saudi Arabia's strategic importance to the United States' national security.

By 1943, Germany's drive into Soviet territory had stalled. A persistent shortage of oil became a major constraint on Hitler's ambitions, prompting Allied concerns about the safety of oil fields of the Persian Gulf.[60] On

February 16, 1943, pursuant to that anxiety, President Roosevelt informed the Lend-Lease Administrator, Edward Stettinius Jr., that "the defense of Saudi Arabia [was] vital to the defense of the United States," and Roosevelt committed to the extension of Lend-Lease aid to that country.[61] On February 14, 1944, Roosevelt secretly met Saudi King Ibn Saud at the Great Bitter Lake in the Suez Canal on board the USS *Quincy*, where they negotiated for five hours.[62] Under this agreement the US pledged that if Saudi Arabia was threatened by another power the US would pursue "energetic measures under the auspices of the United Nations to confront such aggression."[63] After Roosevelt's return to Washington, the *New York Times* editorialist C. L. Sulzberger wrote: "American interest in the area is strongly centered on two subjects of intense national interest to Americans—oil and air bases. The immense oil deposits in Saudi Arabia alone make that country more important to American diplomacy than almost any other smaller nation."[64] The agreement between Roosevelt and Ibn Saud constituted a de facto alliance; the Saudi's agreed to provide cheap oil to the United States and her Allies, and in exchange the US would henceforth guarantee Saudi security from external aggression. This meeting also was the turning point at which the US began to get involved in the turbulent international politics of the Persian Gulf. From this point on, the Persian Gulf becomes increasingly seen as part of the United States' sphere of influence, and US dominance of the region increased with the contraction of Britain's overseas commitments and its gradual withdrawal from the Gulf. The clandestine meeting between Roosevelt and Ibn Saud also serves as the pivotal decision point that permits the subsequent evolution of the Carter Doctrine, in which the US would announce to the world its resolve to protect its allies in the Gulf region. Importantly, this security-based alliance with Saudi Arabia marked a decisive and illiberal turning point in US foreign energy policy. From this point on, the US increasingly became a major supporter of illiberal and draconian oil-producing regimes that engaged in the systematic violation of human rights. Thereafter the US would become increasingly adept at turning a blind eye to political repression abroad, as long as the oil of the Persian Gulf continued to flow to the West.

In hindsight, the two world wars were powerful exogenous shocks that entrenched the path dependence that had been forming in American energy security. By 1945, US military forces were highly dependent on petroleum. That dependence would continue into the twenty-first century.

In the wake of World War II, the United Kingdom and the United States had determined that the Persian Gulf was of enormous strategic significance to the survival of the West, particularly in the face of the emerging Soviet threat. Indeed, such was the fear of Soviet aggression that American policy makers crafted a plan, detailed in National Security Council memorandum NSC 26/2, to destroy the oil fields of the Gulf in order to prevent the USSR from seizing them.[65] This joint recognition of the Soviet threat resulted in increased cooperation between the US and Britain, manifesting in the Anglo-American Agreement on Petroleum. This concord sent a veiled warning to the countries of the Gulf that the Western powers would demand the fulfillment of all existing contracts for the procurement of oil, and that they threatened to use force to see to it that such contracts would be fulfilled.[66]

In 1952, toward the end of Harry Truman's presidency, the President's Material Policy Commission (also known as the Paley Commission) issued a report titled *Resources for Freedom*. The report argued that the moral opposition to the "barbarous violence" of Communism, "must be supported by an ample materials base."[67] "The over-all objective of a national materials policy for the United States," the report stated, "should be to insure an adequate and dependable flow of materials at the lowest cost consistent with national security and with the welfare of friendly nations."[68]

Operation Ajax

In 1953 the United States' involvement in the Persian Gulf region took a decidedly illiberal tack during the Mossadegh Affair. The US Central Intelligence Agency colluded with the British MI6 in orchestrating a coup d'état to remove Iran's democratically elected prime minister, Mohammed Mossadegh, from power. This fundamentally anti-democratic and reactionary coup was known as Operation Ajax. Though the CIA denied its participation in Operation Ajax for decades, it finally admitted US complicity in the affair in 2013.[69]

Mossadegh, a potent reformer of Iranian society and politics, had been the primary force behind the nationalization of the Iranian oil industry, which had been under British control since 1913 through the Anglo-Iranian Oil Company (AIOC). Elected prime minister on April 28, 1951, he soon nationalized all British oil assets in Iran. This nationalization resulted from decades of mistreatment by the AIOC, which had steadfastly refused to provide even remotely equitable royalty payments to the people of Iran. Consequently, the impetus for the strike against Mossadegh resulted from anxiety and anger in Britain (and in the United States) over the decision by the Iranian Majlis and Senate to nationalize the AIOC on March 20, 1951.

At first, the Truman administration thought the British were too heavy-handed in their conduct toward the Iranian people and tried to mediate the growing political discord between London and Tehran.[70] Truman's Secretary of State, Dean Acheson, vociferously opposed British actions, arguing that London was "destructive and determined on a rule or ruin policy in Iran."[71] In October of 1952, Mossadegh declared the British to be enemies of the Iranian people and cut diplomatic relations with London. The election of Dwight Eisenhower as president of the United States in 1952 resulted in a pronounced shift in US foreign energy policy toward the British and away from a position of sympathy for Mossadegh. Eisenhower wrote: "As to Iran I think the whole thing is tragic. ... [Some sources] attach as much blame to Western stupidity as to Iranian fanaticism and Communist intrigue in bringing about all the trouble. Frankly, I have gotten to the point that I am concerned primarily, and almost solely, in some scheme or plan that will permit that oil to keep flowing westward ... ."[72]

The new US Secretary of State, John Foster Dulles, requested that the CIA (headed by his brother Allen) prepare plans to oust Mossadegh. Subsequently, the CIA worked to mobilize factions of the Iranian population to rise against the Mossadegh government, using propaganda to foment domestic unrest. Widespread social destabilization and violence ensued, and on August 19, 1953 Mossadegh was deposed and sentenced to permanent house arrest.[73] Although the CIA has largely taken the blame for this subversion of Iranian democracy, it is clear that President Eisenhower provided direct support for it. According to the scholar Moyara de Moraes Ruehsen, "not only did [Eisenhower] know what was going on with respect to Iran, but he was concerned about it as far back as 1951 after the AIOC was nationalized; he gave a 'green light' to his cabinet advisors to come up with a plan 'which kept Persia in the Western orbit.'"[74]

Operation Ajax clearly illustrates the power of oil to induce the United States (and Britain) to engage in fundamentally illiberal foreign-policy behavior. At the behest of the Anglo-Iranian Oil Corporation, the machinations of the British and the Americans led to the removal of a democratically elected prime minister in Iran and his replacement by Shah Reza Pahlavi, who used the secret police to quell dissent. The imposition of the pro-Western Shah and the crushing of democracy consequently led to rise of Islamic fundamentalism in Iran. Ultimately, this chain of events led to the revolution of 1979, the fall of the Shah, the rise of Ayatollah Khomeini, and the emergence of a fundamentalist Iran that was hostile toward Western countries. Operation Ajax exemplifies the profoundly illiberal policies undertaken by the United States and Britain in order to placate corporate interests and to perpetuate market-based energy security for the West. Counterfactually, one wonders what Iran (and the Persian Gulf) might look like now if Mossadegh had remained in power, and if democracy had subsequently flourished in Iran. Unfortunately, the reality is that Iran is now a revisionist and authoritarian power with significant ideational and geopolitical ambitions. Tehran's Islamic fundamentalism and its nuclear ambitions constitute a threat to the security of the Sunni countries in the region and to Israel. Iran is also a sponsor of international terrorism, with considerable revenues dedicated to the expansion of Hezbollah's activities in the Levant and to the use of that organization to direct violence at Israel.

In the mid 1950s the European powers were contracting their empires and ridding themselves of their colonial responsibilities. Consequently, the United States found itself drawn into the emerging power vacuum in the Persian Gulf, and increasingly adopted the mantle of enforcer of the peace in that region, largely under the banner of a Pax Americana. With the intensification of the Cold War, and growing concerns about Soviet aggression, the Eisenhower administration also created the Interstate Highway System, which certainly augmented domestic economic productivity and interstate commerce but which exacerbated a growing societal and economic addiction to petroleum.

In 1959 the Eisenhower administration erred again when it established mandatory controls on the importing of oil in an attempt to slow the flow of cheap Middle Eastern oil into the US market. Eisenhower dubbed it the Mandatory Oil Import Control Program. The government justified this policy on the basis of national security, but detractors dubbed it the "drain America first" policy.[75] Unfortunately, this policy had the effect of accelerating the decline of US domestic oil reserves, helping the country to pass its peak of oil production in 1970 or 1971, just as the geologist M. King Hubbert had predicted.

The Nixon Doctrine

President Richard Nixon and Secretary of State Henry Kissinger were acutely aware of the problem that rising global oil prices posed for the United States, both in economic terms and in national-security terms. The Nixon administration's attempt to impose price controls on oil in the early 1970s echoed the misguided strategy of the Eisenhower administration's import-control policy. As Michael Graetz notes, Nixon's price controls "decreased the effectiveness of conservation efforts and held down both domestic production of oil and domestic development of alternatives to oil. Perhaps even more important, they dominated the legislative efforts regarding energy policy and tied our political process in knots."[76]

In the context of decolonization and the final departure of the British from the Persian Gulf in 1971, the United States moved in to fill the power vacuum in the region. As a result, the Nixon Doctrine, which held that the United States should use its power in combination with allies in the developing world, was subsequently employed in the Persian Gulf. Thus, the Nixon Doctrine entailed the development of the Twin Pillars strategy, whereby the United States' interests in the Persian Gulf would be facilitated through the pro-Western regimes of Saudi Arabia and Iran. During this phase, policy makers in Washington actively encouraged the Saudis and Iranians to invest in downstream production capabilities (notably tankers and refineries) in the United States. The idea was to increase the economic interdependence of the oil-producing countries and the oil-consuming countries. The Twin Pillars strategy also entailed the provision of huge amounts of US military aid to Saudi Arabia and Iran, a policy that began in the 1960s and persisted thereafter. Kissinger specifically approved the sale of F-4, F-14, and F-15 fighter jets to these countries in order to strengthen their relations with the United States.[77] This strategy was formalized by Kissinger in National Security Study Memorandum (NSSM) 174, dated March 8, 1973. Unfortunately, the Twin Pillars strategy also entailed the political repression of peoples throughout the Persian Gulf region. It exemplifies the illiberal strategy of the United States in using fundamentally authoritarian, even despotic regimes to maintain American hegemony over the oil resources of the Persian Gulf region. Thus, the hegemonic provision of public goods, in the form of oil flows to the West, rested upon the oppression of peoples in Iran and Saudi Arabia. In this manner, the liberal international energy order rests upon a foundation of fundamentally illiberal behavior.

The Arab Oil Embargo

On October 20, 1973 the Organization of Arab Petroleum Exporting Countries (OAPEC) retaliated against the United States for its support for Israel during the recent Arab-Israeli War by initiating a comprehensive embargo on oil exports. The oil shock that ensued was unprecedented. The price of a barrel of oil rose from $3 on October 16 to $11.75 by the end of December.[78] The embargo resulted in soaring fuel costs, in the rationing of both heating oil and gasoline, in severe inflation, and in social disruption. Truckers protested fuel prices by blocking highways and gas stations. Long lines for gasoline resulted in disorder ranging from threats of violence to the occasional shooting. The embargo also initiated the pernicious trend of "stagflation" that would plague the United States throughout the 1970s, wherein high unemployment combined with soaring inflation (primarily as a result of increasing energy costs) to generate a deep recession. The oil crisis of 1973 revealed the new vulnerability of Western countries—particularly the increasingly import-dependent US—to oil shocks.

The historian Bruce Beaubouef argues that "the first oil shock of 1973–74 had the effect of a new tax, as would the second oil shock of 1978–81." "This so-called 'OPEC tax,'" he continues,

drained money and spending power out of the US economy and into the coffers of OPEC nations. The resulting transfer of wealth meant that Americans had less disposable income to buy goods and services. It led to balance-of-payments and trade deficits. ... Rising inflation lowered real wages for US workers. Between November 1973 and March 1975, consumer purchasing power fell by almost 9 percent. Making less money in real terms, US workers bought less and saved less. Rising inflation also took a toll on productivity. ... Soaring energy prices meant a higher cost of doing business. Rising production and transportation costs, in turn, lowered productivity. Falling business productivity, in turn, led to layoffs. Unemployment, which had been roughly 5 percent in 1973, jumped to 9 percent in May 1975, and averaged 8.5 percent for the year. Ultimately, the embargo cost approximately 500,000 American workers their jobs.[79]

In the wake of the OAPEC embargo, President Nixon acknowledged the United States' acute vulnerability to oil-supply disruptions and/or price spikes. Nixon also intimated that the Soviet Union might have designs upon the Arab world, particularly the Persian Gulf. "The entire industrial economy of the West," he wrote in his 1980 book *The Real War*, "now depends on oil, and the entire military machine of the West runs on oil. Control over the West's oil lifeline is control over the West's life. Never has the future of the Persian Gulf been so vital to the future of the world. Never have the nations of the Persian Gulf been so vulnerable to an aggressive power that seeks to impose its will on the world."[80]

Nixon's speech to the American people on November 25, 1973 detailed various mechanisms of adaptation that the administration recommended in order to minimize the disruptive effects of the embargo. Nixon asked the American people to conserve energy by turning down thermostats, reducing driving speeds, and eliminating excess lighting. Of greater significance, Congress subsequently enacted legislation to create the Alaskan pipeline, and Nixon signed it into law on November 16.[81] The rationing of fuel, executed through the Emergency Petroleum Allocation Act of 1973, resulted in inefficient distribution, which only exacerbated the social disruption generated by the embargo. In a subsequent speech, Nixon announced "Project Independence," the country's first attempt to wean itself from its now-recognized dependence on foreign (notably Persian Gulf) oil imports. Nixon concluded the speech by "restating our overall objective":

It can be summed up in one word that best characterizes this Nation and its essential nature. That word is 'independence'. In the last third of this century, our independence will depend on maintaining and achieving self-sufficiency in energy. What I have called Project Independence 1980 is a series of plans and goals set to insure that by the end of this decade, Americans will not have to rely on any source of energy beyond our own. As far as energy is concerned, this means we will hold our fate and our future in our hands alone. As we look to the future, we can do so, confident that the energy crisis will be resolved not only for our time but for all time. We will once again have plentiful supplies of energy which helped to build the greatest industrial nation and one of the highest standards of living in the world. The capacity for self-sufficiency in energy is a great goal. It is also an essential goal, and we are going to achieve it.[82]

Paradoxically, the economic and political dislocation generated by the OAPEC embargo resulted in some marginally positive long-term outcomes for the United States. First, it resulted in the creation of the Federal Energy Administration by Congress in 1974. Two other benign results were the development of Corporate Average Fuel Economy (CAFE) standards for vehicles and the development of alternative fuel technologies. Furthermore, the OAPEC embargo stimulated the creation of an energy regime in the form of the International Energy Agency.[83]

The economic discord wrought by the OAPEC embargo lingered in the minds of members of the Gerald Ford administration. The head of the Federal Reserve, Arthur Burns, presciently argued that soaring energy prices might result in a "permanent decline in our nation's economic and political power in a troubled world."[84] Burns was correct. Increasing prices for oil imports and the transfer of wealth from the United States to oil producers would serve to drain the economic vitality of the United States in the years to come, generating significant imbalances in terms of trade and aggravating deficits and the national debt.

Only rarely has the federal government imposed duties on oil imports, the exceptions occurring during the Eisenhower and Ford administrations. In 1975, the duty eventually amounted to about $2 per barrel. John Duffield argues that this was in fact a "bargaining chip" used by President Ford to ensure that Congress would pass the Energy Policy and Conservation Act (EPCA) in December of 1975.[85] This legislation "granted the president standby powers to impose gasoline rationing and other demand-restraint measures."[86] Beaubouef notes that EPCA did give the president enhanced powers: "[T]he president could require power plants to use coal rather than oil, order the development of new coal mines, and allocate and appropriate domestic oil and gas reserves. The president could also order mandatory conservation measures and oil and natural gas rationing."[87]

The Advent of the Carter Doctrine

The administration of Jimmy Carter confronted a number of significant problems arising in the domain of energy policy, notably the environment of economic stagflation that bedeviled the United States in the wake of the oil shocks of the early 1970s. President Carter followed the Nixon administration's lead in drawing up a National Energy Plan, which was provided to Congress in April of 1977. Just a few years later, in 1978, Congress authorized the Energy Tax Act, which "established a full excise tax exemption through 1984 for alcohol fuels."[88] That was followed by the National Energy Act of 1978 (Public Laws 95-617, 95-618, 95-619, 95-620, and 95-621).

The Iranian revolution of 1979 brought Islamic fundamentalist theocracy to that country and generated yet another pronounced spike in the global price of petroleum. The Soviet Union's invasion of Afghanistan in the same year contributed to American misperceptions that Russia was engaged in a strategic campaign to push southward in order to capture the resources of the Persian Gulf region. The strategic nature of the oil resources of the Persian Gulf was clearly revealed in the president's articulation of what became known as the Carter Doctrine. On January 23, 1980, in his State of the Union Address to Congress, President Carter said: "Let our position be absolutely clear: An attempt by any outside force to gain control of the Persian Gulf region will be regarded as an assault on the vital interests of the United States of America, and such an assault will be repelled by any means necessary, including military force."[89]

The Carter Doctrine has had long-term detrimental effects on the conduct of US foreign policy in the Middle East. The illiberal militarization of the Gulf that began with the Twin Pillars strategy took a huge leap forward with the Carter Doctrine, as it resulted in the establishment of the Rapid Deployment Joint Task Force (RDJTF) in March of 1980. This force was ultimately transformed into the Central Command under the Reagan administration. "To an extent that few have fully appreciated," the political historian Andrew Bacevich argues, "the Carter Doctrine has had a transformative effect on US national security policy. Both massive and lasting, its effect has also been almost entirely pernicious. Put simply, the sequence of events that has landed the United States in the middle of an open-ended war to determine the fate of the Greater Middle East begins here."[90] Bacevich then notes that "each of Carter's successors has reinterpreted his eponymous doctrine, broadening its scope and using it to justify ever larger ambitions. The ultimate effect has been to militarize US policy across various quarters of the Islamic world."[91]

During the early years of the Reagan administration, the United States was once again drawn into the turbulent politics of the Persian Gulf, this time because of a war between Iraq and Iran. That war, which lasted from 1980 to 1988, was fought largely over possession of the oil fields that lay on either side of the Shaṭṭ Al-'Arab River. In 1981, Reagan clearly stated that the United States would not permit turbulence within the Persian Gulf, internal insurrection against Riyadh, or external aggression to diminish the flow of oil from Saudi Arabia to the West.[92] To emphasize the importance of Persian Gulf oil to US national security, the Reagan administration passed National Security Decision Directive 114 in 1983, which included this statement: "Because of the real and psychological impact of a curtailment in the flow of oil from the Persian Gulf on the international economic system, we must assure our readiness to deal promptly with actions aimed at disrupting that traffic."[93]

Again, such policies represented a curious mix of liberal and illiberal thought (and conduct) on the part of American policy makers. The United States vowed to protect the Gulf region against the perceived aggression of external powers (e.g., the Soviet Union) and guarantee the continued flow of Gulf oil to the West. These actions constituted the provision of public goods to Western countries by a benign hegemon. However, US policies also guaranteed continued oppression of the peoples of Saudi Arabia, Kuwait, and Iraq. The US has been complicit as its illiberal allies in the Gulf have systematically crushed domestic political dissent in order to maintain this flow of energy to Western interests.

From 1980 to 1984 the US provided weapons to Iraq in the hope that Saddam Hussein would check the power of a revolutionary, expansionist, and fundamentalist Iran. However, the US approach changed in 1984 when Iraqi forces began to attack Iran's oil facilities at Kharg Island. Thereafter, both Iran and Iraq began a systematic campaign of aggression against non-combatant oil tankers in an effort to deprive the opponent of oil revenues. On March 7, 1987, in a clear attempt to minimize the war's disruption of global oil supplies and markets, the US began to re-flag Kuwaiti oil tankers to help them avoid being attacked. Subsequently, US naval forces deterred Iranian aggression in a campaign to maintain the flow of oil through the Strait of Hormuz in two operations, one named Earnest Will and the other Prime Chance.[94]

The United States' naval involvement in the Persian Gulf intensified when an Iraqi jet fired two Exocet missiles at the USS *Stark* (a guided-missile frigate) on May 17, 1987, killing 37 US sailors. In October of 1987, US forces began to attack Iranian oil platforms in retaliation for Iran's mining of Gulf waters, which had severely damaged many Kuwaiti and American vessels. On April 18, 1988, the US launched Operation Praying Mantis, which resulted in the destruction of several Iranian oil platforms and several gunboats.[95]

The Strategic Petroleum Reserve

The Strategic Petroleum Reserve (SPR) was the brainchild of Senator Henry (Scoop) Jackson, who contrived the idea in April of 1973, just before the OAPEC embargo.[96] The SPR was created as a result of the Energy Policy and

Conservation Act, under Section 151(a), which was signed into law by President Ford on December 22, 1975. The SPR consists of a series of immense reservoirs of crude oil sealed within salt caverns along the Gulf of Mexico. As of May 2011, they contained approximately 726.5 million barrels of crude oil. The system was built to mitigate against significant shortfalls in supply of crude oil to the United States, but it is also is part of the global network of SPRs facilitated by the International Energy Agency, which would work together to mitigate a global shortfall in oil supply. Ostensibly the purpose of the American SPR is to moderate the price of crude oil during periods of disruption of supply, but in actuality the conditions that suffice for a release from the SPR are quite nebulous. Ultimately, the president of the United States has the power to determine if circumstances have generated a severe supply interruption, Congress having given the president the power to authorize limited releases in 1991.[97]

"Perhaps even more important than the actual physical energy security the SPR provided," Bruce Beauboeuf argues, "was the symbolic 'signaling' role it played in the national and international arenas."[98] Moreover, Steve Yetiv posits that the SPR has induced a perception of "structural change" in oil markets.[99] This is true to an extent. Limited releases in 2011 resulted in short-term declines in the price of crude oil on global petroleum markets. In this sense the SPR may be useful in dealing a blow to excessively "bullish" speculation on global oil markets. While this "signaling" function may take the form of unilateral action by the United States, countries also cooperate in multilateral fashion to use their respective SPRs to reduce global crude-oil prices. For example, after Iraq's invasion of Iraq in 1990 the United States coordinated a multilateral release of oil from European and Japanese SPRs through the International Energy Agency, and global oil prices declined rapidly. "There is no doubt," Yetiv writes, "that the SPR release played both a real and psychological role in calming oil markets." Yetiv notes that "the 1991 release made the SPR a major factor in the international energy sector because it transformed it from a theoretical concept to an effective and demonstrated instrument of oil stability."[100] Again, during the Libyan civil war in the spring of 2011, OECD countries conducted a coordinated release of crude oil from their strategic reserves; that reduced the price, though only for a few months.

However, the rise of the international SPR system has not truly stabilized international oil markets. The extraordinary price spike of 2007–08 was due largely to a surge of financial assets into "paper barrels" as a hedge against the implosion of the US real-estate bubble and the subsequent collapse of equity markets. In this case the surge in global oil prices wasn't mitigated by coordinated SPR releases. During the period in question no substantive international coordination occurred to mitigate surging oil prices, the International Energy Agency proved to be a marginal actor at best, and the spike in the price of crude oil helped to drive the global economy deeper into recession.[101] Despite its ineffectiveness in 2008, the SPR system was successfully activated during the spring of 2011 in response to the disruptions to North African oil production witnessed during the "Arab Spring" revolutions, primarily during the Libyan conflict. The civil war in Libya took approximately 2 million bpd of light sweet crude production off line, resulting in significant shortfalls for southern European refineries that were geared to refine this particular type of oil. As a result of the disruption to Libya's exports of crude oil, global oil prices surged again.

President Barack Obama authorized the release of 30 million barrels of oil from the SPR on June 21, 2011, partly in response to the Libyan shortfall and partly in a bid to quell excess speculation and perhaps to spur the Organization of Petroleum Exporting Countries to increase production. The US release was augmented by the release of another 30 million barrels of oil from other IEA member countries. Senator Jeff Bingaman, chairman of the Senate Energy Committee, said "I hope it helps deflate speculative froth in the markets and further settles prices back to levels where most experts believe it should be."[102] In response to the coordinated SPR release, the prices of Brent Crude and West Texas Intermediate fell, but only briefly. Analysts concluded that the release was too small to have much of a sustained effect on crude-oil futures. It probably was the weakening of the European banks in response to the Greek, Italian, and Spanish debt crises of 2011, and the possibility of renewed global recession, not simply the use of the SPR, that reduced the dollar price of Brent oil to the mid eighties in September of 2011.

This historical analysis illustrates that the conduct of the United States in the domain of foreign energy policy has vacillated between liberal and illiberal behavior over the decades. Thus, I argue that the modern "liberal" international order, particularly in the domain of energy, rests upon an often illiberal foundation: the United States overthrew democracy in Iran to protect corporate interests, coddled authoritarian regimes in Saudi Arabia, Kuwait, Iraq, and Iran, and progressively militarized the Persian Gulf region. All of this fundamentally illiberal activity was conducted in order to guarantee the continued flow of oil to the West.

2   The Illiberal Political Economy of Oil

There is no substitute for energy; the whole edifice of modern life is built upon it. Although energy can be bought and sold like any other commodity, it is not "just another commodity" but the precondition of all commodities, a basic factor equally with air, water and earth.

E. F. Schumacher, 1964

In the fall of 2012 the International Energy Agency made the astonishing and ebullient prediction that domestic production of crude oil in the United States would soon equal the production of Saudi Arabia, and consequently the US would soon cease to import oil.[1] The logic of the IEA is based on recent advances in exploration and in fracking technologies that allow for increased production of tight oil from reservoirs across the country, such as the huge Bakken formation of North Dakota. Simultaneously, the IEA predicts great gains in engine efficiency, largely resulting from the aggressive targets recently launched by the Obama administration. Thus, the IEA predicts increasing energy independence for the United States, at least until the year 2030.

Though it is tempting to adopt the IEA's exuberant position, the IEA's report is based on a number of questionable assumptions made by IEA economists. First, they assume that US demand for oil will decline as a result of considerable gains in efficiency, even though a relatively high rate of population growth will result in greater aggregate consumption. It is a bit of a stretch to assume that gains in efficiency will necessarily offset increases in consumption. Second, the IEA economists assume that prices for West Texas Intermediate (WTI) crude oil will remain high enough to justify a steady stream of large investments in domestic production. However, the IEA's report doesn't address the persistent problem of bottlenecks in infrastructural equipment availability (such as a shortage of rigs and drilling ships) that may constrain production. Indeed, such infrastructural bottlenecks were problematic in the years 2000–2014.[2] Third, the IEA's calculations don't account for continued (or increasing) opposition from domestic environmental factions that may slow the spread of fracking and coastal drilling. Thus, although US production has increased remarkably in recent years and will probably continue to do so in the near future, the IEA's projections of American energy "independence" seem a bit far-fetched. Nonetheless, recent technological advances are promising and have led to dramatic increases in US production. One should assume that such technologies will be adopted on a global scale, and that this will result in a global increase in oil production. However, such increases in production may lower global crude-oil prices, and this may combine with global population growth and the rise of the middle class in developing countries to stimulate demand, which will then deplete unconventional sources at an increasing rate. Thus, there is no way of knowing how long this global boom in "unconventional oil" will last.

In this chapter I delineate the foundations of the international political economy of oil, and argue that the global political economy of energy has shifted away from the liberal model toward an increasingly statist and often illiberal model that is currently dominated by the NOCs. The implications of this shift are significant for the United States, as its symbiotic model based on collusion with the international oil companies now seems somewhat archaic. However, the technological revolution in computer visualization and fracking may force many of the NOCs to partner with technically sophisticated IOCs, and this may shift some power away from the NOCs.

Let us turn to the problem of complex interdependence for a moment, noting its capacity to function as a double-edged sword. Archetypal liberal institutionalists tend to articulate complex interdependence as a qualitatively benign phenomenon. However, the political scientist Nazli Choucri alluded to the problematic side of complex energy interdependence in a book published in 1976: "Increasing trade in petroleum and higher prices have given rise to complex economic transactions, providing every state with new opportunities for influencing other states, which makes each more sensitive to the actions of others."[3] Choucri was hinting at the fact that small disturbances in the global web of oil production, occurring in distant countries, can cause major dislocations in the global energy economy.

Thus, disturbances in smaller nodes of energy production or energy transit within the system can result in macro-level destabilization as the price of crude oil soars. Thus, while complex interdependence has allowed the United States and other major economies to feed their oil addictions via the web of global oil production and transport, it also allows for considerable instability in the price of oil, which is exacerbated by demand and supply-induced shocks and by speculative activity.

In the modern globalized capitalist economy it might be fair to say that complex interdependence may exacerbate or even generate systemic crises,[4] whether it is the Asian economic meltdown of the late 1990s, the crash of the global economy in 2008, or the enduring fiscal and monetary crisis in Europe from 2009 to 2014. In classic Schumpeterian fashion, the global economy staggers from crisis to crisis, theoretically rebuilding itself in a perpetual cycle of creative destruction.[5] To the extent that the price of oil assists in such stochastic variance, it is both the lifeblood of the global economy and also (on occasion) a mechanism of profound destabilization. As the global economy lurches into the future, the steadily increasing price of oil will undoubtedly impose ever greater costs upon those economies that suffer from energy inefficiency, and thereby induce greater volatility into the system.

Price

In the twentieth century, oil prices declined from their absolute (inflation-adjusted) peak in the late nineteenth century. Volatility in price is defined as a function of the magnitude and the speed of changes in price.[6] For example, when adjusted for inflation in US dollars the average price of crude oil in 1970 was only 25 percent of the average price in 1870.[7] During the 1950s and the 1960s the price of crude oil was fixed by long-term bilateral contracts between oil-producing countries and the IOCs (also known as the Seven Sisters). The vertical integration of the IOCs allowed the corporations to minimize the instability of oil prices, thereby limiting price volatility to their downstream operations and thus to consumers. Moreover, during those years the rapid frequency of new field discoveries kept pace with rapidly increasing global demand.[8]

Volatility in the price of crude oil increased dramatically during the 1970s. The nationalization of oil reserves observed during that period, particularly in OPEC countries, gave oil-producing countries much greater influence over the price of crude oil. Volatility also increased as a result of the OAPEC embargo, increasing global demand, and the deterioration of the Bretton Woods system of fixed exchange rates.[9] The Iranian revolution of 1979 and the subsequent war between Iraq and Iran (1980–1988) resulted in surging crude-oil prices throughout the early 1980s, but prices then plunged in the mid 1980s as new oil fields came on line and increased the global supply. In absolute terms the inflation-adjusted price of oil in 1980 wasn't reached again until 2007.[10]

On the macro level, price cycles in crude oil are influenced by a number of things, including population growth, urbanization rates, and increasing levels of gross national product per capita. Thus, increasing numbers of people, combined with urbanization and greater purchasing power results in an increasing number of cars on global roadways, which translates into the soaring global consumption of gasoline. These macro-level trends are also driving increasing consumption of other crude-oil distillates, and thus the price of oil continues to remain elevated.

The devaluation of the US dollar over the past few decades may also have influenced increasing prices for a barrel of oil. As Michael Graetz observed, "Nixon's devaluation of the dollar made this task (keeping energy prices low) considerably more difficult. Oil-producing countries lost purchasing power throughout the world as the value of the dollar fell because their oil prices were set in dollars. In September 1971 … at an OPEC meeting in Beirut, its member states increased prices by nearly 9 percent explicitly to compensate for the devaluation of the US currency." As the dollar fell further in value, OPEC continued to raise prices to compensate.[11]

Analysts often argue that the value of the US dollar is not linked to oil prices, as barrels are priced in US dollars. Yet this logic is questionable. In fact devaluation of the US dollar is extremely bullish for commodities prices in general, and for oil prices in particular.[12] This powerful empirical negative association between the dollar and commodities means that a weakening dollar is generally regarded as very bullish for commodities as the latter acts as a hedge; conversely, a strengthening dollar is typically extremely bearish for commodities, and this applies for oil as well.

Furthermore, devaluation of the dollar may also increase the price of a barrel of oil in other ways. First, devaluation diminishes purchasing power, which makes the cost of a given barrel more expensive in US dollars. Example: The Saudis pull a barrel out of the ground and that barrel is worth US$90; however, five years later that same barrel of oil is still worth US$90, but as a result of quantitative easing (i.e., the printing of money) the US dollar is now worth less relative to other currencies. In that case the Saudis probably will want to charge more for that barrel of oil in order to retain their purchasing power in a global market. This is one reason why the members of OPEC and the Russians have increasingly talked about moving toward valuation of barrels of crude oil in non-US currencies (e.g., the euro, the Yuan) in order to offset the declining value of the dollar.

Hence, a declining dollar valuation (relative to other currencies) might actually contribute to the increasing cost of a barrel of oil in US dollars. If the dollar is worth less on international markets, it may take more dollars to purchase that very same barrel of oil. Therefore, multiple iterations of quantitative easing, which stimulates endogenous demand in the United States, may actually be contributing to higher energy prices, which ultimately are inflationary. The economists Mahmoud El-Gamal and Amy Myers Jaffe concur: "The latest bubble in commodity prices was fed by excess liquidity due to low interest rates on Dollar-denominated assets, which were in large part caused by the growing US debt. This lax monetary environment created serial bubbles in recent years: first in technology stocks, then in real-estate and mortgage-backed securities, and finally in commodity prices."[13]

Thus, the long-term decline in the value of the US dollar has incentivized speculators to use "paper barrels" as a hedge against the declining value of the currency. A similar dynamic occurred in 2007 and 2008 as speculators pulled money out of crashing housing and equity markets and invested in commodities (particularly in crude-oil futures) as a hedge. When oil is priced in US dollars, buyers holding foreign currency will find the commodity increasingly attractive as the dollar weakens. "A weaker dollar," Robert Gibbons argues, "can lift dollar-denominated oil prices by making oil less expensive for consumers using other currencies and by drawing investment away from foreign exchange markets seeking better returns."[14]

The Cornucopian school (which arguably includes the IEA) generally assumes that advances in technology will always provide more oil, at relatively cheap prices, or provide efficient substitutes. However, the price of oil is not simply responsive to supply and demand; it is also responsive to misperception and fear, and subject to speculation triggered by the latter. Indeed, the mere threat of production cuts or of internal political instability in oil-producing countries can induce spikes in the price of crude oil, regardless of the actual supply of crude oil on international markets.[15] Such schemes are readily facilitated by international mercantile exchanges, on which traders may deliberately attempt to amplify such signals to increase fear in the global market, which then may lead to dramatic surges in price. The main problem is that there is no solid empirical information on global petrol reserves, just ballpark estimates, and there is widespread concern that certain oil-producing countries may deliberately falsify their estimates in order to unduly influence prices. For example, OPEC countries have perverse incentives to inflate estimates of their reserves in order to allow for greater production quotas, which in turn provide them with more revenue. Collectively, such manipulation generates significant uncertainty, and this uncertainty translates readily into fear, which in turn exacerbates volatility in oil prices.

Geopolitical instability also generates insecurity and fear, which then induce or intensify spikes in oil prices. For example, the first US war against Iraq (1990–1991) initially caused a surge in the global price of crude oil, as did the subsequent US invasion of Iraq in 2003. Similarly, the Arab Spring revolutions of North Africa in 2011 increased the price of WTI crude from $84 in February of 2011 to $108 in April of 2011, an increase of 28.6 percent. This occurred despite the fact that North Africa wasn't a major supplier of the world's supply of crude oil. The spike in global oil prices was based on erroneous speculation that North Africa's instability would translate into widespread political turmoil throughout the Arab world, particularly in the Persian Gulf.

Political disruptions often result in increased spot market prices and in increased downstream prices through the mechanism of the futures markets.[16] El-Gamal and Jaffe argues that political upheavals resulted in oil prices' reaching new highs, and that "this, in turn, allowed the ruling elites in those countries to use the new wave of petrodollars to pacify their populations with a combination of security heavy-handedness and economic relief."[17] Thus, "the [Persian Gulf] region's geopolitical turmoil is … intricately connected to global financial conditions. The region's economic and political problems are typical of regions that suffer from a resource curse, which has now been globalized … ."[18]

Elasticity

Today in the United States there are few effective substitutes for oil distillates in the transportation sector. People travel to work, to school, and to stores, often in fuel-inefficient vehicles. "[Demand] elasticity is low but it's not zero," Adam Simiensky, chief economist of Deutsche Bank, observed. "We've learned in the past that there tends to be a break point somewhere near $4 (per gallon of gasoline)."[19] Crane et al. estimate that, in the short run, "the elasticity of motor-fuel demand in the United States and other developed countries run about −0.1—that is, an increase of 10 percent in the price of gasoline would trigger a fall of 1 percent in consumption, all other factors held constant." To take a recent example, from January through May of 2008 gasoline prices rose 25.5 percent over the same period in 2007, and US gasoline consumption fell 3 percent while incomes more or less stagnated. Using these numbers yields a US price elasticity of demand for gasoline of −0.12. According to Crane et al., "a low-end estimate for the longer-term elasticity of demand for motor-vehicle fuels in the United States is −0.3; an upper-end estimate, −0.7 (Bartis, Camm, and Ortiz, 2008, p. 153)."[20]

To what degree is the global supply of crude oil elastic? Economists tend to argue that there is considerable long-term elasticity in supply. Of course, such economic models often fail to account for variance in time horizons. Short-term supply elasticities are limited because production capacity is relatively inflexible in the near term. On the whole, production capacity is slow to respond to changes in price, primarily because of the high costs and perennial shortages of capital equipment and because of the enormous lead times needed to bring new resources on line. Of course, such inelasticity of supply (and demand) is a significant contributor to the price volatility observed in recent years. Cambridge Energy Research Associates' Upstream Capital Costs Index indicates that "finding and development costs in oil and gas have risen by a startling 210 percent since 2000, adding a significant cost increment to crude supply."[21]

Increasingly sophisticated exploration technologies have allowed for the discovery of vast new reservoirs of crude oil at great depths in the continental shelves of the oceans, in the Arctic, and in still largely unexplored regions such as Eastern Siberia. These discoveries, which are consistent with Yergin's theory of a rolling production plateau effect, undermine quasi-Malthusian claims that the world's great oil reservoirs had been discovered and were close to exhaustion.[22] Indeed, the "easy oil" has been fully exploited, but clearly there are still huge reservoirs of "unconventional oil." The discovery and development of tight oil resources continues to augment

North American oil production. The Bakken formation in the Dakotas is now yielding considerable amounts of crude oil, and the exploration and development of other oil shale deposits is promising. The costs of developing Alberta's oil sands have declined significantly since 2000, and more than 300,000 new bpd of oil-sands production came on line in 2012. Edward Morse argues that most of these new unconventional-oil-source projects make sense at US$60 barrel, a price that is likely to hold for some time.[23] In all likelihood, US domestic production will continue to increase for the foreseeable future. Historically, the greatest obstacles to the discovery and production of "unconventional oil" have been bottlenecks in the availability of capital equipment to tap and extract these resources.[24] However, despite recent advances in discovery and extraction one should remain wary of Panglossian economic models that promise oil in perpetuity.

Economic theories regarding supply elasticity cannot model certain variables that are essentially unknowable, such as the remaining quantities of oil in the sea beds or in tight oil formations, nor the capacity for human ingenuity to progressively locate and tap ever-increasing reservoirs of oil in the Earth's crust. Such models assume that human ingenuity, both technical and social, will *perpetually* succeed in discovering a series of new reservoirs to exploit. Despite the considerable unconventional resources that remain undiscovered, the inescapable logic of geology (not to mention chemistry and physics) holds that Panglossian notions of perpetual discovery are essentially an impossibility. The scientist and policy analyst Vaclav Smil derides the more extreme optimists (such as Julian Simon and Morris Adelman) as naive: "Their enthusiasm about the potential for new discoveries, often shared by some of the industry's managers, is frequently exaggerated."[25]

Improvements in technology have certainly stretched out the time horizons of the hydrocarbon era, but once we have depleted the sea beds and terrestrial unconventional oil sources we will have to switch to other energy sources (something that presumably will be costly and may also be destabilizing). In the face of a growing global population and increasing aggregate energy consumption, new exploration and drilling technologies will only provide a degree of respite, and probably only for a few decades at most. Consequently, one might conclude that supply elasticity will exhibit declining responsiveness to price signals in the decades to come. Short-term supply and demand elasticities are relatively low in the United States and in the rest of the world. Consequently, persistent inelasticity will contribute to continued volatility in the price of crude oil. Thus, minor disruptions in supply or demand can have outsized consequences for the price of crude oil, both positive and negative, as we clearly witnessed in 2008.

Markets

In the early years of the twenty-first century, oil prices have exhibited considerable volatility. The price of a barrel of WTI crude went from $147 in the summer of 2008 to $34 a year later, than back to $111 in April of 2011, exhibiting considerable deviation from the mean over that period. In light of these dramatic swings, stability in oil prices appears rather elusive. Modern telecommunications and electronic trading platforms, in conjunction with the borrowing of large amounts of capital, have enhanced speculative behavior ("paper barrels"). Thus, one class of material variables (computer technology) may actually be exacerbating the price volatility of another class of material variables (oil).

Steve Yetiv contends that processes of globalization have minimized the potential for disruptions in energy flows, arguing that "the global economy has been able to count more and more on sources of oil that can be put on the market to contain the negative effects of a disruption in supply caused by political and security events."[26] This argument is valid insofar as the proliferation of producers of oil means that the chance of an actual supply disruption has been mitigated. Perversely, globalization may also be contributing to identity-based conflicts and to the emergence of criminal and terrorist networks, both of which contribute to global volatility in oil prices. It is clear that political events such as domestic attacks on oil platforms in West Africa, the Arab Spring revolutions of 2011, and the 2011 civil war in Libya induced substantial increases in the global price of oil, though there was no actual shortage in the global supply of crude oil. Thus, even though the Saudis contend that the world is awash in oil, rampant speculation exacerbated by geopolitical tensions has recently driven the prices of oil and of gasoline and other distillates to levels that may damage economies that remain highly sensitive to oil prices.

In contrast to the position adopted by the archetypal liberal school, I argue that complex energy interdependence is a double-edged sword, capable of generating outcomes both benign and malign. Yetiv has argued that the globalization of economic interdependence "has increased the extent to which an oil crisis negatively affects OPEC as much as it does its customers. High prices can trigger economic recession, damage the interdependent global economy, and lower the demand for oil."[27] This is the classic archetypal liberal argument that the OPEC countries would keep oil prices low in order to avoid reducing demand, maintain their own profit streams, and ensure the continuing vitality of the global economy. However, such optimists assume that OPEC retains the "swing capacity" to moderate global oil prices.

"Swing capacity" refers to the OPEC states' ability to curtail production in order to increase the price of crude oil, or conversely to produce greater amounts of crude oil in order to bring down excessively high prices that might reduce demand. Optimists also neglect the rise of the "hawkish" faction within OPEC (particularly Iran and Venezuela, which care more about short-term revenues to maintain domestic power structures than about the vitality of the global economy).

There is an increasing amount of evidence to suggest that OPEC's swing capacity waned a bit in the years 2000–2014. During 2008, OPEC proved largely incapable of moderating the spike in oil prices that was induced by global speculation as cash flowed out of collapsing real-estate markets into commodities that were deemed safer, particularly oil. Concatenating crashes in the real-estate and equity markets, and the consequent spike in energy prices, resulted in a global recession. During the period of deflation that followed, oil prices fell. Neither the price spike (which reduced demand) nor the subsequent crash in prices (which diminished revenues for producer states) would seem to have been in the interests of the OPEC countries, and certainly not in the interests of the historically moderate Saudis.

Modern computing and communications technology, in conjunction with rampant speculation in commodities and the rapidity of capital movements, seems to have increased the volatility in oil prices in recent years. Archetypal liberals fail to acknowledge that such spikes and crashes are occurring *despite* increasing global energy and market interdependence. To the contrary, it seems that the intensification of global trading, the relative deregulation of markets, and the increasing speed of transactions has resulted in this increased volatility. Thus, complex interdependence may have introduced new vulnerabilities into tightly coupled global energy systems. In a sense, then, complex interdependence may result in significant gains at the onset of a system, marginal returns and stagnation as the system matures, and then declining returns beyond a certain threshold point. We may now be in the midst of the era of marginal returns and stagnation arising from our adherence to the carbon-based energy regime, particularly as we begin to factor in the costs of environmental externalities such as climate change.

Markets and State Capacity

G. John Ikenberry's argument that the global oil market augmented state capacity for the United States has proved largely correct.[28] However, the rise of resource nationalism so evident in the national oil companies may be increasingly problematic for US interests. As long as the NOCs ally with the international oil companies (Exxon, Chevron, etc.) in order to develop new fields and put additional quantities of crude oil on the global market, global oil markets will continue to augment the state capacity of the US and other major importers.

But if the NOCs fail to work effectively with the IOCs, or if they engage in deliberate market manipulation through subterfuge, increasing energy prices will undermine the capacity of importing states. Thus, in a scenario where NOCs and IOCs cooperate everyone wins, but such cooperation should not be taken as a given. The economist Dambisa Moyo argues that the Chinese NOCs will have little incentive to cooperate effectively with the IOCs, and that this will generate a climate of increasing energy scarcity for the United States.[29] However, if the IOCs develop advanced technologies that the NOCs don't possess, the latter will have considerable incentive to partner with the former and share the resulting revenues.

Pundits (and many economists) often refer to a "free market" in global energy prices, but such a market is in fact illusory. International energy markets, particularly for crude oil, are subject to enormous distortions generated by the increasing nationalization of industry, and by the widespread subsidization of oil and its distillates to consumers. The "free market" in oil simply doesn't exist in any strict sense, particularly in view of the dominance of the national oil companies. Thus, the oft-repeated mantra that we should just leave oil production to the free market is a canard.

Furthermore, global crude-oil markets have proved to be largely inelastic. Raymond Vernon observes that, with respect to oil, "the short-term elasticities of both supply and demand have been very low," and that "when prices have changed, demand and supply have been slow to respond, so that the price could move a considerable distance before it was checked by market forces."[30] "In the short run," he notes, "price increases have not expanded supply nor have price declines reduced it; the marginal costs of oil and oil products to major suppliers are so low relative to the market price as to be irrelevant to price determinations. On the demand side, price elasticities in the short run have also been very low."[31]

El-Gamal and Jaffe have analyzed the inelasticity of both supply and demand in oil markets. "High rates of economic growth," they write, "increase demand for oil significantly faster than capacity for extraction and refining can respond. In other words, short-term supply and demand are both highly inelastic, and increased demand thus drives prices up very significantly. In the long term, however, higher prices reduce demand, as higher costs lead to economic recession, and increased supply further contributes to falling energy prices."[32]

Thus, there are enormous time lags between increases in the price of oil and increases in the supply. This lag effect is attributable to price inelasticities and to the exceptionally long lead times in developing oil resources—from exploration, to drilling, to production, to refining and transportation. Thus, market elasticity is marginal at best because of the significant lead times involved in the production of crude oil.[33] "The existing system," El-Gamal and Jaffe write, "is wasteful of global resources, because it encourages investment in building excess capacity when the petrochemicals industry has to compete with other thriving sectors of the economy. Moreover, the system amplifies the cycle, because of both adding to investment spending during boom times and reducing investment during recessions."[34]

When oil prices are low, there are few incentives for new investments in the infrastructure of production capacity. Rising prices create incentives for such investments; however, this requires years of sustained price increases, so infrastructural components (rigs, ships, and so on) are chronically in short supply. Furthermore, the inelasticity of oil demand, particularly in the United States, is particularly problematic.[35] Normally, as the price of a good rises, consumers will begin to search for cheaper alternatives. However, the inelasticity of demand in the United States suggests that there is a lack of alternatives—particularly of adequate public transport infrastructure in many of the country's suburbs and exurbs.

In view of the rise of the national oil companies, there is good reason to be skeptical of the notion that markets will automatically guarantee the flow of oil to the United States at reasonable prices. Even the archetypal liberal Joseph Nye concedes that "simple reliance on market forces is not an adequate policy for energy security."[36] "Internationally," Nye continues, "we placed too much faith in the conventional economist's wisdom that high prices would solve the oil problem."[37] According to Fatih Birol, chief economist for the International Energy Agency, "oil prices are entering a dangerous zone for the global economy." "The oil import bills," Birol comments, "are becoming a threat to the economic recovery. This is a wake up call to the oil consuming countries and to the oil producers."[38]

Optimists such as Crane et al. remain undeterred. They argue that "a disruption in the global supply of oil is an economic, not geopolitical, problem." "In the event of a reduction in supply," they continue, "the market as a whole shares the burden of the supply reduction, as prices rise to ration demand. In the event of an abrupt reduction in the global supply of oil, the United States would not face a physical shortage, but US consumers would have to pay the higher market price, which would lead to a fall in consumption. By the same token, as long as the US military is willing to bid high enough, it will have access to fuel."

This logic is flawed on a number of points. First, geopolitical problems clearly can lead to disruptions in the supply of oil. Consider the Yom Kippur War (1973), the Iranian revolution (1979), the Iran-Iraq War (1980–88), the Gulf War of 1991, the invasion of Iraq in 2003, the Arab Spring of 2011, and the 2011 civil war in Libya. The political scientist John Duffield argues that authoritarian modes of governance, in conjunction with inequitable distribution of revenues, increase the probability of internal conflict, which may then entail supply disruptions that reverberate in the region or globally. Duffield argues that "a majority of the global supply disruptions since 1951 have had domestic origins," and that "major supply disruptions are perhaps most likely to be the result of domestic political conflict, whether in the form of civil wars, coups, revolutions, strikes, terrorist attacks."[39]

The second part of the logic of Crane et al. is flawed because of the persistent inelasticity of oil demand in the United States. Fortunately, the domestic price of crude oil will probably plateau in the near future as US production of tight oil continues to accelerate. However, in view of the possibility of significant price increases in the next 10–15 years, a reduction in the consumption of oil by American consumers may take some time, and during the transitional period the US economy may suffer considerable disruption. Additionally, not all citizens of the US have an equal capacity to absorb soaring gasoline prices, particularly in rural areas where mass-transit infrastructure doesn't currently exist. It would take significant time and enormous resources to restructure the entire transportation infrastructure to accommodate soaring oil prices. Thus, the urban-centric mindset that Crane et al. exhibit may apply to the densely populated metropolis of coastal regions, but not to much of the rest of the country.

Moreover, markets aren't perfectly transparent, and market prices don't truly reflect the costs of obtaining petroleum. For example, the prices of oil and its derivatives don't include the exorbitant military costs of "protecting" the Persian Gulf region and ensuring the safety of global petroleum flows. Nor do the prices include the costs resulting from the environmental externalities due to carbon and methane emissions. A considerable proportion of the budget of the US Department of Defense is spent on protecting the flow of oil from the Persian Gulf. This seems a bit odd, since most of the oil the US imports now comes from the Americas, particularly from Canada, Mexico, and Venezuela. Delucchi and Murphy estimated that the Department of Defense spent between $26.7 billion and $73.3 billion protecting oil flows from the Persian Gulf region in 2006.[40] Copulos subsequently estimated that the cost for 2007 was $137.8 billion.[41] Dancs et al. estimated that the cost to the Department of Defense for fiscal year 2009 was roughly $103.5 billion, excluding the direct costs of the Iraq War that would have doubled that figure.[42]

Subsidies

Since 2000 significant subsidization of petroleum production by producer states (including the United States) and subsidization of the production of gasoline and other distillates by governments in developing countries have distorted the price of oil. Widespread state subsidization of gasoline in China, in India, and throughout the Middle East ensures that price feedback mechanisms don't function effectively, and thus subsidies merely reinforce global demand for gasoline and hence crude oil.[43] For example, because Beijing requires the Chinese NOCs to sell gasoline and diesel fuel at specified price levels, often incurring losses, the NOCs have to go cap in hand to the government for reimbursement.

The fact that higher prices for oil and gas are often absorbed by governments and not passed on to consumers encourages increases in domestic consumption. For that reason, the perpetuation of gasoline subsidies in many developing countries has resulted in global price increases in the price of a barrel of crude oil. The IEA has also expressed concerns about the distorting effects of government subsidies on oil prices, particularly in Russia, Brazil, and China. "So long as you have price support in these emerging markets," David Fyfe of the IEA's Oil and Industrial Markets Division argues, "you can still have robust oil demand growth even in the face of $100-plus oil."[44] As a result, subsidies and price controls moderate the effects of soaring global crude-oil prices on demand, and therefore encourage continuing high domestic consumption.[45]

The proliferation of statist energy policy programs has resulted in a decline in the efficacy of liberal energy markets, and we may be witnessing an inexorable shift toward quasi-mercantilist approaches to trade in crude oil. The most significant example of this is China, which is openly engaged in the negotiation of bilateral contracts and in quasi-mercantilist tactics throughout Africa.[46] Even Joseph Nye concedes that mercantilist practices are creeping into China's and India's policies with respect to foreign energy.[47]

Economic Shocks

The OAPEC embargo of 1973 and the consequent spike in oil prices ushered in a period of slow economic growth in the West, and stagnation in many oil-dependent developing countries. In the context of the production plateau, moderate advances in fuel efficiency may be offset by increasing demand from non-OECD countries. If that happens, there will be a moderate rise in global oil prices.

A shortfall in global oil supplies relative to rising demand resulting from increases in global population and consumption, or excessive speculative activity (as occurred in the years 2003–2008), may result in a considerable increase in world market oil prices. Despite recent increases in production, the United States will probably remain a net importer of oil for some time, and so increasing oil prices may undermine US terms of trade and consequently diminish consumers' purchasing power. Higher costs for transportation of both workers and goods would diminish economic activity and reduce macro-level demand. Such a reduction in the demand for goods and services would, in all likelihood, result in more unemployment.[48] "A rapid, sustained doubling of oil prices," Crane et al. argue, "could lead to a decline in GDP of 1 to 5 percent, all other factors being equal. This decline would be superimposed on baseline economic growth: If the economy were growing at 2 percent per year, the shock could translate into growth of 1 percent to a decline in output of up to 3 percent."[49]

The situation is complex, because even as US domestic production of crude oil increases, it doesn't guarantee the vitality of the global economy, which remains somewhat at risk as a result of macro-scale energy demand pressures. According to Deutsche Bank AG, a prolonged $10 increase in the price of oil would shave 0.5 percentage point off US growth over the subsequent two years.[50] According to the International Monetary Fund's April 2007 *World Economic Outlook report,* a doubling of oil prices would result in a decline of 1.4 percent of global GDP, and an increase of 1.5 percent in global inflation.[51] Because the US economy derives much of its strength from exports, the fragility of the global economy would inevitably sap the United States of some economic vitality. Thus, even as US domestic oil production continues to surge, the global economy may be subject to the constraints of the plateau effect. Such constraints on the global economy may then slow the expansion of the US economy. Ultimately, this means that the global economy may periodically knock its head against the ceiling imposed by constraints on oil production.

Volatility

Volatility in the price of crude oil may cause destabilizing shocks to the global economy. Arguably, 1998–2013 was a period of exceptional volatility in the price of crude oil.[52] This runs contrary to the assumptions of the optimists who argued that "longer-run political, security, technological, and market developments interact in the crucible of history to yield a counterintuitive outcome: enhanced oil stability."[53] Oil prices have been particularly unstable since 2005. Why?

First, OPEC members' and Russia's secretiveness about their crude-oil reserves and the inscrutable intentions of consumers such as Beijing have created profound uncertainty. Consequently, relatively small disturbances (economic or political) at the international or domestic level may induce enormous volatility in the price of crude oil.[54] Regime change in oil-producing countries also may result in more volatility. According to

El-Gamal and Jaffe, "regime change, or the danger thereof, poses a number of threats for oil-exporting countries. One is the financial risk of freezing the *ancien regime*'s dollar-denominated assets, thus robbing the new regime of a primary source of investment financing. Another ... is the potential for technocratic brain drain, which in turn results in lower long-term productivity. Generally speaking, regime change is associated with reduced oil production for roughly five to ten years."[55] Moreover, the intensity of globalization, particularly in financial and energy markets, has only exacerbated the problem of volatility. According to El-Gamal and Jaffe, "the increased contagion in financial markets will exacerbate rather than ameliorate the propensity for speculative bubbles and crashes."[56]

Speculators

The role of speculators in influencing global markets is also a double-edged sword. On a positive note, futures markets are a useful mechanism for the hedging of risk, and long-term increases in the cost of oil (as long as they aren't overly stochastic) are useful in causing a reduction in demand, and incentivize the creation of alternative sources of energy. On the negative side, speculators bear primary responsibility for the oil-price spike of 2007–08, and for surges in the price of oil in early 2011. These price spikes have resulted in huge transfers of wealth from consumer to oil-producing countries, and have greatly enriched highly leveraged speculators on Wall Street.

The role of speculators in the generation of price spikes is a pernicious problem for the United States and other consumer countries. The economist James Hamilton argues that there is a strong positive correlation between price spikes and subsequent recessions in OECD countries.[57] Of course, such shocks exhibit some degree of endogeneity, insofar as much of the trading of oil occurs on global markets that are based in New York and London, and the traders themselves are largely drawn from OECD countries. Clearly this is an example of a privileged transnational elite making profits at the expense of the vast majority of the global citizenry. The legal scholar Michael Graetz concurs:

[O]il price volatility and uncertainty is greater than ever, due not only to ongoing conflict in the Middle East, but also to the speculative market in oil futures. The quantity of trades in oil futures on the New York Mercantile Exchange every day is ten times the world's daily oil consumption. Oil is no longer just a fuel; it may also serve as financial protection against declining value in the dollar. Around the world, the total daily trades in oil on paper are often as much as thirty times greater than the consumption of oil in barrels. Fluctuations in oil prices are quick and frequent. They often have little or nothing to do with the fundamental relationships of oil supply and demand. Dramatic price swings and the uncertainty about the future of both supply and demand, coupled with the necessity of large long-term capital investments, exacerbate the problems of creating sound policy.[58]

The Commodity Futures Modernization Act of 2000 has proved problematic, inspiring increasingly dodgy conduct in the futures markets, particularly in oil ETFs (exchange-traded funds). For example, the presence of non-commercial traders in oil markets increased by a factor of 15 from 2000 to 2008. Furthermore the percentage of open contracts held by non-commercial traders increased from 20 percent in 2000 to 55 percent during the spike of 2008.[59] As of the time of writing, oil trading remains highly leveraged with investors having borrowed significant capital, and traders often are required to put only a minimal amount down, sometimes enjoying leverage ratios as high as 100 to 1. In fact, it is now commonplace to use considerable amounts of borrowed capital invested in ETFs to speculate in oil prices.[60]

In theory, there are mechanisms in place to inhibit rampant speculation that could generate global economic damage: coordinated releases from the IEA's SPR system in concert with increases in production from "swing producer" states (if possible). This particular strategy was employed in 1990–91 during the Desert Shield and Desert Storm operations, in order to moderate global prices; and again by the Clinton administration in the mid 1990s. However, it wasn't employed during the 2007–08 spike in oil prices, perhaps because of the Bush administration's insistence on free-market dynamics and its disdain for multilateral cooperation through international institutions. The Obama administration employed it in 2011, with some short-term success.

In 2007 and 2008, the economist Amy Myers Jaffe notes, "governments around the world ... engaged in building strategic stockpiles, as oil prices rose from $65 per barrel to $125. This policy signaled to oil markets participants and OPEC that governments would not use strategic petroleum stocks to ease prices under any circumstances except major wartime supply shortfalls. This allowed speculators to confidently expand their exposure in oil market futures exchanges without fear of repercussions and revenue losses from a surprise release of US or IEA strategic oil stocks."[61]

In the mid 2000s, as investors grew concerned about the perceived bubble in real estate, they began to pour their money into commodities, which were seen as a hedge against real estate. Of course, this strategy only served to create bubbles in commodity prices, particularly in oil, which is relatively price inelastic. This was facilitated by the rise of commodity ETFs that made ownership of "paper barrels" relatively easy. El-Gamal and Jaffe concur that rampant speculation caused the price spike of 2008, which then triggered a recession. "Like other manias before it," El-Gamal and Jaffe write, "the rise in prices attracted trend-following speculative traders, who bought oil futures because prices were rising, and of course oil prices were rising because they were buying. ... Oil exporters themselves were baffled by the price levels reached by mid 2008, which they attributed to speculative trading."[62]

On June 22, 2008, Saudi Arabia held a global summit of oil-producing countries in Jeddah. During the ensuing discussions of how to deal with the rapidly inflating bubble in oil prices, King Abdullah blamed speculators for the surge in prices and castigated the Bush administration for its denial that speculators were driving it. The bubble burst in July of 2008 after the price of crude oil peaked at $147 a barrel. Bildiricci et al. argue that in both the 1974 crisis and the 2008 crisis "budget and current account deficits" induced depreciation of the US dollar, which in turn fostered increases in the price of oil. "With the onset of the collapse of several of the major US investment banks in the fall of 2008," they write, "the long-standing access to huge margin accounts contracted, and there was an overall outflow of money from the commodity markets."[63]

Speculators are capable of driving oil prices up very rapidly, as happened in 2007–08 and in early 2011 (when the price of oil went from $102 to $127 in only nine weeks). Of course, the oil industry's capacity to meet surges in demand is limited by the long lead times for exploration, drilling, and the development of infrastructure to bring new resources on line. Thus, in the interim period, price spikes may benefit managers of hedge funds but do significant harm to the economy. Thus, speculators are capable of inflicting real damage on the body politic. Rampant energy speculation may ultimately contribute to recession, sapping the financial resources of the people and depleting the coffers of consumer states while transferring enormous wealth to producer states.

In May of 2011, in a New York court, the Commodities Futures Trading Commission of the United States charged several traders with engaging in improper trading practices. The traders' artifice included deliberate hoarding of oil in order to convince the market there was a scarcity, which produced an artificial price spike. The traders then "shorted" the price of oil, then suddenly released their stocks onto the market, making $50 million in illegal profits.[64]

The multinational investment banking firm Goldman Sachs estimated that the actions of speculators had added roughly 20–25 percent ($21.40–$26.75) to the cost of a barrel of oil in early 2011. Goldman Sachs also estimated that every million barrels of oil held in futures contracts by speculators drives the price of a barrel of oil up by 8–10 cents. According to the CFTC, as of April 5, 2011 "hedge funds and other financial traders held a total net-long positions in U.S. crude contracts equivalent to a near record 267.5 million barrels."[65] According to El-Gamal and Jaffe, "statistical evidence was mounting to support the thesis that financial players were fueling a speculative bubble in oil, which was increasingly treated as an asset class that diversifies away from the Dollar and other deflating assets."[66] Such concerns were raised in the wake of comments in late April 2011 by several OPEC leaders that global oil markets were fundamentally oversupplied.[67]

The rise of hedge funds and sovereign wealth funds has added volatility to global markets for crude oil. In a hearing before the US Senate on May 14, 2011, Rex Tillerson, CEO of ExxonMobil, admitted that on the basis of supply and demand the price of a barrel of oil should be in the $60–$70 range. Instead it tends to be in the $90–$100 range. Apparently, this is primarily attributable to international oil companies' locking in high prices through futures contracts and to the high-frequency trading practices of hedge funds.[68] El-Gamal and Jaffe argue that "standard portfolio management … may encourage managers of large hedge and sovereign wealth funds to construct portfolios that they will need to unwind quickly once any of a number of assets in the portfolio experiences a large negative shock," and that "in this sense … they contribute significantly to perpetuating the crisis and introducing correlations where none had existed previously, through their simultaneous rebalancing and trading patterns."[69]

National Oil Companies and the New Statism

Alliances between the state and the corporate sector are nothing new, particularly in the US. Energy corporations, particularly oil companies, have influenced US foreign policy to a considerable degree. International oil corporations often act hand in glove with the US government in a quasi-symbiotic relationship, the former exercising considerable (and often undue) influence on the latter.

Despite its protestations of support for free-market capitalism, the US has long practiced a form of quasi-statism in the domain of energy foreign policy, the federal government aggressively interceding to provide greater opportunities for the IOCs. Though the earliest overt manifestation of this dynamic was Operation Ajax in Iran, one might argue that frequent US interventions throughout the Middle East also exhibit this often illiberal and statist pattern of intervention. As I will argue below, this quasi-statist and interventionist character of American energy foreign policy is clearly evident in US relations with the states of the Persian Gulf region, particularly in the 2003 invasion of Iraq. Moreover, I will argue that the intensification of corporate-state alliances around the world, in polities ranging from China to Russia to Brazil, presages increasingly mercantilist and illiberal behavior in the domain of energy and may bode ill for international cooperation in the long run.

The history of the national oil companies dates back to the interwar period (1919–1938), beginning with the British pursuit of oil in the Persian Gulf. As was noted above, one of the first NOCs resulted from the British government's acquisition of the Anglo-Persian Oil Company. In the years that followed, prominent NOCs such as ARAMCO (Saudi Arabia), PDVSA (Venezuela), and Pemex (Mexico) were established for the purpose of capturing rents from the sale of crude oil on international markets, and revenues were subsequently redistributed, often in the form of public goods to the societies in question. By the late 1970s, Raymond Vernon notes, the NOCs were beginning to gain ascendancy over the multinational oil corporations, "selling over 40 percent of the world's oil by the end of the 1970s, leaving a greatly curtailed sphere of operation for the multinationals."[70] The IOCs now appear to be marginalized in terms of the total reserves they lay claim to, a result of years of declining reserves relative to the reserves claimed by the NOCs. NOCs now possess the majority (over 80 percent) of the known global reserves of crude oil,[71] and the IOCs have unhindered access to only 6 percent of those reserves.[72]

The rise of the NOCs, in conjunction with a growing international trend toward energy nationalism,[73] has contributed to increasingly mercantilist behavior in recent years. "For China's leaders," Mikkal Herberg writes, "energy security is too important to be left to the markets, and so far its approach has been decidedly neo-mercantilist and competitive."[74] The global rise of energy neo-mercantilism indicates that China and India increasingly view access to oil and gas as a zero-sum game of seeking to acquire equity oil rights to fields in Africa and Latin America.[75]

The UNOCAL Affair

Recent decades have seen the rise of powerful new national oil companies, particularly Chinese corporations such as Sinopec and the China National Offshore Oil Corporation (CNOOC). Although these companies purport to be autonomous from the government in Beijing, they are in fact quasi-crown corporations, and consequently they often operate as direct agents of that government. Many policy makers in Washington suspect that these NOCs are powerful mechanisms of a Chinese foreign policy that is geared toward locking up global energy resources while cutting competitors out.

In 2005, CNOOC attempted to acquire the US-based UNOCAL Corporation, but the transaction was blocked by Congress on the basis of fears that the United States would lose strategically valuable petroleum reserves to China. Representative Joe Barton, a Republican from Texas, raised the national-security implications of the deal in a letter to President Bush: "We urge you to protect American national security by ensuring that vital US energy assets are never sold to the Chinese government."[76] Ultimately, a bipartisan group endorsed House Resolution 344, which defined oil and gas reserves as strategic assets and stated that the sale of Unocal to the Chinese would jeopardize the national security of the United States.[77] Policy makers concerned with the deal subsequently invoked the Exon-Florio Amendment (1988), which permits the executive branch to review any foreign investments in the US that might have potential implications for national security. Under that amendment, should the executive branch determine that investment in a US corporation constitutes a significant threat to national security, the president may block investments deemed injurious to national interests.[78]

Investment by Chinese NOCs in projects beyond the Chinese mainland has increased oil supplies on the global market. These actions have augmented China's energy security, but whether the NOCs can supply enough oil to satiate China's surging demand isn't clear. The rise of the Chinese NOCs also contributes to the very illiberal oppression of peoples in Iran, in Sudan, and in other oil-producing states. Klare asserts that "China has allegedly armed and provided military support to a Sudanese government accused of the wholesale slaughter of civilians in Darfur and the non-Muslim south in return for privileged access to Sudanese oil."[79] Even as the NOCs bolster China's energy security, such neo-mercantilist behavior may be simultaneously eroding China's soft power. Chinese oil ventures in Sudan have been accompanied by extensive human-rights abuses carried out by China's partners in Khartoum, and have thereby undermined China's international image.[80] Moreover, China's disputes with its neighbors in the South China Sea result from contested claims to oil and gas fields. This bellicose behavior also undermines China's soft power.

With the rise of the statist NOCs, the United States' historical model of energy security, as based on the premise of continuing dominance by IOCs, has become increasingly divorced from reality. However, recent advances in exploration and drilling technologies may begin to tilt the global playing field back toward the IOCs to a degree. One would expect that the IOCs would use this proprietary technology to open up considerable reserves of "unconventional oil" around the world, which could expand the reserves held by the IOCs and consequently increase their share of global reserves relative to the NOCs. As the world's conventional reserves are depleted, the technological sophistication of the IOCs will force the NOCs either to partner with them or to compete with them by developing their own technologies. In the case of Russia, it appears that the Putin regime has decided that limited IOC-NOC partnership may be preferable to outright competition. For example, Exxon has recently partnered with Rosneft of Russia in a series of joint ventures in the Kara Sea and the Black Sea.[81] In the case of China, it would appear that a preference for equity oil abroad may also convey some elements of technology transfer through the NOCs to Beijing.

I have argued several points in this chapter. The first is that during the twentieth century the United States engaged in a symbiotic corporate-statist partnership with the international oil companies, a partnership that led the US to engage in some illiberal behavior in the domain of US energy foreign policy. The second is that the supposedly liberal international system of energy trading is sullied by subsidies and is subject to increasingly egregious speculative behavior through the mechanisms of "paper barrels" and ETFs, which drive global price volatility. The third is that the once-dominant international oil companies have now been largely marginalized by the rise of the NOCs, which have been locking up the greater part of the remaining oil reserves on the planet. Fourth, the rise of the NOCs is associated with an increasing level of mercantilism and zero-sum thinking in the domain of energy (oil) foreign policy, particularly in Beijing. Despite the mythology, on a fundamental level the international political economy of oil is not dominated by "laissez-faire" markets, is increasingly statist and mercantilist, and therefore is much more illiberal, in many ways, than most casual observers would expect.

3   Oil, American Diplomacy, and Weak Institutions

Whether one calls it sensitivity or solicitousness or simply "reality," is there any doubt that our allies listen more carefully to kings and rulers who supply them with energy than to those who do not?
Assistant Secretary of Defense Richard Perle, 1981[1]

One can understand current international energy governance, particularly its long-standing institutions (e.g., the International Energy Agency), as an extension of American power. These institutions were created during the Cold War with two principal goals: maintaining US hegemony in the international system and maintaining a stable and prosperous global economy that would enhance the stability of the NATO polities and of the international system. Thus, international institutions in the domain of energy illustrate and reinforce the United States' ability to guarantee the flow of energy to Western countries and thereby enhance the national security of the US. However, even as international institutions directly reflect American power and security interests, and provide a secondary goal of global economic and political stabilization, these very institutions appear to be increasingly sclerotic and dysfunctional. Assumptions that international organizations will possess both the will and the capacity to ameliorate demand-induced increases in the global price of crude oil are naive at best and perhaps dangerous. The evidence presented in this chapter supports the archetypal liberal narrative to a degree, although this finding must be placed in the proper regional context. Even as the United States acted as a benign hegemon in the creation of energy public goods for postwar Europe, and created international institutions to guarantee such energy flows, it was engaged in rather illiberal behavior elsewhere (prominent examples being Operation Ajax and the Twin Pillars strategy in the Persian Gulf).

Thus, regionalism and contextualization are important. Viewed through a European lens, the actions of the US appear to be the actions of a benign hegemon and to fit the archetypal liberal narrative. However, beyond the European context the actions of the US in the domain of energy appear increasingly illiberal.

In this chapter I argue that global energy institutions and regimes dealing with crude oil exist, but that they are extremely weak and often ineffectual. Thus, the archetypal liberal internationalist perspective is correct in that institutions (OPEC and IEA) have formed and in that they exhibit considerable "stickiness," but unfortunately these institutions have been very feeble for several decades. Furthermore, these institutions may be increasingly powerless in the face of the increasing global demand for crude oil—particularly in light of the fact that much of the increasing demand emanates from China and India, which aren't members of the IEA. Proponents of archetypal liberal optimism often exaggerate both the capacity and the efficacy of these institutions.[2]

A History of International Energy Institutions

The strategic value of oil was recognized during World War I, and the subsequent rise of intense Anglo-American rivalry over oil resources provides us with the first outlines of international energy diplomacy. The initial call for an international treaty regarding the sharing of oil supplies occurred in 1920 when Van H. Manning, director of the US Bureau of Mines, called for the development of an international regime to ensure the "equitable development of world oil resources."[3] After the discovery of a significant oil field in Iraq on July 31, 1928, American, French, and British oil corporations drew up the Red Line Agreement to divide the oil resources contained within the former Ottoman Empire. This was a clear case of quasi-statism in international energy politics. Corporations pressed for an international accord, and their home governments backed their corporate interests.[4]

On September 17, 1928, the international oil companies held a meeting at Achnacarry Castle in Scotland in order to devise an international system allocating oil (and products derived from it) so as to maximize profits, eventually devising what came to be known as the As-Is Agreement.[5] Thus, the earliest diplomatic initiatives in the domain of energy weren't purely "statist" in origin. Rather, such initiatives resulted from negotiations between international corporations, and from negotiations between corporations and their respective national governments, all meant to force the governments involved to adopt positions favorable to corporate actors.[6]

After World War II, Europe experienced a severe energy crisis. The war had demolished much of the Continent's energy infrastructure, including oil refineries, coal mines, and transportation networks. Dire shortages of coal threatened to strangle the nascent economic recovery, and to foment social destabilization in Western Europe. Thus coal, and therefore energy, became an issue of high politics throughout postwar Europe.[7] In order to head off the widespread economic and political destabilization that would result from an energy crisis, the European Coal Organization was established on May 18, 1945, with the United Kingdom, the United States, France, Belgium, Denmark, Netherlands, Norway, Greece, Turkey, and Luxembourg as members. Although the ECO is often thought to have been simply an economic mechanism, it is important to recognize that its roots were in the US military, specifically in the Solid Fuels Section of the Supreme Headquarters Allied Expedition Forces. The objective was to restore production from the damaged coal mines of Aachen and the Ruhr rapidly in order to increase energy flows and enhance economic vitality.[8] Thus, the benign hegemony of the United States, and specifically the projection of US military and economic power in order to stabilize Western Europe, set the stage for the emergence of the first international institution in the domain of energy. Thus, the ECO was first multilateral organization created to deal with energy shortages. Although it was only an advisory organization, countries often heeded its counsel.

"The ECO," Ethan Kapstein notes, "was founded on the principle that during shortages states should not scramble for available fuel supplies, and that coal should be allocated equitably." "By providing a central information source on coal markets," Kapstein writes, "the organization lifted some of the uncertainty regarding supplies and prices. (Further) by allocating coal on a multilateral rather than bilateral basis, the ECO helped to create an atmosphere of trust, and to legitimate US leadership."[9] Thus, the ECO was an expression of US hegemony through the formation of a nascent energy regime, and given its legitimation of American stewardship over a shattered European continent, it also enhanced the "soft power" of the United States in Europe over the longer term.

Clearly the United States recognized that the provision of energy as a public good reinforced the economic base that underpinned regional security.[10] The elevation of energy to the level of high politics accelerated with the Schuman Declaration of 1950[11] and the treaty (signed on April 18, 1951) that launched the European Coal and Steel Community. "The gathering of the nations of Europe," the Schuman Declaration proclaimed, "requires the elimination of the age-old opposition of France and Germany … . The solidarity in (coal and steel) production thus established will make it plain that any war between France and Germany becomes, not merely unthinkable, but materially impossible."[12] Thus, the European Coal and Steel Community wasn't only a political and economic mechanism for European integration; it was based on a security mechanism designed to foster transparency and consequently prevent bellicose behavior. Building steel weapons required energy from coal, and the transparency granted by the ECSC would prevent either Germany or France from secretly conducting a large-scale re-armament campaign. By promoting transparency and trust, the ECSC helped to prevent conflict between Germany and France by providing both countries with access to the mineral resources they had historically fought over in the Saar, Ruhr, and Alsace-Lorraine regions.[13] Moreover, fostering economic interdependence as a mechanism to prevent war provided the foundation for the emergence of the European Union and a means of moving beyond the nation-state.[14]

Public Goods

The United States' backing of the European Coal and Steel Community constitutes a public good. Mancur Olson argues that "*the achievement of any common goal or the satisfaction of any common interest means that a public or collective good has been provided for that group*," and that "the very fact that a goal or purpose is common to a group means that no one in the group is excluded from the benefit or satisfaction brought about by its achievement."[15] Public goods are therefore defined as non-rivalrous and non-exclusionary, and global (or regional) public goods are typically provided by a hegemonic power or a coalition of dominant powers.

The British Empire provided a global public good in its relentless campaign against piracy on the high seas, as piracy constituted a historical "public bad" or hazard that bedeviled all seafaring countries.[16] Ultimately all countries benefitted from the British actions, even though the hegemon (and thus the British people) ultimately had to pay for it. In the modern era, the US and British fleets' campaigns against piracy provide an extension of this global "public good."[17] However, the primary reason the US combats piracy is not some ideational commitment to global altruism; it is that maintaining a benign and stable global milieu for international trade directly serves the interests of the US. The generation of such public goods in the domain of energy, particularly as they contributed to increased global trade and investment, has certainly benefitted the US, and the US has used its asymmetrical power advantages to craft treaties and other mechanisms that ensure its continued dominance.

Beyond providing information and reducing transaction costs, international energy organizations have promoted "development of emergency energy allocation schemes and the coordination of member state energy policies."[18] Thus, the founding of these international organizations by the United States served multiple functions, including economic stabilization, political stabilization, and the legitimation of the United States in its role as one of two emergent hegemons.[19] Moreover, such institutions were largely effective in linking regional economies together, and in helping to bring a cessation to the internecine violence that had dominated Europe during the first half of the twentieth century.

In view of the United States' provision of energy to Western Europe during the Cold War and its long-standing protection of flows of crude oil from the Persian Gulf, one could argue that the US has long been involved in the provision of global public goods in the form of energy flows. Similarly, one could argue that one of the central missions of US force projection since the 1930s (particularly the use of naval forces) has been the protection of global flows of energy, and particularly of oil.[20] Insofar as the US seeks to maintain its status as the incumbent hegemonic power, the provision of global energy public goods makes sense as the US continues to benefit from the international status quo. The maintenance of US hegemony benefits from the provision of global energy public goods through the following mechanisms: First, the US economy remains energy intensive, particularly when it comes to the oil distillates that fuel the vast majority of US transportation networks, and so oil imports will remain integral to the functioning of the US economy. Second, the US economy is highly dependent on exports, which benefit from a strong and stable global economy, and this global economy remains highly dependent on the continued flow of energy (particularly oil) at relatively low and stable prices. Thus, the direct and indirect networks of dependence on this global flow of energy contribute to the United States' willingness to provide this global public good, which is often maintained through the illiberal projection of military force.

The rise of illiberal China and its bid for East Asian hegemony, in conjunction with the intensification of nationalization represented in the rise of the national oil companies, makes the United States' provision of global energy public goods increasingly problematic. In perverse fashion, the United States' policy of using its naval power to guarantee the safe transport of oil from the Persian Gulf to East Asia is directly facilitating the rise of a peer competitor in Beijing. Moreover, the US now borrows money from China to pay for this projection of power, which only increases our national debt and makes us increasingly beholden to Beijing. Paradoxically, the net effect is to facilitate the rise of a regional hegemonic power in China that may actually become a substantive challenger to US dominance on a global scale. Thus, to put it bluntly, the United States is literally engaged in a policy of strengthening a potential strategic rival.

Humanity's reliance upon carboniferous technologies (including oil) generates externalities or "public bads." A classic example of a global public bad is air pollution, which typically spreads throughout the global atmospheric commons in a non-rivalrous and non-excludable manner, affecting all peoples to varying degrees by undermining their health and imposing costs on ecosystems. For example, several centuries of industrial production have released large quantities of carbon dioxide and other greenhouse gases into the atmosphere, some of this CO_2 is then absorbed into carbon sinks such as forests and oceans. As carbon is absorbed into the oceans, it makes the waters more acidic.[21] This progressive acidification damages the biological chain of life in the oceans, destroying fish stocks, and damaging fishing and tourism industries around the world. This widespread ecological destruction is therefore distributed among the countries of world, resulting in widespread and diffuse biological (and economic) damage—a global public bad.

Pandemic disease is yet another example of a global public bad that spreads fear, economic dislocation, morbidity, and mortality across polities. For example, the SARS epidemic of 2003 saw the spread of a novel pathogenic coronavirus from its biological reservoir in the bats of Guangzhou in southeastern China. The coronavirus then spread throughout China, to

Hong Kong, throughout East Asia, and then jumped to Canada. The SARS epidemic caused about $20 billion in economic damage as a result of lost trade throughout the Pacific Rim from 2003 to 2004. This example shows that disease can radiate outward as a public bad (or externality) that undermines the economic productivity and socio-political stability of countries.[22]

The formation of the European Coal Organization and the European Coal and Steel Community entailed a recognition that energy shortages and crises constituted public bads, or externalities, that could radiate to damage many actors in an increasingly interconnected system, regardless of the specific origin of the externality. "During an energy crisis," Kapstein writes, "states may lack information regarding the duration and scale of shortages, and about alternative supplies and prices. This uncertainty may lead states to hoard fuel, strike bilateral deals, and take other actions that raise energy prices for all states; the result is a collective bad."[23]

Embargoes

In the realm of international energy diplomacy and security, the use of embargoes has proved problematic, often producing unanticipated consequences for both initiators and targets. The first major oil embargo occurred in the wake of Fascist Italy's invasion of Abyssinia (now Ethiopia) in October of 1935, as the League of Nations sought to embargo the sale of oil and petroleum products to Rome in an attempt to curtail Benito Mussolini's aggression. "In Ethiopia," F. P. Walters writes, "the Italians were fighting with planes, tanks, and mechanical transports against levies that moved on foot and were armed only with rifles and machine-guns. Deprived of their oil supply the Italians would have had no choice but to retreat."[24] Similarly, Daoudi and Dajani write that "the one sanction that could have been most effective, had it been implemented properly, was the oil sanction," and that "oil was an absolute necessity to the Italian war machine; deprived of their oil supplies the Italian army would have had no choice but to retreat."[25] Unfortunately, Germany and other polities friendly to Rome didn't honor the League's embargo, and weakness within the British and French Foreign offices also contributed to the failure of the League's efforts. Thus, the oil sanctions against Rome ultimately failed.[26]

As was noted above, both Japan and Germany exhibited significant concerns about their oil supply in the determination of their strategic objectives leading up to, and during the conduct of, World War II. Since the United States and the Dutch East Indies were the primary sources of oil for Japan during the 1930s, the United States' embargo on oil to Japan in 1941 (in an attempt to force a Japanese withdrawal from Manchuria) proved decisive in influencing the Japanese decision to strike at Pearl Harbor.[27] The embargo was meant to strangle the Japanese military (particularly the navy's capacity to project power throughout East Asia) and force Japan to withdraw its forces from Manchuria. No one in Washington foresaw that the Japanese high command would perceive the embargo as an imminent threat to Japan's survival, requiring a direct strike against the United States' Pacific Fleet.[28] Perversely, even though its purpose was to reduce the ability of the Japanese to make war, the embargo served to intensify the security dilemma between the US and Japan. Paradoxically, then, the United States' oil embargo and the paranoia it generated in Japan contributed to the aggression that the embargo sought to contain.

After the military campaign by France, Britain, and Israel to wrest control of the Suez Canal from Egypt in 1956, Saudi Arabia embargoed oil shipments to Britain and France. The effects of the embargo were limited. France and Britain were able to procure oil from alternate sources, and therefore neither of them experienced significant shortfalls. The European powers and Israel ultimately agreed to withdraw from Suez, but the Saudi embargo played only "a minor role in this decision."[29] During the Six-Day War of June 1967, the Arab countries placed an embargo on exports of oil to countries that provided military and/or political backing to Israel. Though the United States, the United Kingdom, and West Germany were the main targets of the embargo, their oil supplies weren't curtailed significantly. The Khartoum Resolution resulted in the end of the embargo on September 1, 1967. Though this first Arab oil embargo was largely ineffective in changing the behavior of Israel's allies, this collective action mounted by Arab oil producers against Western consumer countries set an important precedent.[30]

In October of 1973 the Organization of Arab Petroleum Exporting Countries embargoed oil exports to the West in retaliation against the United States (and others) for providing support to Israel during the Yom Kippur War. During that embargo, OAPEC states cut production by 25 percent, and consequently oil prices increased from $3 per barrel in 1972 to $11.65 per barrel in the spring of 1974. The embargo was intended to compel Israel to withdraw from the Occupied Territories it had claimed after the 1967 war and the United States to curtail its support for Israel.[31] It ended in March of 1974, and the wave of diplomacy that followed resulted in the Camp David Accords of September 17, 1978. According to Hans Morgenthau, "the embargo on oil by the oil-producing states in the winter of 1973–74 together with the drastic rise in the price of oil have clarified like a stroke of lightning certain basic aspects of world politics which we might have understood theoretically simply by reflection but which were brought home by the drastic change in power relations which these two events imply."[32]

The OAPEC embargo can be seen as an exogenous shock that induced the great powers (particularly the United States) to adopt a series of policy measures and international mechanisms (e.g., treaties and international organizations) to minimize the future vulnerability of Western countries to such oil crises. Consequently, the US, with the collaboration of the European countries, formed the International Energy Agency to offset the rising powers of another international organization: the OPEC cartel.

The Rise of OPEC

The Organization of Petroleum Exporting Countries was the brainchild of Juan Pablo Perez Alfonso, a Venezuelan. Perez Alfonso argued that oil-producing countries would find it expedient to cooperate in order to maintain reasonable prices, and to conserve their resources in order to maintain substantial revenue streams.[33] On September 10, 1960, delegations from Venezuela, Iraq, Kuwait, Saudi Arabia, and Iran met to "study and formulate a system to insure the stabilization of prices by, among other means, the regulation of production."[34] The organization was primarily a response by developing countries to the historical patterns of exploitation by the Seven Sisters (the international oil companies), which had systematically extracted oil from oil-producing countries while giving them a pittance in the form of royalties. Many of the oil-producing countries felt that such inequities could not be tolerated any longer. OPEC was officially formed in Baghdad in September of 1960.

Initially OPEC found it difficult to enforce price discipline among its members, and the organization remained feeble and dysfunctional throughout the 1960s. "The United States barely noticed OPEC," according to Stephen Rabe. "During the 1960s, the Department of State never felt compelled to issue a major statement on the organization. Indeed, the department, responding to budgetary constraints, actually abolished its petroleum affairs section. US officials and oilmen considered OPEC not only impotent but also irrelevant."[35] However, this changed in the early 1970s with a war in the Middle East. "The Middle East war of 1973," Joseph Nye writes, "gave OPEC a boost, a signal that now it could use its power. The Arab countries cut off access to oil during the 1973 war for political reasons, but that created a situation in which OPEC could become effective. At one point in the crisis, Secretary of State Henry Kissinger said that if the United States faced 'strangulation,' military force might have to be used. Fifteen percent of traded oil had been cut, and the Arab embargo reduced oil exports to the United States by 25 percent."[36]

OPEC was clearly weakening again by the late 1980s, in part because of the Iran-Iraq War. By forcing prices up during the 1970s, OPEC had caused demand to decrease in consumer countries, mobilized exploration resources in a global search for non-OPEC reserves, and stimulated the development of infrastructural capacity to tap those non-OPEC reserves. The results were a global glut of petroleum in the late 1980s and a corresponding decline in the global price of oil. "In these conditions," Freedman and Karsh write, "OPEC had found it difficult to function as an effective cartel in setting quotas and prices, which had been one of the main stimulants to the Iraqi-Kuwaiti dispute."[37]

That OPEC acts with a clear and monolithic degree of agency is a dramatic oversimplification. Historically, OPEC has had a "hawk" faction and a "dove" faction. Since the 1950s the Saudis have adopted "dovish" positions, largely because they have possessed the greatest degree of economic interconnectivity with global markets, particularly through their investments in global equity markets. This pragmatic approach derives from the diversification of Saudi assets into the global economy, and of course it means that the Saudis have a vested interest in a stable long-term oil price that will allow the global economy to flourish.[38] OPEC's "hawkish" faction now includes Venezuela, Iran, and Algeria; in the past, it included Iraq under Saddam Hussein.[39]

One might argue that global excess capacity is a significant determinant of price stability. However, because the excess (or swing) capacity of major producers has diminished as a result of the depletion of major oil fields, prices have been increasingly volatile. Arguably, Saudi Arabia's swing capacity hit a nadir in the years 2006–2008, when the Saudis argued that they no longer had the capacity to increase oil production.

OPEC has been less than cohesive in designing and implementing policy on the production of crude oil. A historical analysis of OPEC negotiations finds numerous examples of the cartel's breaking down, particularly when certain members cheated by exceeding their production quotas. Such cheating consequently diminished revenues for OPEC members who abided by the quotas, and introduced a considerable degree of political acrimony into the cartel's decision making.[40]

Kuwait's persistent cheating during the late 1980s was one of the primary reasons given by Iraq to justify its invasion of that country in 1990. Since 2011, oil prices have again been a source of conflict within OPEC. Ardent "price hawks" (notably Venezuela and Iran) now openly rebel against the historically conservative Saudis. In a departure from the scripted tranquility of most OPEC negotiations, the OPEC meetings of June 12, 2011 collapsed in discord as a result of disputes between "hawks" and "doves." OPEC, which has historically functioned to moderate and stabilize oil prices, now finds itself riven with discord.

Though OPEC members certainly retain the capacity to increase prices, particularly by fostering uncertainty and fear in global oil markets (as Iran sought to do in early 2012), they no longer possess the requisite swing capacity to unilaterally moderate volatility in the price of crude oil. Thus, a significant component of OPEC's power has vanished. Moreover, the recent surge in North American oil production, largely as a result of technological advances by the IOCs, will strengthen the United States' hand relative to OPEC by diminishing the United States' dependence on oil imported from OPEC countries. The sharp decline in oil prices in late 2014 resulted from a surge in production in the US, from OPEC's desperation to maintain its share of the market, and from economic weakness in East Asia and in Europe.

The International Energy Agency

Organizations have at least two aims: to get something done and to maintain themselves as organizations. Many of their activities are directed toward the second purpose.

Kenneth Waltz

Since most international organizations are manifestations of the interests of the current hegemonic power (or powers), the International Energy Agency was (and remains) primarily a reflection of American and (to a lesser degree) European interests and concerns. This recognition that international institutions serve the interests of the powers that created them is nothing new, but this doesn't preclude such institutions' gaining a capacity for efficacy and a degree of autonomy from their member states.

Before the oil shocks of 1973, the energy committees of the OECD countries had typically governed matters of energy in the international sphere. The OAPEC embargo thrust energy into the realm of high politics, where it would remain until the early 1990s. The IEA was deliberately fashioned by Secretary of State Henry Kissinger as a counterbalancing mechanism to OPEC for the purpose of warding off future oil shocks to the OECD countries. The IEA took its explicit form in the Agreement on an International Energy Program of November 18, 1974, which was adopted by 16 OECD countries and which formally established the organization.[41] The treaty was designed to ensure security of energy supplies, and to avoid competitive scrambles for energy supplies that could undercut international cooperation and damage the global economy. Furthermore, the IEA was meant to foster collaboration among its member states in the formulation and execution of energy policies, and thereby to deter the use of oil as a weapon by oil-producing countries.[42]

The principal goals of the IEA are to mitigate or minimize possible supply disruptions through a system of emergency oil sharing between member states, to promote effective and collaborative energy policies among countries, to maintain an information exchange system regarding global oil reserves, production and markets, to promote sources of alternative energy and augment energy efficiency, to augment the development and exchange of energy technology on a global scale, and to promote integrated environmental and energy policies.[43] As of 2008, 28 countries were members of the IEA, all of them also members of the OECD. Requiring OECD membership is increasingly problematic, as it precludes China and India. For the United States, membership in the IEA entailed some domestic institutional changes, among them the creation of the US Department of Energy in 1977. The federal government also enacted a number of domestic laws (notably the establishment of the CAFE standards in 1975[44]) in order to diminish the energy intensiveness of the US economy and reduce the burden of the country's increasing dependence on foreign oil. Perhaps the greatest domestic consequence resulting from membership in the IEA was the creation of the global Strategic Petroleum Reserve system, each national reserve holding 90 days' worth of crude oil. The establishment of such domestic reserve systems required the IEA to develop two formal modes of response to oil shocks: the International Energy Program and the Coordinated Emergency Response Mechanism.[45]

Under the provisions of the International Emergency Program (IEP), founded in 1974, all IEA members are required to devise measures of oil demand restraint to reduce ultimate rates of consumption during a crisis. According to the political scientist John Duffield, "whenever the group as a whole sustains an oil supply reduction of at least 7 percent, each country must reduce its consumption by that amount."[46] In 1979 the IEA established the Coordinated Emergency Response Measures (CERM) system, that involved a new set of procedures to permit a rapid response to those supply disruptions that were significant yet failed to reach the 7 percent threshold.[47] The system was used successfully by the United States, Germany, and Japan during the Gulf War of 1991, and again in 2006 after Hurricane Katrina.[48]

Another mechanism that was adopted was the Emergency Sharing System. As Duffield notes, the ESS consists of "treaty-based, obligatory measures for preparing for and responding to short-term supply disruptions. In particular, it requires members (1) to build and maintain substantial levels of oil stocks; (2) to plan and implement, if necessary, measures to reduce oil consumption during interruptions, and (3) to allocate available oil supplies equitably among IEA members in an emergency."[49] The sharing mechanism would be the first line of defense, although it would be accompanied by measures to reduce demand and by attempts to use alternative fuels. Interestingly, the sharing mechanism implies that during a global shortfall in stocks of crude oil the United States might be obliged to share its domestic oil supplies with other participating countries.[50]

Although this burden of sharing is specified in the language of the ESS, expectations of such sharing by the United States during a time of extreme crisis is not politically realistic. Simply put, to ask one of the greatest oil addicts on the planet to share its hoard with others during a time of extreme scarcity reflects a profound misunderstanding of US domestic politics. Any elected representative, even the president, would be vilified for sharing American energy reserves with other countries, presumably by both Republicans and Democrats.

The IEA also functions as a global clearinghouse for information regarding the reserves, production, and pricing of oil. The database of the International Energy Forum was created to enable energy producers and energy consumers to share information, to promote informal dialogue, and thereby to lower transaction costs. It allows "market players" to "enhance their knowledge about present and (expected) future national, regional and global consumption levels, thus fostering planning security."[51] However, the IEF's function is increasingly problematic, given that many oil-producing countries (particularly members of OPEC) have a significant economic incentive to exaggerate their reported reserves. Exaggeration of reserves allows OPEC countries to increase their allowable production levels under OPEC quota agreements. Moreover, data are reported to the IEA by those same governments without any significant third-party oversight, so data may be readily manipulated and/or falsified. On any given day the IEA is simply a data mine for consumer countries, and an occasional forum for discussion. Unfortunately, the high levels of cooperation that were supposed to occur between countries, in order to help them formulate and implement a more efficient allocation of global energy resources, haven't been seen. Cooperation has been sporadic at best.

Academic proponents of the IEA trumpet the success of international cooperation in the domain of energy. For example, the archetypal liberals Goldthau and Witte argue that "the consumers' quest for supply security is met by the producers' quest for demand security. And while new consumers have an interest in overcoming the disadvantages they experience as latecomers on the global market, old consumers have an interest in accommodating them at least possible cost, which means in a conflict-free manner."[52] Goldthau and Witte assume that existing consumers can and will accommodate new entrants to the field simply by adjusting internal consumption patterns, and that producers will readily respond with increased production. Such logic is intrinsically flawed because it assumes that consumers can readily alter their path-dependent domestic infrastructure and institutions, and that producers can *always* generate an adequate supply of oil to meet inexorably increasing global demand. In view of the limited elasticity of demand for oil and gasoline and rigid domestic path dependencies, it is not at all clear that the US could simply and rapidly adjust its internal consumption patterns to deal with global supply shortfalls or surges in demand. In view of the inelasticity of the supply and the long lead times

associated with developing new oil fields, it is not at all clear that producers—not even the Saudis—can simply increase the supply of oil.

Furthermore, the use of mechanisms such as the SPR to moderate global
spikes in oil prices can be problematic. During the Libyan uprising against
Colonel Moammar Qaddaffi in the spring of 2011, President Obama used
the IEA's SPR mechanism to encourage a number of states to release oil from
their respective SPRs, in order to compensate for Libya's lost production of
crude oil. On June 23, 2011, when the Obama administration announced
the collective coordinated SPR release, the price of a barrel of Brent Crude
was $116.79 and the price of a barrel of WTI was $98.97. As a consequence
of the release, the price of WTI dropped to $78.32 per barrel on August 9, but
then it rose rapidly, hitting $90 per barrel on September 13 and $102.59 on
November 16.[53] The price of Brent hit a nadir of $106.26 per barrel in Decem-
ber of 2011, but then surged back to $126 per barrel in March of 2012.[54]

Despite the SPR-release-induced decline in the prices of Brent and WTI,
speculators gradually bid the price up again over a matter of months. Thus,
the efficacy of the SPR mechanism seems rather contingent on the time
span. Coordinated SPR releases can be quite effective over a relatively brief
span of time, but such releases aren't likely to moderate price increases over
the longer term. Whether targeted and random periodic SPR releases could
effectively dampen speculative activity in crude-oil futures over the longer
term is debatable.

NAFTA and Oil

Since the 1980s the United States has sought permanent access to Canadian
energy reserves in order to secure both energy security and national security.
The US ensured such access through the mechanism of the North American
Free Trade Agreement, concluded in 1988 between the Reagan administration and the Mulroney administration. This was executed through Article
904. According to the historian Stephen Randall, this clause "stipulates that
while either country might restrict energy resources if required to conserve
resources or to deal with a short-supply situation, as permitted under GATT,
it could do so only if the restriction did not reduce the proportion historically available, impose a higher export than domestic price, or disrupt
the normal channels of supply or the mix of energy products supplied to
the other country."[55] Put simply, it obligates Canada to provide continual

energy (i.e., petroleum) exports to the US, prohibits Canada from enacting tariffs on external sources of energy, and ensures that Canadian export prices of petroleum are consistent with Canadian domestic prices. Another complexity of the NAFTA agreement is the "proportional sharing rule," which appears in both Article 315 and Article 605(a). According to this rule, Canada is obligated to continue both the proportional quantity, and the equivalent quality, of energy exports to the United States, even in times of scarcity. Further, this rule makes no exception for a global supply shock. Such protocols don't apply to Mexico, which shrewdly sought exemptions:

Subject to Annex 605, a Party may adopt or maintain a restriction otherwise justified under Article XI:2(a) or XX(g), (i) or (j) of the GATT with respect to the export of an energy or basic petrochemical good to the territory of another Party, only if:

(a) the restriction does not reduce the proportion of the total export shipments of the specific energy or basic petrochemical good made available to that other Party relative to the total supply of that good of the Party maintaining the restriction as compared to the proportion prevailing in the most recent 36-month period for which data are available prior to the imposition of the measure, or in such other representative period on which the Parties may agree.[56]

In the face of a global supply crunch (not probable in the near future), this protocol would undoubtedly significant generate economic losses and political tensions in Canada, and mobilize Canada's political elites to protect the country's economy. Thus, in the face of a future demand shock, the NAFTA accords could sow a considerable degree of political discord between the United States and Canada. NAFTA further undermines Canadian energy sovereignty by providing US multinational corporations with their own enforcement mechanisms. Specifically, chapter 11 of the NAFTA accords provides a mechanism for these corporations to sue the federal governments for alleged violations of NAFTA rules. All suits are adjudicated by NAFTA tribunals, whose decisions take precedence over domestic laws of the member countries.[57]

Institutional Efficacy

International institutions exhibit properties of "stickiness" in that they tend to persist, regardless of need or efficacy. In this sense the IEA is certainly sticky, but we can legitimately ask whether the organization is in fact effective. The persistence of an institution doesn't necessarily mean that it is useful. Perhaps the greatest problem with the IEA's mechanism for the sharing of oil is that it wouldn't come into play unless countries experienced a shortfall in oil supplies of at least 7 percent in imports of crude oil. Thus, a global supply disruption that resulted in a shortfall of 6 percent (which would generate considerable price increases and economic dislocation) wouldn't trigger the sharing mechanism.[58] Duffield also points out that the international response under the current architecture of the ESS might be slow: "As many as 24 days could transpire between the necessary finding by the secretariat and the implementation of emergency measures, during which affected states might have to use a substantial share of their oil stocks."[59] The Emergency Sharing System has failed in the past—notably in March of 1979, when Sweden suffered a supply shortfall of about 17 percent and asked for activation of the ESS. Unfortunately, the ESS secretariat declined to rule that this exigency required activation of the sharing mechanism, arguing that Sweden's problems were the product of "special conditions."[60]

Furthermore, the IEA failed abjectly to remedy the crude-oil price spike of 2007–08 by using any of the mechanisms at its disposal. During that episode, IEA countries resolutely refused to release stocks from their SPR systems in order to contain the rampant speculation that dominated global oil markets, or even to issue verbal signals to the market that they would take action to contain the speculation. As the Saudis pointed out at the time, soaring crude-oil prices didn't reflect any empirical physical scarcity of crude oil in the face of soaring global demand. Rather, the price spike was simply a function of speculators' diverting their money into commodities as a hedge against the collapse of the housing and equity markets. Beaubouef concurs that this is a problem with the IEA in general, and the SPR mechanism in particular, arguing that "oil crises should be viewed through the lens of price, not volume," and "thus the policy of waiting for shortages ... was fundamentally flawed."[61]

Furthermore, as with most international organizations, the IEA can only act in an advisory capacity; it has no enforcement mechanism to ensure that member countries comply with its rulings. As Kohl notes, "the IEA cannot force its members (which are sovereign governments) to adopt policies. It can only make recommendations. The additional function that it can occasionally perform is the issuance of 'report cards' on country behavior."[62] Thus, the IEA's enforcement mechanisms amount to nothing more than a slap on the wrist for noncompliance. In the event of a global oil supply shortfall, the IEA secretariat could order a mobilization of the ESS; however, the US could simply refuse to comply with that ruling, and the mechanism wouldn't function properly. Vernon also expressed doubt that the ESS would be effective: "[T]he ideological reluctance of the US government to consider how the sharing formula might actually work in an emergency practically guarantees that it will not work very well. Besides, only an interruption of the first magnitude ... would bring the plan into play."[63] Despite the fact that multilateral sharing is a rational course of action during a global demand shock, states may not adopt such a policy, often because of political games played by powerful factions at the domestic level. A lack of sharing between sovereign states in a crisis situation is certainly not inconceivable, as the US has often found the strictures of international law to be rather inconvenient to its interests.[64]

With its current mandate and structure, the IEA is limited in its capacity to address the rapacity of new energy consumers, particularly China and India. Because they are excluded from membership in the OECD, China and India remain excluded from the IEA's institutional framework that deals with management of short-term supply disruptions; they are also removed from the SPR and ESS mechanisms.[65] The exclusion of these rising consumers also poses challenges for integrity of the data shared by the IEA, "given that new consumers and major producing countries fail to publish crucial data on market fundamentals, markets are characterized by increasingly significant uncertainty."[66] Thus, a sensible course of action that the US should propose to the OECD would entail an expansion of the IEA to include China and India. The US should certainly consider the inclusion of Brazil as well, in view of its recent enormous petroleum discoveries and its impressive capacity to produce cellulosic ethanol.

The IEA faces additional problems in containing excess volatility and turbulence in global crude-oil markets, notably with respect to "paper barrels" and speculative activity. During a conversation at the University of Texas in Austin, I asked Ethan Kapstein "Is the IEA capable of effectively dealing with the problem of speculation?" Kapstein answered:

No, because there is an economic problem there regarding the optimal use of a stockpile. And there is a fundamental problem, if you are in the midst of a shortage where prices are increasing, and you believe that you are on that trajectory, then you may actually add to your stockpile—rather than deplete it. So, in a sense, a stockpile is pro-cyclical in a way, rather than counter-cyclical. Then you'll buy the oil when it is very cheap, but you won't necessarily release it when oil is dear. Because if you believe it is becoming even more expensive, or because of a political crisis or war, then it's going to become scarcer, and you are not going to release it. So, when do you release the oil? And I don't believe they have solved that question. Then there are free-rider problems. I think there are these very fundamental, foundational issues that they've never managed to resolve, as far as I can tell. It seems that if the IEA has changed over time, it's become much more of an informational institution, and it's become the authoritative institution in terms of energy statistics. And maybe that is a useful function.[67]

In defense of the IEA, Goldthau and Witte argue that "price stability through national or even international policy intervention is an unattainable goal."[68] Perhaps so, but the increased volatility in oil prices of the early twenty-first century represents a challenge to the stability of the global economy. Even if we can't ensure a modicum of global oil-price stability (something that the Saudis want as well), we can at least work to minimize the price volatility that generates boom-and-bust cycles and induces major recessions. Setting minimum global prices (price floors) may begin to reduce volatility, create incentives for longer-term sustained capital investment, and eventually create incentives for the development of alternative fuels.

The IEA is, essentially, a mechanism to counterbalance the formation of the OPEC cartel. Both oil-producing countries and oil-consuming countries manufactured international organizations to protect their national and collective interests. OPEC was originally intended to offset the power and depredations of the international oil companies and the Western developed countries that had originally backed them, particularly the United States and Britain.[69] The IEA then was a counter to that alliance of developing non-Western producer states, and it is best conceptualized as a mechanism of collective energy security to counter the machinations of OPEC. One might equate this behavior to the concept of "balancing" in the realm of international relations, which posits that states will create coalitions to balance against powerful states or alliances. In this particular case, coalitions or factions of sovereign states created international organizations to balance (in a macro sense) against corporations, and then against other sovereign states.

Thus, the dynamic of tension between the IEA and OPEC is an interesting example of *competing* international organizations that are often (and increasingly) working at cross-purposes—particularly when the "hawks" dominate the policy-making process within OPEC.

The IEA has produced a degree of international cooperation, but largely in the field of data sharing. Unfortunately, it has generated little in the way of proactive adaptation by its member countries. This is particularly true of the United States, as it remains addicted to oil, with few gains in fuel efficiency to report. Even though the Obama administration has mandated significant improvements in domestic engine efficiency, that initiative has little to do with the desires of the IEA.

Energy Regimes

It can be argued that the ECO, the ECSC, OPEC, and the IEA constitute a nascent international energy regime. Stephen Krasner's classic definition holds that regimes are explicit or implicit "principles, rules, norms, and decision making procedures around which actor-expectations converge in a given issue area."[70] On the nature of regimes, Joseph Nye writes: "When generally accepted rules, norms, or procedures exist in a given issue area, we speak of an international regime governing the issue. Regimes generally reflect the power of states at the time of the regime formation, and they tend to erode or change as the structure of power changes in general or in the specific issue area."[71]

Goldthau and Witte argue that a global energy regime does in fact exist, and that it is robust. I concede that a global energy regime exists, but that it is focused primarily on nuclear energy and on containing the risk of nuclear proliferation. The energy regime is much weaker in the domains of crude oil and renewable energy; indeed, one is tempted to relegate this non-nuclear mechanism to the status of a quasi-regime at best. Pursuant to that, the United States is party to ten international protocols in the domain of oil, notably the following:

• the International Convention for the Prevention of Pollution of the Sea by Oil (1954, signed by US in 1961)

• an agreement regarding levels of Canadian oil exports and the proposed looping of the Interprovincial Pipeline via Chicago (1967)

• the International Convention Relating to Intervention on the High Seas in Cases of Oil Pollution Casualties (1969)

- the Agreement Relating to the Establishment of Joint Pollution Contingency Plans for Spills of Oil and Other Noxious Substances (1974)

- an implementing agreement for a program of research, development, and demonstration on enhanced recovery of oil (1979)

- an implementing agreement for a program of research, development, and demonstration on coal/oil mixtures (1981)

- the Protocol Concerning Co-operation in Combating Oil Spills in the Wider Caribbean Region (1983)

- an agreement relating to jurisdiction over vessels utilizing the Louisiana Offshore Oil Port (1984)

- the International Convention on Oil Pollution Preparedness, Response and Co-operation (1990)

- a memorandum of agreement concerning an oil supply arrangement, with related understanding (1979; amended and extended 2004)

Five of these ten protocols explicitly deal with oil pollution and therefore are also elements of the global environmental regime.

The patterns of institutions, norms, and rules that govern global movements of oil and energy flows have changed significantly since the formation of OPEC. The 1960s were characterized by conditions of oligopoly as the "seven sisters" determined how much oil would be produced, set prices, and maintained close ties with the governments of consumer countries (particularly the US and the UK). The great powers often maintained the unequal structure of the oil markets through military intervention.[72] Although OPEC was formed in 1960, the most significant transition in the regime governing global oil markets occurred after 1971, when there was a tremendous shift in wealth from affluent to poor states. Nye explains how decolonization affected this process:

In 1960, half the OPEC countries were colonies of Europe; by 1973, they were all independent. Accompanying the rise in nationalism was a rise in the costs of military intervention. The relative symmetry of economic power in oil markets also changed. During the two Middle East wars of 1956 and 1967, the Arab countries tried an oil embargo, but their efforts were easily defeated because the United States was producing enough oil to supply Europe when it was cut off by the Arab countries. Once American production peaked in 1971 and the United States began to import oil, the power to balance the oil market switched to such countries as Saudi Arabia and Iran.[73]

Thus, the period 1971–1973 saw a major shift of economic power away from the United States and toward OPEC and other major oil producers. Not coincidentally, the "seven sisters" lost a considerable degree of power after 1971, ceding much of the world's remaining reserves of crude oil to the national oil companies. Nye concurs that a weak quasi-regime has emerged, but that it has "eroded and not been replaced."[74] Under this quasi-regime, "supply was assured by efficient operations of the companies under a Pax Americana that involved only an occasional diplomatic assurance of access, or antitrust measures to assure a modicum of cooperation."[75] However, Nye conveniently omits the illiberal actions of the Western powers that buttressed this quasi-regime, specifically the odious Operation Ajax and the oppressive Twin Pillars strategy.

Other components of this existing quasi-regime include the Energy Charter Treaty of 1994, which focuses on the energy sector and which links open investment regimes with free-market policies. Unfortunately, many of the signatories have failed to ratify the treaty, and it is observed only by certain countries (and not by the US). Thus, the ECT remains an extremely weak mechanism of global energy governance. The quasi-regime also contains institutions such as the International Energy Forum (IEF), which was created in 2003 under the Lisbon Treaty to serve as a ministerial-level forum for discourse between consumers and producers. According to Kohl, the Lisbon Treaty "contains a strong basis for a common energy policy,"[76] although, like the Energy Charter, it has yet to be ratified by most member states. The problem for the liberal optimist camp is that an energy quasi-regime (particularly those aspects that deal with oil and its distillates) appears to be primarily a result of hegemonic power structures. As such, the existing quasi-regime merely reinforces the status quo of political and economic power distributions that existed during its formation.

In view of the waning power of the international oil companies, which now control only 5 percent of the world's remaining reserves of crude oil,[77] the United States' policy of reliance on the IOCs is fraught with uncertainty. American energy security is based on the archaic model of the IOCs as agents of price moderation, but the IOCs no longer possess such capabilities. However, I argue that IOC-led advances in technology should lead to IOC-NOC partnerships that may make the American model more feasible.

Goldthau and Witte, emphasizing the "rules of the game," suggest that international norms, codes of conduct, organizations, and markets have created an orderly dynamic within which international energy markets operate: "These rules of the game—that is to say, the institutional architecture that underpins global energy—govern central aspects of financing, trading, and hedging oil and gas ventures via financial markets, investment treaties, and trade agreements. These rules also address short-term supply risks in the event of market failure or disruption."[78] This concept is valid to an extent, yet Goldthau and Witte all too frequently neglect questions of political power in their framework. For example, many treaties and trade agreements are valid only as long as the signatories choose to observe them.

For example, Russia has often found it expedient to abrogate its written energy trade agreements with Ukraine, and with the various international oil companies that assisted in the development of new fields such as those at Sakhalin. Hence, the rules of the game would only seem to apply to the weaker parties in the international system, and the great powers (or hegemonic aspirants) often play by their own sets of rules.

This is not to adopt the realist position that norms and regimes don't matter; that is simply incorrect. Rather, I argue that regime formation and regime compliance are often simply functions of the distribution of political power and of the efficacy of enforcement mechanisms. The international energy quasi-regime that developed after 1914 is based upon the interests of the dominant or hegemonic powers, primarily the US. In this sense the articulation of a darker variant of liberalism accepts that norms, treaties, and regimes can encourage cooperation between sovereign states, but that they illustrate the distribution of power and capacity *ex ante*. Thus, such norms and regimes may not be honored by powerful states whose interests diverge from the treaty, institution, or regime in question.

Illiberalism and Power

The crisis of governance in the West that has persisted since 2007 presents a challenge to the international liberal order that was fashioned in the aftermath of World War II. One finds evidence of this in the pervasive fragility and ineffectiveness of international institutions—the near economic collapse of the European Union in the years 2011–2013, the inability of the United Nations to broker substantive and progressive climate accords, and the continued weakness of the International Energy Agency. The unilateral and often bellicose behavior of the United States in the first decade of the twenty-first century also presents a profound challenge to archetypal liberal assumptions that the US acts consistently as a benign hegemon.

I have argued that even though the US played the role of the benign hegemon generating public goods in Europe after 1945, it simultaneously pursued a strategy of illiberalism in many developing countries. In doing so, it supported authoritarian regimes throughout the Persian Gulf, Latin America, and South Asia from 1945 to 2013. In this sense, arguments that characterize the US as a benign hegemon (particularly in the domain of energy) are largely contextual and apply only to Europe. In the wake of the attacks of September 11, 2001, the US again engaged in some extremely illiberal behavior, such as the invasion of Iraq in 2003.[79] Thus, the portrait of the US as a benign hegemon, as a fundamentally liberal power, is some-what at odds with its actual behavior *outside of Europe* in the early years of the twenty-first century.

In the twenty-first century, the United States is not subject to the self-restraint that it demonstrated at various times in the twentieth century. Kapstein argues that there are problems with archetypal liberal arguments that the US is party to the norms of self-binding and cooperation with other polities—arguments frequently articulated by Nye, as in this passage:

There are positive problems and normative problems, if you will. The normative problems are that there is an implicit assumption in that literature that the US high-ly values cooperation with other countries. To me that's an assertion that may not be grounded empirically. My impression is that cooperation is very fitful, very contex-tual, very contingent, and if the US had a longer term policy of cooperation as with some of the international institutions like the IMF, GATT, that was because of the confluence of domestic interests which supported those kinds of institutions, which favored their creation. So, I think to believe that there is some transcendent value in cooperation that the US has, I just don't know how well grounded in historical truth that is. From the positive angle, if you look at various issue areas, you will see how US policy was decisively shaped by domestic interests, and oil policy is a classic example of that. Basically the US created a two-tier market in the 1950s. That was purely for reasons of domestic politics. If you look across issue areas these no longer become exceptions to the rule, they become the rule.[80]

A New Cooperation?

Daniel Yergin argues that we have seen "a larger shift in relations among oil-importing and oil-exporting countries, away from the confrontation of the 1970s to what has become known as consumer-producer dialogue."[81]

Through the emergence of this dialogue, he asserts, we have reached a new level of international cooperation in the domain of energy. This claim is consistent with the archetypal liberal position that cooperation is the dominant mode of interaction between countries in the sphere of global energy resources.

Yergin's ebullient claim is problematic for several reasons. First, it ignores the increasingly hawkish behavior exhibited since 2004 by two major OPEC producers, Iran and Venezuela. Their apparent hostility toward the dovish Saudis manifested in open diplomatic confrontation during OPEC meetings in 2011, and has contributed in recent years to the very high price of crude oil, which has arguably dampened the global economic recovery. Though OPEC has always had "hawkish" and "dovish" factions, and its members have habitually engaged in cheating on quotas, recent tensions within the organization point to a new level of discord among the producers. Thus, Yergin's assertion of a constructive dialogue is a bit overstated, insofar as the producers can't even seem to agree among themselves on optimal oil prices or on production targets. In 2014 the Saudis argued against OPEC production cuts, presumably to drive North American producers of unconventional oil out of business and perhaps also to harm Russian and Iranian interests.

On the consumer side, divisions have emerged over which model is most effective: the classic American model (based on IOCs and global markets), or the neo-mercantilist Chinese model (based on NOCs and bilateral contracts with oil-producing countries). To argue that the US and China share a vision of energy resource development, based on free market dynamics, is either extraordinarily naive or ethnocentric. Despite the optimistic claims of Yergin and Nye regarding substantially increased levels of international cooperation in the issue area of oil, solid evidence of cooperation, much less of its efficacy, is lacking. Certainly there is more cooperation between producers and consumers than there was during the acrimonious 1970s, but in the twenty-first century cooperation doesn't seem any more robust than it was in the 1980s or in the 1990s. Therefore, the talk of a "new dialogue" and new levels of cooperation seems exaggerated.

This is not to argue that the realm of international energy politics is utterly anarchic, or that it is exceptionally competitive and prone to the rancorous scrambles for energy that occurred during the first decades of the twentieth century. There are strong incentives for countries to cooperate on the basis of their shared interests, and on any given day the system tends to exhibit what Hedley Bull, in his book *The Anarchical Society*, called a "society of states." Wars over energy resources are still exceedingly rare, and there have been no wars between the great powers over energy resources since the 1940s. There is a basic congruence of interest in this "society of states," and the dominant mode of interaction in the domain of energy is generally pacific, though punctuated by occasional conflicts.

Despite the wars that have occurred in the Persian Gulf since 1980, dire predictions of resource-based conflict between the great powers have not been fulfilled. However, it is similarly incorrect to adopt archetypal liberal arguments that a robust global energy regime exists, underpinned by strong institutions and norms. The existing institutional architecture of the energy quasi-regime is quite frail and may not be capable of mitigating demand shocks, the negative effects of prolonged supply shortfalls, and/or the price spikes that often threaten the resilience of the global economy.

4 Oil and International Security

For I have sworn thee fair, and thought thee bright,
who art as black as hell, as dark as night.
William Shakespeare, Sonnet 147

Energy and National Security

The United States has long recognized the strategic importance of oil to its
national security. Energy resources power the engines of the economy and
provide for the national defense, and thus are crucial to both the vitality of
the body politic and the capacity of the state. Because of the centrality of
energy to national power, the availability of cheap oil was instrumental in
the rise of American power in the twentieth century, propelling the might
of the American economy and offering a significant advantage to US military forces in both world wars.

On the surface, the mechanisms of maintaining US energy security, as
expressed through global markets, international institutions, and the work-
ings of the international oil corporations, appear to be highly liberal. The
archetypal liberal explanation for the United States' behavior is rooted in
the ideological construct that the US simply acts as a benign hegemon that
seeks to maintain global flows of energy (particularly petroleum) as a global
public good. However, I argue that the core of US foreign energy policy frequently exhibits a fundamentally illiberal character, and this is particularly
true of US military actions taken in the domain of energy.

In this chapter I advance several further arguments:

• Material forces exert an enormous (but often ignored) influence on the
United States' security decision making and on its grand strategy. Purely
ideational explanations that ignore the role of the material (*physis*) are
insufficient.

- Perceptions and misperceptions regarding the availability of energy (e.g., oil) may affect decision making in a substantive fashion, and may result in deviations from rationality that contribute to the onset of conflicts, such as the United States' problematic decision to invade Iraq in 2003.

- Oil acts as a mechanism that exacerbates the security dilemma in the Persian Gulf. Oil resources serve as a target of aggression, and revenue flows from oil foster militarization and intensify a regional arms race that has sporadically resulted in powerful manifestations of inter-state violence.

- The United States' various interventions in the Persian Gulf (Operation Ajax, the Twin Pillars strategy, Desert Storm, the Iraq War) are significant manifestations of its often illiberal behavior in the domain of foreign energy policy. Such interventions illustrate the United States' desire to maintain its hegemony over the energy resources of the region and to prevent the rise of a regional hegemon that could attain dominance over much of the world's oil supply.

- Although the Iraq War (2003–2012) wasn't entirely about oil, oil was a significant factor in the decision by the Bush administration to undertake the invasion of Iraq in 2003.

Historically, inter-state wars over petroleum resources have been driven by the material/psychological combination of perceptions of scarcity and the empirical reality of scarcity. For example, during World War II the Axis powers experienced an empirical scarcity of oil that drove them to undertake risky (and ultimately irrational) decisions. As was noted above, the United States' oil embargo of 1941 was a central factor in Japan's decision to attack Pearl Harbor in December of that year. The physical scarcity of oil in Central Europe figured in Nazi Germany's decision to invade the Soviet Union (Operation Barbarossa) in June of 1941, as Berlin sought to control the oil fields of the southwestern USSR. Ultimately, those decisions proved highly self-destructive to Japan and to Germany.

Energy security has long been a central theme of older strains of realist thought, particularly in the work of Hans Morgenthau, James Schlesinger, N. J. Spykman, and David Deese.[1] The role of petroleum was also given considerable weight in the literature on hegemonic stability. Robert Gilpin argued that "there are three sources of power in the modern world: nuclear weapons, monetary reserves, and petroleum."[2] Kenneth Waltz wrote that oil was "the only economic interest for which the United States may have to fight."[3] Despite the earlier emphasis on energy by the classical realists, oil has all but disappeared from the writings of the modern structural realists, but it appears in the quasi-realist works of Stokes and Raphael, Stulberg, and Klare.

As was noted above, the United States has been cognizant of the nexus between oil and national security since World War I, but such concerns intensified as a function of the Arab oil embargo of 1973. As the Yom Kippur War drew to a close, the OAPEC embargo resulted in considerable economic dislocation for the US. At the time, Henry Kissinger briefly discussed the possibility of using US military force to seize control of the oil fields of the Persian Gulf, and the Department of Defense went so far as to create contingency plans to intervene in the region.[4]

By the early 1980s, the manipulation of oil in order to assert power asymmetries was clearly an established mechanism of political power, and was increasingly a threat to international security. In the wake of the oil embargoes of the 1970s, liberal internationalists were also cognizant of the dangers arising from the denial or manipulation of energy resources. Joseph Nye argued that acute energy vulnerability constituted "a clear and present danger to the security of individual nations and to the international order."[5] Robert Keohane argued that the attainment of hegemony required a "preponderance of material resources,"[6] particularly energy reserves, in order to foster economic productivity and to maintain military dominance. Such positions weren't confined to academe. "Ever since the industrial revolution," former Secretary of Defense and Secretary of Energy James Schlesinger argued, "energy and the need to secure its supply have been fundamental to any position of power in the world."[7]

One of the earliest academic proponents of the linkages between natural resources and conflict was Arthur Westing. He posited that a lack of resources, particularly energy resources, threatened the vitality of the state, as "essentially all nations depend upon external sources of at least some natural resources for their continued development, and even for their survival."[8] Furthermore, Westing argued,

A number of wars ... have been fought over oil. For example in the Chaco War of 1932–35, Paraguay annexed a region of Bolivia in the mistaken belief that it contained oil deposits. ... France was reluctant to lose Algeria in the latter's war of independence of 1954-62 partly because of Algeria's oil deposits, but was unable to prevail. ... Similarly, Nigeria was reluctant to lose Biafra in the latter's bid for independence in 1967–70 in large part owing to local oil deposits, and was able to thwart Biafra's attempt at secession. The Paracel (Hsi-sha) Island Clash of 1974, in which China routed Vietnam in re-establishing its claim to this island group in the South China Sea, was apparently motivated chiefly by the presumed offshore oil deposits ... .[9]

The national security of the US is now inextricably linked to global energy markets, as expressed through the dynamics of complex interdependence. The US continues to act in benign hegemonic fashion to guarantee the protection of global energy-supply lines; however, the provision of such global public goods helps to maintain its structural economic power. "By acting as the ultimate guarantor of global energy security," Stokes and Raphael argue, "US hegemony is consolidated, with potential rivals to its position forced to be (and in some instances content to be) reliant upon American power."[10] Thus, US actions in the domain of energy foreign policy exhibit properties of both liberalism and illiberalism, and thus defy simplistic categorization as either liberal (in the archetypal sense) or realist.

Scholars of offensive realism (e.g., John Mearsheimer) and of structural realism (Kenneth Waltz) argue that US actions abroad are primarily driven by the balance of relative power between sovereign states, within the overarching context of competitive anarchy that forces all states to seek survival. Survival is consequently ensured through the maximization of power, typically through the development of military force. However, structural realist conceptualizations of international politics fail to explain the actions of the US in international energy politics. A realist argument could be made that the US-led war against Iraq in 1990–91 was an attempt to contain Iraq's aspirations for regional hegemony, and that such hegemony over the Persian Gulf might threaten the global economy and hence US interests. However, structural realist arguments can't explain the invasion of Iraq in 2003, as Iraq was quite incapable of any such bid for regional (let alone global) hegemony at the time. No stretch of structural realist logic could possibly conclude that Iraq in 2003 was a rising power with aspirations to peer-competitor status, and therefore a serious threat to US hegemony.[11] Thus, the distribution of power in the international system has little if any explanatory capacity regarding the United States' military incursions into the Persian Gulf since 2000. Nonetheless, certain elements of classical realist thought[12]—particularly the security dilemma and the emphasis on materialism—remain valuable in explaining the sporadic outbreaks of conflict, and US military intervention, in the Persian Gulf region.

Archetypal liberals typically argue that the provision of such global public goods illustrates the benign hegemony of the United States.[13] However, one must note that this modern "liberal" architecture of energy interdependence was deliberately fostered by hegemonic powers (first Britain, then the United States) in order to maintain their respective positions of military and economic dominance. With the contraction of the British Empire through processes of decolonization after 1945, and consequently Britain's withdrawal from the Persian Gulf region (circa 1971), a power vacuum ensued in the region. In the context of the Cold War, the United States' informal guarantees to Saudi Arabia, and the debacle of Operation Ajax in Iran, it was hardly surprising that the US chose to fill the vacuum left by Britain's retreat. Since then, the US has been deeply involved in the turbulent geopolitics of the Persian Gulf region.

Consequently, what appears on the surface to be the liberal behavior of a benign hegemon often masks illiberal motives, and in this sense the behavior of the United States is quite consistent with the tenets of shadow liberalism.[14] Thus, the US uses its significant capacity to project military power to maintain global energy flows, largely in order to maintain its economic and hegemonic power. It then casts its behavior as benign, through the provision of global public goods for the benefit of all peoples, which is a carefully honed artifice. By focusing the perceptions of the American public on the United States' provision of global public goods, rather than on the United States' preservation of its hegemonic power through often illiberal tactics, this artifice is maintained.

This combination of the liberal and illiberal aspects of US hegemony infuses the history of US energy foreign policy. All hegemonic powers have, at various times, claimed to have crafted international laws and treaties, provided international public goods, and projected military and economic power in various forms, in order to guarantee the stability of the current "order." US policy makers often fail to see that the maintenance of hierarchy required by such hegemony inevitably results in increasing inequities of power and wealth and in increasing resentment by weaker countries toward the hegemon.

The Energy-Security Nexus

The national security of the United States may be damaged by disruptions to the energy supply, which may occur through several mechanisms. Economic security may be impaired by the transference of riches to producer countries as a result of oil imports, and through an inflationary effect on the price of goods (particularly foodstuffs). However, disruptions to the energy supply may also engender threats to public order, and to health when energy isn't available at a price that by the majority of the body politic can afford.

One is reminded here of the work of Hendrik Spruyt and Charles Tilly regarding their analysis of the extraction-coercion cycles that led to the rise of the modern state.[15] The military (the apparatus of coercion) initially requires access to energy in order to gain and maintain dominance over competitor countries. To slake its thirst for oil, the state must then work with the apparatus of energy extraction (industry) under a set of favorable conditions (e.g., subsidies) maintained by the bureaucracy. However, in order to reinforce the state's capacity for extraction, which entails expansion beyond the physical boundaries of the country, ever more military power must be deployed to protect the flows of energy. This, in turn, increases the very amount of energy required to project power abroad. Since 1914 we have seen the intensification of this ever more powerful (and problematic) feedback loop, as it has drawn the US military into regions of the world that it might wisely have avoided.

The energy pessimism of the early 2000s, as reflected in the works of the neo-Malthusians (among them Matthew Simmons, Michael Klare, and Thomas Homer-Dixon), predicted a world of increasing oil scarcity, increasing statism, and inter-state conflict. Paradoxically, the adoption of such Malthusian beliefs by American policy makers in the first decade of the twenty-first century, and the filtering of perceptions through such belief structures, may have contributed to the some of the bellicose actions of the United States under the Bush administration, particularly the invasion of Iraq. The illiberal currents that have permeated US energy foreign policy for decades may be exacerbated under future scenarios of declining oil production, but these projected declines in domestic (and global) production may not be imminent. The rise of new technologies to extract oil from unconventional sources, and increased domestic oil production, may reduce Americans' perceptions of energy insecurity. Consequently, these factors may begin to mitigate the United States' illiberal tendencies to some degree.

In 2005, the Bush administration and National Commission on Energy Policy conducted a simulation called Oil Shockwave and determined that even a relatively minor disruption in the global oil supply could generate exponential economic damage, in this case resulting in a 177 percent increase in the global price of oil.[16]

With increases in the world's global population and in consumption, Michael Klare argues, oil will revert to a strategic commodity that will generate scrambles and inter-state rivalry. "In the emerging international power system," he writes, "we can expect the struggle over energy to override all other considerations, national leaders will go to extreme lengths to ensure energy sufficiency for their countries, and state authority over both domestic and international affairs to expand."[17] Perhaps, but the picture painted by Klare ignores recent technological developments that have resulted in global increases in the production of oil; it also ignores the variable of time.

Contrary to Klare's assertions, a global crash in oil-production capacity is hardly imminent, thanks to the development of new exploration and drilling technologies. The period of enhanced extraction from unconventional sources and incrementally increasing prices that began in 2009 will presumably persist at least until 2030. However, this new era of extraction from unconventional sources will continue to be burdened with statist and often illiberal tactics in the domain of energy, led by China and its statist tactics of energy neo-mercantilism.

Oil as Goal and as Mechanism

The political scientist Gregory Gause argues that, because oil is a constant in the Persian Gulf, the frequent outbreaks of inter-state conflict in that region can't be attributed to it. He posits that "oil was not the primary driver of any of the Gulf wars."[18] But that logic ignores the role of oil as an antecedent variable that acts as a latent driver of conflict throughout the region; it also ignores the fact that oil reserves are often targets of conquest. Oil, and the enormous wealth that it generates for oil-producing countries, is a material factor that operates not only as a strategic goal but also as an enabler of conflict. In the Persian Gulf, oil is in fact a primary cause of conflict. The accretion of enormous oil revenues by Gulf states throughout the 1970s spurred the regional arms race, which in turn contributed to the multiple wars that shook the Gulf from 1980 through 2011.

Gause later conceded that "the oil revolution of the 1970s provided numerous incentives for more grandiose ambitions." "Each of the major regional states," he noted, "was much richer and more capable of contemplating an aggressive foreign policy, and all built up their militaries at staggering rates. The weaker Gulf states were much more attractive targets, as the oil on which they sat was a much more precious prize than it had ever been before."[19] Thus, the seemingly pacific 1970s provided the material basis for an intensifying regional security dilemma that would explode in periodic fits of intense violence. The influx of petrodollars, combined with dynamics of militarization, fueled an arms race in the region. This desire for the possession of oil fields in the region was the primary cause of the War of the Cities between Iraq and Iran, which claimed more than a million lives.[20] Thus, oil is a strategic goal in itself and also a mechanism (through petrodollar revenues) that enables inter-state conflict in the Gulf. The energy resources of the Persian Gulf structure the distribution of regional power, inform the goals and gambits of the players in the region, and draw external hegemonic powers into the area. Thus, oil wealth has clearly exacerbated and intensified the security dilemma in that tumultuous region.

If one takes into account the realist maxim that the survival of the state is paramount, then oil wealth (which is fungible) is a mechanism that is readily translated into military power. Thus, for the autocratic regimes of the Gulf, oil allows for the survival of the state through the maximization of power, primarily through militarization that is accomplished though the purchase of weapons systems by petrodollars. Oil wealth leads to militarization for the purposes of protecting the oil supply, but military forces often give the state both offensive and defensive capabilities. The militarization of the region, in conjunction with international anarchy and the inability to know the intent of "the other," results in increased insecurity for all countries in the region. Thus, all the countries in the Persian Gulf region seek increased security through militarization, but this spiral of militarization simply leads to greater perceptions of insecurity by all parties, which in turn fosters a regional arms race. In short, the region exhibits an intense security dilemma that is driven by the material interests of oil wealth.

The United States' military presence in the Persian Gulf region is now practically recognized as a given, at least among elites in Washington. The long history of US involvement in the region that began with the deal between Franklin D. Roosevelt and Ibn Saud intensified with Operation Ajax, the Carter Doctrine, Reagan's Tanker War, Desert Storm, and the Iraq War that began in 2003—an astonishing degree of political and military intervention in a relatively remote part of the world. The only substantive reason for such activity is that the region possesses considerable strategic utility because of its oil. Imagine a counterfactual scenario in which the Persian Gulf didn't possess vast amounts of oil. The great powers would have no compelling interest in the region. In the absence of oil, the economies of the Gulf States would have no significant source of revenue, and the countries of the region would have no opportunity to purchase or develop weapons systems or otherwise develop any consequential military capacity. Thus, oil is the reason for great powers' interest in the region, and the reason for the autocracy, the militarism, and the security dilemma in the region. Ultimately, the political scientist Christopher Fettweis is correct in arguing that "the presence of petroleum was a necessary, if not sufficient, condition for both Gulf wars, and is the main reason for great [powers'] interest in [a] barren, violent, and tyrannical region."[21]

Operation Desert Storm (1990–91)

The War of the Cities, waged between Iraq and Iran from 1980 to 1988, effectively shattered the economies of both countries. At the outset of hostilities, President Saddam Hussein of Iraq had pledged to protect the other Sunni states in the Gulf from the aggressive intentions of a revolutionary Shiite Iran. In return, the Kuwaitis and the Saudis had pledged to provide economic aid to Iraq to rebuild its shattered infrastructure at the war's close. However, at the conclusion of that war both the Kuwaitis and the Saudis reneged on their pledge to assist Iraq with reconstruction. Iraq, put in the position of relying on revenues from oil exports in order to rebuild its economy, then channeled a considerable proportion of those monies into a program of re-armament.

In order to accelerate the restoration of its economy, Iraq then actively sought to limit OPEC's production so as to drive the international price of oil up and consequently increase flows of revenue. However, the Kuwaitis insisted on exceeding their production quotas substantially, which kept the price of crude oil on international markets from increasing as much as it might have and consequently diminished the flow of revenue to Iraq.[22] Saddam was further incensed by the revelation that the Kuwaitis were using new "slant" drilling technologies to pump oil from the disputed Rumailah oil field, which straddles the Iraq-Kuwait border.[23] Kuwait's actions depressed Iraqi revenues from oil sales and consequently slowed Iraq's economic reconstruction.[24] "In January 2001," according to Steve Yetiv, Deputy Prime Minister Tariq Aziz "would reflect back and assert that Kuwait 'got what it deserved' in 1990 because it had undermined Iraq's oil prices and undertaken slant-drilling."[25] Moreover, Saddam Hussein claimed that the entirety of Kuwait's territory (and thus its oil) was a former province of Iraq that had been cut off from Iraq by the British for the purpose of securing oil rights. The Iraqi claim centered on the argument that Kuwait had formerly been part of the Ottoman Empire, specifically part of the province of Al-Basrah. In this case, the ruling al-Sabah family of Kuwait had cut a deal with London in 1899, and thereafter Kuwait had become a British protectorate.[26] Thus, Saddam posited that Iraq had a legitimate (and irredentist) claim to Kuwaiti territory.

Tensions between Iraq and Kuwait reached a boiling point in the summer of 1990. Late in July, armored divisions of the Iraqi Republican Guard took up positions on the Kuwaiti border. Iraq invaded on August 2, seizing all of Kuwait's territory within 24 hours. The presence of significant oil reserves, and the prospects of manipulating its extraction and its price, had made Kuwait a target of Iraqi aggression. Saddam Hussein's desire to capture the oil fields of Kuwait, and presumably those of Saudi Arabia too, were the principal reasons for the invasion. Doubtless there was also an element of revenge involved, as Saddam desired retaliation against the Sunni regimes that had abandoned Iraq after its war with fundamentalist Shiite Iran.

In the weeks that followed, the United States announced that the Iraqi invasion would not stand and assembled a coalition of powers under the auspices of the UN Security Council in order to drive Iraq out of Kuwait.[27] President George H. W. Bush declared that the UN Coalition forces were upholding international law (and a new post–Cold War international order) in repelling Iraq from Kuwait, in classic liberal fashion. Yet a deeper critical reading of the matter suggests that the US was simply upholding the principles established in the Carter Doctrine, namely protecting the oil fields of the Gulf from hostile powers with hegemonic designs over the region and protecting Saudi Arabia from further Iraqi aggression.

Iraq's *fait accompli* was widely derided in the West and prompted President Bush to call for an international economic embargo on Iraq. That position was reiterated by the UN Security Council on August 6 in Resolution 661. As a consequence of the embargo of oil from Iraq and the disruption of oil flows from Kuwait, approximately 7 percent of the world's consumption of crude oil (roughly 4.3 million barrels per day) was removed from global markets. Resolution 661 also proved to be authorization for the military action undertaken by the US-led coalition of UN forces in order to force Iraq to retreat from Kuwaiti territory.

Predictably, the global price of oil surged as a result of the disruption caused by Iraq's aggression. "The psychological shock of the invasion," Beaubouef notes, "initiated a wave of panic buying by refiners, retailers, wholesalers, and marketers … . As before, anxiety, uncertainty, and fear led oil-purchasing companies to husband stocks and aggressively bid for additional supplies, beyond normal levels, as a hedge against future shortages and price increases."[28] In seizing Kuwait, Iraq had gained control of approximately 20 percent of the world's known reserves of crude oil, and exports of about 4 million barrels per day. The crisis posed a considerable challenge to global oil markets, since two oil producers (Kuwait and Iraq), accounting for roughly 7 percent of global oil production, were excluded from the world oil market as a result of sanctions.[29] After the invasion, the price of a barrel of Brent Crude surged from $18 in late July of 1990 to $40.27 in mid October,[30] a 223.7 percent increase over a period of three months.

In 1990, in contrast with the United States, the European countries and Japan remained highly dependent on Persian Gulf oil. However, global economic interdependence made the US *indirectly* dependent on oil from the Gulf region. The Bush administration understood that any rapid increase in the global price of crude oil would stifle the global economy's nascent recovery from the recession of the late 1980s and consequently damage the prospects of economic recovery in the US. Such fears reflected a long-standing mindset of Western powers with regard to the Persian Gulf, one defined by the strategic nature of Persian Gulf oil. According to the political scientist L. Carl Brown, "today's belief that the industrial nations must have uninterrupted access to Middle Eastern oil is in the tradition of the British (and Western) thinking concerning the Suez Canal."[31]

The seizure of Kuwait proved economically problematic for the OECD countries (including the United States), and the prospect of Iraq's seizing the vast oil wealth of Saudi Arabia generated enormous concern in Washington. "If you allow someone like Saddam Hussein to get a stranglehold on oil production," Representative Ted Weiss (a member of the House Foreign Affairs Committee) commented on August 13, 1990, "it gives him control of our economy. If you give that kind of control to a person such as Saddam Hussein, the consequences would be very, very dire."[32]

Oil came to be seen as a mechanism of power by both the United States and Iraq. Saddam Hussein calculated that a disastrous "oil shock" to the global economy would weaken the resolve of his adversaries in the West. The US, and the UN coalition that it led, argued that multilateral sanctions against Iraq would deprive it of its revenues from oil exports. Thus, in the fall of 1990 the Western powers hoped that this sanctions regime would compel Iraq's compliance with the Security Council's resolutions.

Representative Patricia Schroeder (a member of the House Armed Services Committee) reiterated the United States' interests in Persian Gulf oil: "Basically, our main interest in Saudi Arabia and Kuwait comes down to a three-letter word, oil. It is oil, oil and oil. We don't seem to have any capacity as a nation to think long term: anyone who looked at the region could tell it has not gotten any more stable, and we certainly know the entire industrialized world relies heavily on oil. The world economy is quirky enough without a massive oil shock. That's why we didn't have any time to play around in dealing with this crisis ... ."[33] On a strategic level, soaring oil prices in late 1990 also threatened to destabilize the precarious economies of the post-Communist countries of Eastern Europe, which were emerging from decades of socialist misrule in the shadow of Soviet hegemony. An oil shock, and the economic destabilization that such a shock would entail, might have led them back into Russia's orbit and threatened the consolidation of democracy in that region.[34] World Bank estimates at the time concluded that the crisis would deprive the post-Communist countries of approximately $15 billion a year, roughly 5 percent of their GDP.[35]

According to Freedman and Karsh, the meeting of the National Security Council on August 2 "confirmed that at issue were US interests as well as international law. Quick calculations revealed that Iraq now had access to 20 percent of the world's known oil reserves. As this could be doubled by taking over Saudi Arabia, the vulnerability of that kingdom was identified as the most pressing security question."[36] "If it were not for oil," Freedman and Karsh argue, "Kuwait would not have been invaded in the first place, nor would the Americans have moved so resolutely to defend Saudi Arabia. In view of the United States' dependence on foreign oil, it was not a complete caricature to suggest that troops were sent initially to the desert to retain control of oil in the hands of a pro-American Saudi Arabia, so prices will remain low ... ."[37]

President Bush initially characterized the Iraqi invasion as a threat to "world order." However, on October 22 he told the American people "our jobs, our way of life, our own freedom, would all suffer if control of the world's great oil reserves fell into the hands of that one man, Saddam Hussein."[38] "After invading Kuwait," Yetiv writes, "Iraq controlled 19 percent of the world's oil. A potential invasion of Saudi Arabia would raise that to approximately 44 percent. If left unopposed, Iraq might gain enough capacity to blackmail other Arab states into supporting its inflated foreign policy agenda, to threaten Israel, and to push global oil prices higher, which would allow it build weapons of mass destruction (WMD). Thus, while the United States received only 8.7 percent of its oil from Iraq and Kuwait combined, Iraq's invasion still posed a serious threat in a world of global interdependence."[39]

Operation Desert Storm began on the morning of January 17, 1991. US forces employed concentrated artillery fire and aerial sorties to soften up Iraq's air defenses, and then to destroy the armored vehicles of the Iraqi Republican Guard. The war itself was brief, an utter mismatch between the poorly trained, poorly equipped, and demoralized Iraqi forces and the determined and well-trained Allied forces led by the United States. US combat deaths due to the war numbered only 172.[40] In the aftermath of the war, the Defense Intelligence Agency estimated that about 100,000 Iraqi soldiers had been killed during the battle, with another 300,000 wounded in combat.[41] It was a truly ferocious display of American military power.

Ultimately, the archetypal liberal justifications for the United States' intervention in Operation Desert Storm as an intervention to preserve world order ring a bit hollow. The United States' claims that the war was undertaken to preserve principles of international law (notably the principle of sovereignty) and the "new international order" of the post–Cold War era are problematic insofar as the US itself has a long history of aggressive intervention in other sovereign states, much of it unilateral. Perhaps the preservation of the principle of sovereignty was a part of the reason for the military action against Iraq, but it was far from being the principal cause of the intervention against Iraq. Moreover, the United States' arguments that the war was conducted in order to preserve democracy were truly mendacious, particularly in that Kuwait had never been democratic before the Iraqi invasion and in that Kuwait has never developed into a democracy in the decades that have passed since the war. Simply put, much of the chatter about the preservation of international order, sovereignty, and democracy masked illiberal behavior based on national interests. The primary motivation for the United States' actions in Desert Shield and Desert Storm was simply to prevent Iraq from achieving regional hegemony, and obtaining a decisive hold on the oil resources of the Persian Gulf. Such an outcome, in conjunction with Saddam's known position as a price hawk within OPEC, was simply strategically unacceptable to the US and other Western countries.

Thus, the balance of historical evidence shows that the United States' declarations of the use of force in defense of the emergent "international order" were a largely a canard, and that complex interdependence in the domain of energy, combined with Iraq's aggression, posed both direct and indirect threats to US economic interests. The US disguised national interest in the form of its continued hegemony over the Gulf, and the protection of Gulf oil flows, under the pretense of the protection of "world order." In this manner, a war to protect US hegemony over the energy resources of the Gulf region was ultimately cloaked in a veneer of liberal internationalism. During this period, General Anthony Zinni admitted that the role of Central Command (the successor to the Rapid Deployment Joint Task Force sent to the Persian Gulf region by President Reagan in 1983) was "basically energy driven" and that the gigantic oil deposits of the region were "one of the prime considerations in determining our interests."[42]

Between Desert Storm and the Iraq War

In the years that followed Desert Storm, American forces garrisoned the northern border region of Saudi Arabia in order to protect its oil fields from potential Iraqi aggression. Coalition forces also established no-fly zones over significant portions of southern and northern Iraq in order to protect Kurdish Shiite populations in those regions (who had risen up against Saddam in late 1991 at the urging of the US)[43] from Saddam's wrath. Throughout the 1990s, the United States' actions were clearly in line with the agreement that President Roosevelt had concluded with King Ibn Saud in 1944 to protect Saudi Arabia's territorial integrity, and with the Carter Doctrine's central goal of maintaining US hegemony over the region. During the period 1991–2003, the intense militarization of the oil fields of northern Saudi Arabia provided intellectual fodder that intensified the activities of al-Qaeda, which used the

presence of "the infidel" near Mecca and Medina as a psychological mechanism to actively recruit jihadist followers. Ultimately, the militarization of
the Gulf region by Western powers (in order to protect oil supplies), and the
ensuing backlash by Islamic fundamentalists through the formation of al-
Qaeda, contributed to the attacks of September 11, 2001.

The Iraq War (2003–2011)

Men are so simple of mind, and so much dominated by their immediate needs, that
a deceitful man will always find plenty who are ready to be deceived.
Niccolo Machiavelli

It isn't possible to provide a compelling and rational explanation for the
United States' invasion of Iraq in 2003 without attributing considerable
weight to the United States' long-standing desire to maintain its hegemony
over the oil resources of the region, consistent with the Carter Doctrine.
One cannot understand the Iraq War of 2003–2011 as a discrete event,
as the shadow of the past exerts a profound influence on present-day US
involvement in the region. Simply put, one must understand the United
States' invasion of Iraq in 2003 as an extension of the conflict that began
with Iraq's invasion of Kuwait on August 2, 1990. Thus, the Iraq War must
be understood as an extension of the United States' historical aspiration
to exert hegemony over the Persian Gulf region, from Operation Ajax to
Desert Storm.

Few scholars would argue that oil was the only cause of renewed hostilities between Iraq and the US, resulting in the 2003 invasion. The balance
of evidence suggests that the George W. Bush administration had decided
to remove Saddam Hussein before the attacks of September 11 for a variety
of reasons. One reason was the personal animus between the Bush family
and Saddam Hussein, based on evidence that Saddam had sought to assas-
sinate the elder Bush in 1993[44] in retaliation for the humiliation of Iraq
during Desert Storm and its aftermath. Persuasive arguments have also been
made that neoconservatives in the George W. Bush administration invoked
a Kantian rationale and sought to crush the despotic regime of Saddam
Hussein in order to establish a beachhead for democracy in the region.[45]

Others have surmised that Iraq posed a growing threat to Israel and
therefore Saddam had to be eradicated before he could use weapons of mass

destruction against Tel Aviv.[46] For example, John Mearsheimer and Steven Walt have argued that "the Israel lobby" pressured the Bush administration to undertake 2003 Iraq War.[47] Perhaps, but one must then ask a fundamental question: Why did Israel perceive Iraq to be a substantive existential threat in the first place? The argument that the Israel lobby drove the invasion neglects the empirical fact that petrodollars derived from Iraq's crude oil supported the country's militarization in the preceding four decades and its aggression against its neighbors. It was exactly this petro-militarization that allowed Iraq to become a menace to the other countries of the Persian Gulf, and eventually to Israel.

The argument that the Israel lobby was the primary force that pushed the US into the Iraq War isn't terribly compelling, for several reasons. First, we must return to the material importance of oil in order to explain Israel's fear of Iraqi aggression. The oil in the region, specifically the oil wealth that Iraq possessed, allowed Iraq to amass the military capabilities that made it a significant threat to Israel. In the absence of oil revenues to fill the coffers of the state, Iraq would have remained impoverished and militarily weak and would have not presented any substantive threat to a well-equipped and highly disciplined Israeli military. Thus, one cannot separate the material-contextual importance of petroleum to the regional security dilemma from the fact that the US sought to attack Iraq from the earliest days of the George W. Bush administration.

To lay all the blame for the United States' 2003 invasion of Iraq at the feet of the Israel lobby seems both reductionist and ahistorical, and ignores the fact that oil exacerbated the regional security dilemma and induced a regional arms race that resulted in the rise of Iraq as a threat to Israel. Realistically, however, Iraq was a far greater threat to its Shiite and Sunni neighbors in the Persian Gulf than it ever was to Israel. Iraq's threats against the Israeli state were, for the most part, a public-relations campaign to placate the "Arab street," punctuated with the errant Scud missile attacks of 1991. Conversely, Iraq's aggression toward Iran, and then Kuwait, clearly illustrated its ambitions for regional hegemony.

Oil as a Necessary but Insufficient Condition

Some aspects of the arguments recounted above may have contributed to the Bush administration's decision to invade Iraq in 2003, but it stands to reason that monocausal explanations for the Iraq War will be insufficient.

The above arguments often omit the role of oil in the Iraq War, and thus are also analytically insufficient. I argue that oil was a significant if not a primary factor in the Bush administration's decision to invade Iraq in 2003, and thus was a necessary but not sufficient condition for the Iraq War.

Admittedly, the argument I present here is circumstantial and is largely based on the historical processes of US foreign energy policy in the Persian Gulf region. I argue here that the Iraq War was *not* a significant departure from long-standing US foreign policy in the region, that it was in fact quite consistent with the Carter Doctrine, and that the Bush administration merely put a neoconservative (or hawkish Kantian) twist on the Carter Doctrine. In view of the historical strategic importance of Persian Gulf oil to the US, and insofar as the Iraq War was the culmination of a lengthy process of hostilities, it stands to reason that oil was a significant factor in the planning of the invasion.

The United States didn't seek direct control over Iraq's oil, as a classic imperial power might have. Rather, the Bush administration employed a degree of subtlety as it sought to free up Iraq's enormous latent supplies of crude oil in order to put them on international markets. First, the US readily defeated the Baathist regime of Saddam Hussein in the early days of the war; it then employed NOCs and (to a lesser degree) IOCs as mechanisms to extract the oil and put it onto international markets. Through the mechanism of the "global bathtub," this would reduce global oil prices in the face of soaring demand from China and India. Thus, it was a war to provide a global public good in the form of augmented global oil flows that would limit global oil prices and bolster the global economy, which would in turn enhance the export-led US economy. Thus, the Bush administration employed a fundamentally illiberal means (war) to attain a liberal end (the provision of global public goods). It goes without saying that the provision of this public good, as it maintained the global economy (and the US economy), was also directly in line with US economic interests.

Former Secretary of Defense Donald Rumsfeld vigorously protested that the Iraq war had nothing to do with oil. Yet the evidence, circumstantial as it may be, would seem to suggest otherwise. Gregory Gause argues against the view that oil was the predominant reason for the Iraq War, asserting that no declassified documents support such a view. However, Gause later acknowledges that "oil is why the outside world cares about the Persian Gulf" and "fully concede[s] that oil is a necessary (just not a sufficient) condition for that war to have occurred." "Absent the strategic importance of the Gulf, a product of that oil," he writes, "there wouldn't have been an American invasion of Iraq in 2003 or an American military effort to turn back the Iraqi invasion of Kuwait in 1990–91. So oil undoubtedly increases the likelihood of regional conflict, because it attracts the attention of the great powers."[48]

What evidence do we have, then, to support the hypothesis that the Iraq War resulted from the United States' desire to maintain hegemony over the oil supplies of the Gulf? First, it is important to recall that the Iraq War was actually a continuation of the hostilities initiated between the United States and Iraq during the Gulf War of 1990–91. That conflict, which was most certainly about oil, ended in a temporary cease-fire. However, violence between the two protagonists soon resumed, the US conducting sporadic air strikes against Iraq throughout the 1990s in order to keep Saddam "bottled up."[49] Mindful of the importance of time, of path dependence, and historical processes, one should then consider the Iraq War as an extension of the processes of conflict initiated during the Gulf War of 1990–91. Thus, it is fundamentally inaccurate to see the Iraq War as a distinct and discrete event divorced from the historical exercise of US hegemony over the energy resources of the Gulf region. The United States' desire for mastery over the region echoes across time, from Operation Ajax through the Carter Doctrine to the Gulf War and the Iraq War.

Andrew Bacevich argues that the Bush administration, "hewing to a tradition that extended at least as far back as Jefferson," "intended to expand American power to further the cause of American freedom. Freedom assumed abundance." "Abundance," Bacevich continues, "seemingly required access to large quantities of cheap oil. Guaranteeing access to that oil demanded that the United States remove all doubts about who called the shots in the Persian Gulf. It demanded oil wars."[50]

Indeed, it seems that the George W. Bush administration sought to liberate Iraqi oil for international oil consortia long before the invasion of 2003. In the earliest days of the administration, Vice President Richard Cheney convened the first meeting of the National Energy Policy Development Group,[51] the purpose of which was to integrate the policies of the state with that of energy corporations—specifically the international oil companies and oil service firms. The existence of this group reveals the historical symbiosis between the US government and corporate entities in the domain of energy.

The NEPDG's report confirms that the Bush administration was extremely concerned that US and global oil consumption was rising while US domestic production of crude oil was steadily declining and global oil production had plateaued.[52] Thus, throughout the report Cheney et al. invoke a quasi-Malthusian mindset that supports their calls for increased offshore drilling and the opening of new resources in regions such as Iraq. During the deliberations of the NEPDG, state and corporate officials pored over charts of known Iraqi oil reserves, various corporate entities delineating which areas were of greatest interest to them. A suit brought by Judicial Watch resulted in the release of various maps and documents that the NEPDG used, many of which indicated the locations of oil reserves that were of significant interest to corporate entities on the task force.

As can be seen from figures 4.1–4.3, as of March 2001 the Department of Defense had designed a list of international corporations that sought access to the rich and largely undeveloped oil fields of Iraq.[53] Note that none of these corporations was American, thus there was concern within the administration that the international sanctions regime against Saddam was deteriorating, and that American corporations might be shut out of the process as Saddam continued to sign deals with foreign corporations. That was, of course, before the attacks of September 11, 2001, and some time before the 2003 invasion of Iraq.

Furthermore, former Secretary of the Treasury Paul O'Neill specifically confirmed that control over Iraqi oil was a significant objective of the administration in its drive to war, and that preparations to invade Iraq were well underway in 2001.[54] Additionally, from February 2002 to March 2003 members of the Working Group of the Department of State's Future of Iraq Project argued in meetings that Iraq "should be opened to international oil companies as quickly as possible after the war."[55] In January of 2003, executives from the oil industry were already meeting with US government officials to divvy up the spoils from a "possible war." Specifically, these executives met with officials from the White House, the Department of State, and the Department of Defense.[56] Moreover, Ibrahim Bahr al-Uloum, who had been a member of the Department of State working group, was appointed Iraq's oil minister in the weeks after the invasion.[57]

After the invasion, one of the first things US forces did was protect the Iraqi oil ministry and Iraqi oil installations and infrastructure. Yetiv argues that the US military carried this out at the start of the war by "seizing

Iraqi Oilfields and Exploration Blocks

35AS0713

Figure 4.1
source: http://www.judicialwatch.org/oldsite/IraqOilMap.pdf

Foreign Suitors for Iraqi Oilfield Contracts
as of 5 March 2001

Country	Firm	Iraqi Oil & Gas Projects	Comments/Status
Algeria	Sonatrach	Tuba	Discussions. PSC.
		Blocks 6 & 7	Collecting data.
Australia	BHP	Halfaya	Discussions. PSC.
		Block 6	Collected data.
Belgium	Petrofina	Ahdab	Technical/economic studies (China's CNPC awarded PSC).
		Block 2	Collected data.
Canada	Ranger	Block 6, other	Signed MOU with Baghdad.
	Bow Canada	Khurmala	Joint proposal w/Czech Republic's Strojexport
		Hamrin	Joint proposal w/Czech Republic's Strojexport
	Alberta Energy	Unidentified	None
	CanOxy	Ratawi	Discussions. PSC.
		Block 5	Collected data.
	Chauvco Res.	Ayn Zalah	Advanced talks by late 1996. Service contract for advanced oil recovery (gas injection project) in this aging field.
	Escondido	Ratawi	Discussions. PSC.
		Block 5	Collecting data.
	Talisman	Hamrin, E. Baghdad	Service contract negotiations October 1999.
	IPC	Hamrin	Discussions. Service contract.
	PanCanadian	Unidentified	None
China	CNPC	Ahdab	Production Sharing Contract (PSC) signed June 1997.
		Halfaya	Bid for $4 bn, 23-year PSC.
		Luhais & Subba	Discussions. Service contract.
		Block 5	Collected data, discussions.
	Norinco	Ahdab	PSC signed June 1997 (CNPC consortium partner).
		Rafidain	Discussions. PSC.
	Sinochem	Rafidain	Discussions. PSC.
Czech Republic	Strojexport	Hamrin	Joint project with Bow Canada. Sent team to Iraq in Sept 1997.
		Khurmala	Joint project with Bow Canada
Finland	Neste Oy	Unidentified	None
France	Total Elf Aquitaine	Majnoon	PSC "agreed in principle" January 1997.
	Forasol SA	Saddam	Feasibility study presented to Baghdad in 1997, updated in 1998.
	IBEX	Hamrin	Technical discussions.
	Perenco	Rafidain	Discussions. PSC.
	Total Elf Aquitaine	Nahr Umr	PSC "agreed in principle" January 1997.
Germany	Deminex	Block 1	Collected data.
	Preussag	Ahdab	Technical/economic studies (China's CNPC later awarded PSC).
		Block 2	Collected data
	Slavneft	N. Rumaylah	Subcontractor to Lukoil consortium.
Greece	Kriti	Gharraf	Discussions. PSC.
Hungary	Hanpetro	Block 3	Collected data.
India	ONGC	Tuba	Advanced contract talks in October 1999 (ONGC drilled at least four wells in Tuba in the 1980s). PSC.
		Halfaya	Discussions. PSC.
		Block 8	Collected data.
	Reliance	Tuba	Discussions.
Indonesia	Pertamina	Tuba	Finalized discussions for a PSC in late 1997.
		Block 3	Collected data
Ireland	Bula	Block 4	Discussions.
Italy	Agip	Nasiriya	PSC initialed Apr 97. $2 bn, 23-year project (w/partner Repsol).
		Iraq-Turkey gas pipeline	Discussions.
		Block 1	Collected data, discussions.
	Snamprogetti	Luhais & Subba	Discussions. Service contract.

Figure 4.2
source: http://www.judicialwatch.org/oldsite/IraqOilFrgnSuitors.pdf

Country	Firm	Iraqi Oil/Gas Project	Comments/Status
Japan	Japex	Gharraf	Bid and technical/economic oilfield study submitted to Baghdad. March 1997. PSC.
	Mitsubishi	Luhais & Subba	Discussions. Service contract.
Malaysia	Petronas	Ratawi	Discussions. PSC.
		Tuba	Discussions. PSC.
		Block 2	Collected data, discussions
Mexico	Pemex	Unidentified	None.
Netherlands	Larmag	Subba & Luhais	Discussions. Service contract.
	Dutch Royal Shell	Ratawi	Discussions.
		Block 8	Collected data.
Norway	Statoil	Block 1	Collected data.
Pakistan	Crescent	Ratawi	Discussions. PSC.
		Block 5	Collected data.
Romania	Petrom	Khurmala Dome (Karkuk)	Apparently awarded service contract, project in advanced technical infrastructure design phase (setting equipment & materials specifications for project).
		Luhais & Subba	Discussions. Service contract.
		Block 4	Collected data, discussions.
		Qayyarah	Contract talks. Service contract for well drilling and engineering.
	Mol	Block 3	Discussions.
Russia	Kond Petroleum	Rafidain	Discussions. Russian firm Sidanko a possible partner. PSC.
	Lukoil	W. Qurnah	PSC signed March 1997. Topographic surveys in 1998.
		N. Rumaylah	Service contract negotiations to upgrade water injection facilities, develop additional geologic reservoirs.
	Zarubezneft	W. Qurnah	PSC signed March 1997 (Lukoil consortium partner).
		N. Rumaylah	Service contract negotiations (w/Lukoil consortium).
		Hamrin	Invited to bid in mid-1997. Service contract.
	Mashinoimport	W. Qurnah	PSC signed March 1997 (Lukoil consortium partner).
		Luhais, & Subba	Discussions. Service contract.
		N. Rumaylah	Service contract negotiations (w/Lukoil consortium).
	Tatarneft	N. Rumaylah	Subcontractor to Lukoil consortium.
	Rostneft	N. Rumaylah	Subcontractor to Lukoil consortium.
	Sidanko	N. Rumaylah	Subcontractor to Lukoil consortium.
S. Korea	Sangyong	Halfaya	Bidding for $4 bn, 23-year PSC. Seoul in June 1997 invited Iraq Oil Minister to S. Korea for signing ceremony.
	Samsung	Halfaya	Bidding (part of Korean consortium). PSC.
	Pedco	Halfaya	" " "
	Hambo	Halfaya	" " "
	Yukong	Halfaya	" " "
	Daewoo	Rafidain	Discussions. PSC.
Spain	Repsol	Nasiriya	PSC initialed Apr 97. $2 bn, 23-year project (w/partner Agip).
		Block 4	Collected data.
Taiwan	CPC	Gharraf	Discussions. PSC.
		Rafidain	Discussions. PSC.
		Tuba	Discussions. PSC.
Tunisia	Setcar	Unidentified	None
Turkey	TPAO	Gharraf	Bid for PSC. Oilfield study completed January 1997.
		Mansuriya Gas Field	Service contract signed May 1997 to develop field, purchase gas.
		Block 4	Reprocessed seismic data, conducting laboratory studies.
UK	Branch Energy	Gharraf	Discussions. PSC.
	Pacific Resources	Rafidain	Discussions. PSC.
Vietnam	PetroVietnam	Amara	Service contract. Near signing Oct 1999

35AS0713

Figure 4.3
source: http://www.judicialwatch.org/oldsite/IraqOilGasProj.pdf

oil-export facilities north of Kuwait, two major Iraqi oil terminals, Iraq's southernmost oil fields of Basra, and the Oil Ministry in Baghdad."[58] Despite the protestations of Rumsfeld (and others in the Bush administration) that the war had nothing to do with oil, the president ultimately tipped his hand to Peter Baker of the *Washington Post* in late 2006, admitting "the war is about oil." Trying to justify the continued US occupation of Iraq, Bush said "You can imagine a world in which these extremists and radicals got control of energy resources."[59]

"It is politically inconvenient," Alan Greenspan wrote in his book *The Age of Turbulence*, "to acknowledge what everyone knows: The Iraq War is largely about oil."[60] Equally damning were comments made in 2007 by General John Abizaid, the former head of US Central Command and Military operations in Iraq: "Of course it's about oil; we can't really deny that." "People say we're not fighting for oil," Senator Chuck Hagel wrote in 2007. "Of course we are."[61]

The invasion of Iraq began on March 19, 2003. The casualties included 4,480 deceased US soldiers, 3,400 deceased US contractors, and 31,928 US soldiers wounded in action. Brian Jenkins of the RAND Corporation estimates that between 110,000 and 150,000 Iraqis were killed during the war.[62] In the end, the economic costs of the war were prodigious. Linda Bilmes and Joseph Stiglitz estimated that the costs of the war to the republic would exceed $3 trillion.[63] Adjusted for inflation, it would be second only to World War II in terms of total US expenditures.

No weapons of mass destruction were ever found, nor was there ever any concrete evidence that the regime of Saddam Hussein was working with al-Qaeda. In hindsight this isn't terribly surprising, as it would be highly unusual for a Baathist Arab regime to be in collusion with a network of Wahhabist Islamic fundamentalists. Thus, we are left with the uncomfortable conclusion that the war resulted from a misperception that Iraq had weapons of mass destruction, a neoconservative (Kantian) desire to spread democracy through warfare, and/or a misperception of looming oil scarcity accompanied by a desire to enable greater access to Iraqi oil for international oil firms and global markets. I suspect that the evidence supports a mixture of these three motives, though the proportions remain in question. Regardless, I have argued that the oil motive was an extremely important factor in the Bush administration's decision to launch the war.

The narrative of events in the later years of the war supports the conclusion that oil played a substantive role in the decision to go to war in Iraq. Although the first round of Iraqi oil exploration rights went to non-American firms, the international oil companies are now very much present in Iraq. In 2009 the Iraqi government awarded the exploration and development rights to the vast West Qurna-1 oil field to a consortium led by ExxonMobil and Royal Dutch Shell. The field is estimated to possess between 8.6 billion and 43 billion barrels of crude oil, making it one of the largest oil fields on the planet.[64] In 2010, Exxon then awarded a contract for drilling in the West Qurna-1 field to the energy services provider Schlumberger.[65] In 2013 local Iraqis began to protest against Exxon's exploration and development strategies. In November of 2013, Exxon began to sell 25 percent of its stake in the West Qurna-1 field to the Chinese NOC PetroChina,[66] which would leave Exxon with a still considerable 35 percent stake. Another Iraqi field was awarded in 2009 to a consortium led by BP in partnership with the Chinese national oil company CNPC.

In July of 2012, Chevron signed deals with the quasi-autonomous Kurdish authority in northern Iraq for development of the vast oil resources there. This was due primarily to the perception by most IOCs that Kurdish northern Iraq is far more politically stable than the south.[67] Chevron now has rights to the exploration and development of three significant blocks in Kurdistan.[68]

The moves by Exxon and Chevron to dominate oil exploration in northern Iraq makes sense, insofar as they hope to export crude oil through pipelines to Turkey and thence to international markets, avoiding much of the chaos and violence that still plague southern Iraq.

BP has been involved in developing a number of fields in southern Iraq, including vast fields at Rumaila, West Qurna, and Kirkuk. BP and CNPC signed a deal with the Iraqi government in 2009 to commence extraction in the Rumaila field.[69] In its desire to tap the wealth of these fields, BP has signed contracts with the international energy service firms Schlumberger and Baker Hughes. In November of 2013, local Shiite populations in southern Iraq stormed a Schlumberger operations camp that was developing the Rumaila field.[70]

The war would also serve to enrich several international energy service corporations that provided infrastructure and management services to the Iraqis, and other oil firms that entered Iraq after the war (among them the Halliburton subsidiary KBR). In 2006, KBR was cited for egregious practices by the Inspector General's office, which determined that an egregious amount of the funds paid to KBR by the US government paid for overhead costs rather than actual work undertaken in Iraq. Auditors for the special investigator general determined that KBR had routinely overcharged the US government for services, and often had billed for services not actually performed.[71] A 2013 investigative report argued that KBR profited from the war and the subsequent occupation to the tune of roughly $39.5 billion, primarily financed by US taxpayers.[72] The extensive use of private contractors by the US military has resulted in the privatization of war. Yetiv also notes this collusion between the federal government and oil services firms: "[I]mmediately before the attack on Iraq in early 2003, Halliburton's subsidiary, Kellog, Brown, and Root, did receive a multi-billion-dollar contract from the Defense Department to repair oil fields and import consumer fuels in Iraq."[73] This veiled collusion between government and the oil industry, in the US and in other OECD countries, constitutes the illiberal core of US foreign energy policy. Alas, the illiberal use of power by many developed nations undergirds the structures of modern liberalism, particularly in the domain of energy.

Michael Klare argues that the invasion was part of a policy of "maximum extraction"[74] that saw both Iraq and Iran as hostile to the United States and as price hawks in OPEC. The Bush administration may have viewed the Saudi regime as fragile and as increasingly incapable of balancing against the growing ambitions of Iran and Iraq. In order to rectify this situation and place a much greater amount of crude oil on global markets, the US sought regime change in Iraq. Ultimately this thesis was borne out; in 2012, Iraq's production of crude oil surpassed Iran's. Specifically, Iraq's output of crude oil reached 3 million bpd in July of 2012, whereas Iran's output had declined to 2.9 million bpd from its zenith of 3.6 million bpd.[75]

Critics of the argument that oil was a significant factor in the Bush administration's decision to invade Iraq cite the fact that the majority of Iraqi oil-production contracts didn't go directly to American-based IOCs. Yet such arguments ignore the subtle reality of the global markets for crude oil. According to the "bathtub theory," it doesn't matter which country or firm puts crude oil on international markets; all producer states contribute to filling a global bathtub of crude oil (represented by global markets for crude oil) from which all consumer nations ultimately draw their supply.

Thus, even if firms from other polities (e.g., China and France) extract Iraqi oil, it will still place a much greater supply of crude oil on global markets, which will consequently moderate global oil prices, and enhance global energy security in the short to the medium term. Logically, then, US corporations need not be *directly* involved in processes of extraction in order to enhance aggregate global supplies of crude oil. Over the longer term, this increased supply of crude oil from Iraq would directly enhance the global supply, and the lower energy prices would consequently stimulate the US economy. Furthermore, lower global energy prices would also stimulate the global economy and consequently strengthen foreign markets for American goods. Former Secretary of State Colin Powell inadvertently confirmed this argument in July of 2003: "We have not taken one drop of oil for US purposes. Quite the contrary. We put in place a management system to make sure that Iraqi oil is brought out of the ground and put onto the market."[76]

The legacy of the US invasion of Iraq has been disastrous. Unfortunately, the government of Nouri al-Maliki persistently rewarded Iraq's Shiite population, marginalized the Kurds, and systematically excluded the Sunni minority from political power and sharing in the country's oil riches. The spring of 2014 saw a dangerous new threat to Iraqi stability in the rise of ISIS (Islamic State of Iraq and Syria), a fundamentalist Sunni militia that was formed in 2004 and was originally associated with al-Qaeda. ISIS gained power and momentum during the chaos of the internecine Syrian civil War. In June of 2014, ISIS rapidly expanded from its bases in eastern Syria to seize much of northern and central Iraq, and consolidated its hold over Anbar province in western Iraq. The rapid gains made by ISIS are attributable largely to disaffected Sunnis' joining (or at least not opposing) ISIS because of their long-standing resentment of the increasingly sectarian Shiite Maliki government. ISIS's goal is to establish a fundamentalist Islamic caliphate incorporating much of modern Iraq and Syria, stretching from Baghdad to the shores of the Mediterranean.[77] To complicate matters, in the summer of 2014 the Maliki government called upon Iran for military assistance, and Iran responded by sending two battalions of elite Quds forces to defend Baghdad against the Sunni revolt.[78]

As of late 2014, the Middle East was faced with a widening sectarian war that threatened to engulf much of the Middle East in chaos and violence. The Obama administration had few palatable options at its disposal, but it elected to send about 300 "military advisors" to the region in order to assist with the defense of Baghdad.[79] This potentially puts the United States in the extraordinarily awkward position of having its troops fighting alongside Iranian Quds units in order to support the tottering regime in Baghdad. During the fall of 2014, the US military began an extensive aerial bombing campaign against ISIS across northern Iraq.

The Iraq War has proved to be a costly farce. Attempts to install a robust democracy in Iraq have proved illusory, and we are now witnessing a brutal sectarian war that threatens international security from the Levant to Iran.

Patterns of Deception

Critics of the hypothesis that oil motivates US intervention in the Persian Gulf region argue that, aside from the Carter Doctrine and George W. Bush's rare admission, the US has never openly admitted that oil is the reason for its deep involvement in the Persian Gulf. The only reasonable conclusion one can draw is that US policy makers employ disingenuous strategies to mask the material basis of US foreign policy in the region with the liberal rhetoric of benign hegemony. In other words, many US leaders have grown quite comfortable in their mendacity (particularly to the American public) with regard to the United States' true materialistic intent in the region. John Mearsheimer argues that American political elites have become extremely comfortable with lying, and that such elites lie to their own publics with great frequency.[80] In the domain of US foreign energy policy, the practiced deception of the American public began with Roosevelt's secret meeting with Ibn al Saud and continued through the CIA-backed coup against the Mossadegh government in Iran and the support of illiberal regimes in Iran and Saudi Arabia under the Nixon Doctrine. The disclosures made in the Carter Doctrine marked a rare moment in truth telling about the United States' intentions in the region, but soon Carter's successors would once more bury the truth under rhetorical flourishes about upholding international law and enforcing global peace.

Mearsheimer's pithy analysis of the history of lying in international politics exposes the fact that policy makers in Washington have become very comfortable with the politics of deception, particularly when it comes to fabricating truths about US foreign policy for domestic consumption. Mearsheimer argues that the Bush administration deliberately told four significant lies in order to sell the Iraq War to the American people. "Key figures in the administration," Mearsheimer asserts, "falsely claimed that they knew with complete certainty that Iraq had WMD. They also lied when they said they had foolproof evidence that Saddam was closely allied with Osama bin Laden, and they made various statements that falsely implied that Saddam bore some responsibility for the September 11 attacks on the United States. Finally, various individuals in the administration, including President Bush himself, claimed that they were still open to peaceful resolution of their dispute with Saddam, when in fact the decision to go to war had already been made."[81]

It appears that the Bush administration was very comfortable practicing mendacity in order to gain (and consolidate) public approval for going to war against Iraq in 2003. For example, the administration explicitly linked Saddam Hussein to al-Qaeda in the aftermath of the September 11 attacks. Anyone with even a basic knowledge of the history and culture of the peoples of the Persian Gulf would question an alliance between the relatively secular Baathists of Iraq and the Wahhabi fundamentalist base of al-Qaeda. In fact, on several occasions Osama bin Laden had railed against the relatively secular Baathist regime of Saddam Hussein. A 2008 study commissioned by the Department of Defense found no evidence of any concrete linkages between Iraq and al-Qaeda.[82] Perhaps even more important, substantive evidence suggests that the decision to invade Iraq was made in the earliest days of the Bush administration, before the events of September 11 and well before the supposed discovery that Saddam was developing weapons of mass destruction. These disturbing allegations come directly from Paul O'Neill, who served as Secretary of the Treasury during the Bush administration.[83] Thus, there was an established pattern of deceit within the administration with respect to Iraq.

Notwithstanding the unusual candor of the Carter administration in its admission that the United States would fight to protect its hegemony over the oil fields of the Persian Gulf, why the long-term pattern of deception in US foreign energy affairs? Mearsheimer argues that "leaders appear to be more likely to lie to their own people about foreign policy issues than to other countries. That certainly seems to be true for democracies that pursue ambitious foreign policies and are inclined to initiate wars of choice."[84] But how could the Bush administration have been able to lie about such an important matter and get away with it? "It is relatively easy for policymakers to lie to their publics," Mearsheimer writes. "For starters they control the state's intelligence apparatus, which gives them access to important information that the public does not have and cannot get ... . Policymakers, therefore, can manipulate the flow of information to the public in various ways, and most people will be inclined to trust what their leaders tell them unless there is hard evidence that they are being deceived."[85]

The Bush administration engaged in a spectacular display of deception in selling the Iraq War to the American public, engaging in the illiberal use of force while cloaking its activities in the language of liberalism. Examples of such "spin" include the administration's initial attempt to justify the invasion of Iraq to prevent that country from developing and using of weapons of mass destruction. When such weapons failed to materialize, the *raison d'être* for the campaign metamorphosed into a neo-Kantian mission dedicated to the democratic liberation of the Iraqi people. Yet in all these explanations the administration avoided any discussion of the principal strategic commodity in the region, and a central reason for the deployment of US forces in the Persian Gulf since the middle of the twentieth century: oil.

Indeed, this is the heart of the argument, as under the Bush administration the United States acted in a highly illiberal fashion, employing deception and engaging in a pre-emptive war even as it cloaked its behavior in liberal gestures, rhetoric and mythology. "In an earlier age," Andrew Bacevich writes, "Americans saw empire as the antithesis of freedom. Today, as illustrated above all by the Bush administration's efforts to dominate the energy-rich Persian Gulf, empire has seemingly become a prerequisite of freedom."[86]

Patterns of Conflict

Historically, shortages of oil have been among the causes of several major interstate conflicts. As Henry Kissinger observed, "competition for access to energy can become the life and death of many societies."[87] Oil has played a multifaceted role in the onset of conflicts, functioning as both a strategic target of aggression and as an amplifier of power for those countries that have possessed it. During the first half of the twentieth century, the unmistakable pattern of conflict over energy resources was one of great powers attacking each other, and great powers attacking weaker powers, in order to seize oil assets. As was noted above, during World War I German forces pushed eastward to capture the Romanian oil fields at Ploesti, primarily because Germany was beset by an acute scarcity of domestic petroleum resources, which in turn inhibited the speed and range of the German war machine. During World War II Germany again drove eastward to capture Ploesti. It then pushed into the Soviet Union during Operation Barbarossa (June–December 1941), largely in order to capture the oil fields of the Caucasus and specifically the oil-rich region around Baku. Japan's expansion throughout the Pacific region during World War II was congruent with its attempts to seize resources, particularly petroleum, throughout East and Southeast Asia, which ultimately led to Japan's invasion of the Dutch East Indies. Furthermore, the strike against the US Navy's base at Pearl Harbor resulted from fear that the oil embargo imposed by the Roosevelt administration would strangle Japan into submission.

During the Cold War period this pattern of aggression over oil changed. The second phase was marked by stronger powers (particularly the United States, the Soviet Union, and the United Kingdom) using strategies of subterfuge to maintain their hegemonic dominance and ensure the flow of cheap oil to themselves and their allies. This pattern is particularly evident in the events of Operation Ajax, wherein the United States and the United Kingdom used their intelligence services to precipitate a coup against the fledgling democracy of Mohammed Mossadegh in Iran. One must also consider that the Nixon administration openly discussed the use of coercive power to seize the oil fields of the Middle East in 1974, although it ultimately declined to do so.[88] The Reagan administration subsequently invoked the Carter Doctrine in 1987 to protect Kuwaiti tankers from attack during the War of the Cities between Iran and Iraq. Further, as I have argued above, oil was a central factor in the United States' decisions to embark upon the Desert Storm campaign of 1990–91 in order to repel Iraqi forces from Kuwait and to protect the Saudis from further aggression by Iraq.

In the post–Cold War era, the evident pattern is one of greater powers attacking weaker powers in order to attain mastery over energy resources, or to prevent potentially hostile actors from interrupting the flow of crude oil. As delineated above, oil has contributed to frequent bouts of inter-state aggression in the Persian Gulf, notably between Iraq and its neighbors Iran and Kuwait. Further, it has manifested in the destructive periodic US military interventions in the Persian Gulf, in both 1990–91 and from 2003 to the present. Thus, asymmetries of power, particularly military power, contribute to energy-based conflicts in the post–Cold War era, as stronger powers attack weaker countries in order to attain (or maintain) dominance over energy resources in a region.

Iraq's invasion of Kuwait in August of 1990 illustrates this dynamic of power asymmetries driving conflict, as Iraq's bid for regional hegemony entailed a rapid strike against Kuwait and the seizure of its vast oil assets. Operation Desert Storm also illustrates this dynamic of power asymmetry, as the United States struck at a much weaker Iraq in its desire to maintain hegemony over the distribution of energy resources in the Gulf. Despite the fact that justifications for the Iraq War of 2003 were couched in the language of liberalism and benign hegemony, the United States' actions were quite illiberal, and further illustrate this asymmetrical dynamic of greater powers attacking weaker powers. This pattern of asymmetrical conflict over energy isn't peculiar to the US. For example, Russia invaded the diminutive country of Georgia in 2008, ostensibly in order to protect Russian ethnic minorities in enclaves of South Ossetia and Abkhazia. However, viewing these events through the lens of material interests, one might argue that Russia also sought to deal a blow to Georgian elites that had actively worked with the US to build the Baku-Tbilisi-Ceyhan (BTC) pipeline,[89] thereby bypassing Russia's historical monopoly on the flow of oil and natural gas from the Caspian region to the West.

During the Obama administration we have witnessed US-led NATO strikes against the Libyan state, ostensibly to protect the Libyan population from genocide. As I argued above, although the Obama administration sought to cloak these actions in the benign mantle of liberalism internationalism, the intervention was undertaken primarily to ensure that the flow of Libyan light sweet crude oil to Southern European refineries would resume. The restoration of Libyan oil flows was crucial to the economic vitality of Southern European economies.

This empirical pattern of asymmetrical conflicts over energy since 1990 calls into question the validity of Michael Klare's argument that an increasing scarcity of oil may generate conflict between the great powers.[90] Clearly the pattern that we have witnessed since 1990 is one of great powers attacking lesser powers, and middle-tier powers attacking one another. We have observed no instances of direct or indirect conflict between the great powers over energy resources since World War II.

For several reasons, one might expect the current pattern to continue. First, most of the great powers possess arsenals of nuclear weapons, and other countries (e.g. Japan) are allied with nuclear powers. The heightened tensions between China and Japan over the Senkaku/Diaoyu Islands and their energy resources suggests that skirmishes are quite possible; however, a full-scale conventional war between China and Japan over possession of these islands seems improbable. Furthermore, Japan falls under the protection of the United States' nuclear umbrella, and so China would have to consider the dangerous possibility (however remote) that a skirmish or a conventional conflict with Japan over resources might escalate to a point where the US would be drawn in by its collective-security agreements with Japan. The exorbitant costs of war between China and the US outweigh any potential gains from in the prosecution of warfare, particularly over energy resources. One can imagine that a resource war between the US and China would easily consume the very energy resources that China had sought in the first place. Thus, war between the great powers over energy would be highly irrational.

But when a great power sees an opportunity to gain energy resources by taking military action against a middle power or a lesser power, it may conclude that the spoils of aggression may outweigh the risks of war. For example, Saddam Hussein made the calculation that Iraq's superior relative power would translate into an easy victory over Kuwait in 1990, giving Iraq dominance over the Persian Gulf's oil resources. However, despite his initial success in capturing Kuwait, Saddam made a grave miscalculation. The United States, Britain, and other Western countries perceived his aggression as a bid for regional hegemony, and as a threat to the global energy economy, and intervened with overwhelming military force to reverse Iraq's occupation of Kuwait.

The dynamic of petro-militarization in the Persian Gulf has also impelled Iran's development of a nuclear weapons program, which is in turn largely a response to the persistent and intense security dilemma of the Persian Gulf region. Again, petrodollars have infused and exacerbated the regional security dilemma, and have made Iran a credible threat to the Sunni peoples of the region and to Israel. Oil revenues permitted the rapid and extensive militarization of Iran, which now possesses an increasing capacity to project military power throughout the region. Moreover, military interventions in the region by Iraq, the United States, and Israel have increased the insecurity of certain countries, particularly Iran. This historical background of external interventions has spurred Iran's nuclear initiative, which has in turn fostered greater insecurity in Israel. Thhe entire region exhibits a positive feedback loop of insecurity, militarization, and fear—a dynamic familiar to scholars of the security dilemma.

Another mechanism that limits the probability of war between the great powers over energy flows is the recognition of the great powers' spheres of influence. The recognized sphere of influence of the United States now encompasses much of the Persian Gulf (excluding Iran). China's sphere of influence encompasses Sudan and, to a lesser extent, Iran, which may help to explain the lack of US military intervention in those polities. Russia's sphere of influence still encompasses parts of Eastern Europe, the Caucasus, and Syria, which may partially explain the recent reticence of the US to intervene in Georgia and Syria. The great powers' recognition of these spheres of influence, particularly in the domain of energy, minimizes the risk of war between them, though considerable potential for misunderstanding remains.

Intra-State Violence

Oil-induced violence between sovereign states remains quite rare; however, the tendency of oil to generate intrastate violence is increasingly recognized in the post–Cold War era. To what degree does intra-state conflict occur over energy resources, and how does such conflict affect the national-security interests of the United States? Certainly intra-state wars within oil-producing countries can jeopardize international energy flows, which in turn can destabilize global oil markets and thereby undermine the sovereign interests of other countries. However, one must be careful to delineate which intrastate conflicts over energy resources threaten the interests of the US and which do not. At present the US considers many intra-state conflicts in which energy resources are involved to be issues of national security that often demand US military intervention, either overtly or covertly. Unfortunately, this has led to the costly militarization of global energy infrastructures,[91] and to the unfettered expansion of US military and intelligence interests abroad.

The political scientist Kalevi Holsti has argued that the locus of war has shifted over the centuries from between sovereign states to within sovereign states. In light of this transformation, systems-level theory's exclusive focus on inter-state war has become somewhat archaic. According to Holsti, "strategic studies continue to be divorced from the practices of war," and "the assumption that the problem of war is primarily a problem of the relations *between* states has to be seriously questioned."[92] Holsti then provides an empirical analysis of the frequency of war (both inter-state and intra-state), concluding that "the trend is clear: the threat of war between countries is receding, while the incidence of violence within states is on an upward curve."[93]

Holsti's findings present structural realists with a significant empirical problem. Realism, particularly structural realism, predicts that under conditions of competitive anarchy the international system should witness wars between sovereign states with some degree of regularity.[94] Yet, contrary to realist suppositions, Holsti's data clearly indicate that the frequency of war between sovereign states has declined over the centuries.[95] Moreover, the frequency of war between the great powers since 1945 is essentially zero. This is not to say that wars between sovereign states don't occur (recent US invasions of Afghanistan and Iraq and NATO actions in Libya attest that they sometimes do); it is to say that such conflicts exemplify the asymmetrical nature of war in the twenty-first century.

Since much of the violence (at least in frequency) that does occur appears to be at the intra-state level, we must try to determine whether oil exploration, oil production, and rents derived from oil contribute to domestic conflicts. At present the balance of evidence indicates that resource rents derived from petroleum often contribute to internal political instability, and even to the onset of civil war.[96] In the majority of oil-producing countries, oil and gas revenues are controlled by the state, which typically reinforces corruption and exacerbates economic inequities within the country, and these mechanisms tend to fuel intra-state violence. The probability of internal conflict (rebellion, civil war) may be increased by one or more of the following: increasing levels of deprivation of the body politic, low or declining levels of state capacity, avarice, and perhaps socio-ethnic segmentation.

Thus, oil wealth would seem to trigger intra-state conflict in three ways. First, oil prices exhibit high levels of volatility, and therefore oil-producing countries tend to be subject to periodic cycles of boom and bust. As governmental dependence on oil rents increases, particularly as such rents are used to provide public goods to the body politic, one also sees a corresponding increase in the probability of socioeconomic chaos when oil prices drop and revenue flows ebb. Second, oil wealth may generate economic instability in a polity, in the form of inflation and the stagnation and/or contraction of non-oil related sectors of the economy (a phenomenon known as Dutch disease).[97] As the ranks of the unemployed swell, they may exhibit frustration with their government and experience deprivation (relative and perhaps absolute). In the context of inflation and the state's declining ability to provide public goods, the dispossessed may find themselves increasingly vulnerable to being recruited by factions that challenge the legitimacy of the state.

NATO and the Libyan Civil War of 2011

The NATO intervention during the Libyan Civil War of 2011 is a curious event in that it exhibits manifestations of both liberal and illiberal behavior by the United States. Moreover, it also exhibits "intermestic" characteristics wherein domestic discord generates externalities that radiate beyond the state. Victor Cha describes the phenomenon of "intermestic issues" as "an interpenetration of foreign and domestic ... issues such that national governments increasingly operate in spaces defined by the intersection of internal and external security."[98] The civil war in Libya, and the consequent destabilization of that country's oil supply to Southern Europe, drew France, the United Kingdom, and the United States into the civil conflict through the mechanism of NATO. The despotic regime of Moammar Qadaffi sought to quell the domestic uprisings associated with the Arab Spring revolutions of 2011, and directed exceptional violence against those elements of the Libyan population that sought reform. In the resulting warfare between insurgents and Qadaffi loyalists, several major Libyan oil-production centers were damaged and/or taken off line.

Because of its proximity to Europe, Libya is the third-largest supplier of crude oil to the European Union. It exports a light sweet crude that is ideal for Southern Europe's refineries. Before the conflict of 2011, Libya accounted for about 10 percent of Europe's imports of crude oil. The sudden cessation of this supply of oil to European refineries threatened the economies of Italy, France, and Spain, which were already suffering from high levels of unemployment, monstrous debt, and increasingly frequent "bear raids" by international bond traders. The conflict-induced decline in Libya's output of crude oil had the potential to exacerbate the destabilization of Southern European economies. Ultimately, this threat to European energy security resulted in multilateral intervention by several great powers (the US, the UK, and France) through the mechanism of NATO, as authorized by UN Security Council Resolution 1973.[99]

However, the roots of the recent NATO intervention in Libya are unintelligible without an understanding of historical processes. The Qaddafi regime was infamous for its history of aggravating British, French, and American interests, particularly in the domain of energy. This particular story begins in September of 1970, when Qadaffi announced to the international oil companies that he was unilaterally imposing a price hike of 30 cents per barrel on all oil extracted from Libyan sources by the Occidental Petroleum Corporation. In retrospect, it isn't unreasonable for a country to demand a fair price for non-renewable resources that will be depleted over time. Michael Graetz argues that Qaddafi's successful shakedown of Occidental Petroleum in 1970 marked a shift in power away from the Seven Sisters (and thus the West) toward the oil-producing countries (particularly OPEC members).[100] In the years that followed, Libya became a strident price hawk within OPEC, an opponent of US interests in North Africa and the Middle East, and an odious sponsor of international terrorism. Interestingly, just before the civil war of 2011 Qadaffi had also mentioned his plans for the "Libyanization" of his country's oil supply, with the clear implication that he intended to deny it to Western countries.[101]

In early March of 2011, the Libyan revolution had propelled global oil prices (courtesy of rampant speculation) to $119 for Brent Crude. The rapid rise in oil prices resulted in declines in global stock markets as investors worried that the violence witnessed in North Africa might spread to Saudi Arabia and Iran. The Libyan situation provoked the UN Security Council to authorize Resolution 1973 to facilitate an intervention in Libya against the Qadaffi regime, both to prevent atrocities and to restore the flow of Libyan oil in order to calm world markets. The rising price of oil also threatened to induce inflation throughout the global economy, and perhaps to push the world back into recession. The NATO intervention was legitimized under Resolution 1973, which imposed a no-fly zone over Libya (the NATO operation known as Operation Unified Protector).

In the wake of the Arab Spring, Ben Bernanke, chairman of the Federal Reserve System, conceded that "sustained rises in the prices of oil and other commodities would represent a threat both to economic growth and to overall price stability, particularly if they were to cause inflation expectations to become less well anchored."[102]

Again oil interests appeared to play a significant role in the NATO intervention in Libya. The involvement of NATO wasn't simply about the protection of human rights; rather, the intervention was spurred primarily by national economic interests, and by the strategic considerations of the United States and the European powers.[103] National interests in the domain of energy combined with a desire to provide humanitarian relief, and the latter clearly provided moral cover for an operation that was primarily based on material economic concerns.

Conversely, the interminable and appalling Syrian conflict, wherein oil interests don't provide a powerful incentive for intervention, clearly illustrates the ambivalence of the West when energy interests aren't part of the calculus of intervention. Syria doesn't produce very much oil in the grand scheme of things (only 60,000 barrels per day), and its exports have been subject to sanctions by the United States and Europe in recent years.

The Syrian conflict has claimed more than 100,000 lives and driven millions from their homes, resulting in an enormous and complex humanitarian emergency.[104] However, the destabilization of Syria doesn't threaten the energy security (and thus the economic vitality) of Europe to the extent that the Libyan crisis did, though there were initially fears that it might destabilize other major oil-producing countries nearby.[105] The regime of Bashar al-Assad has committed atrocities against the Syrian people, and there is a general international desire for humanitarian intervention to stop them; however, there are no substantive strategic energy interests (and therefore no national strategic interests) that would incline the NATO powers to intervene. The situation is aggravated by Russia's support for Syria as one of its historical "client states" in the region. The long-standing presence of Russian military and diplomatic personnel in Syria complicates any prospects for NATO intervention, as Syria lies within Russia's historical "sphere of influence" and therefore falls under Russia's protection to a degree. Consequently, Russia has repeatedly used its veto power in the UN Security Council against substantive resolutions that would provide for multilateral intervention. In the context of Russian obstruction and a lack of strategic energy interests in Syria, the Western powers have shown little interest in upholding the supposed responsibility to protect that President Obama voiced during the Libyan intervention. Since the Syrian debacle is a matter of widespread human-rights abuses, not energy security, the US has been predictably hesitant to take any substantive action to stop the barbarous behavior of the Assad regime.[106]

Dynamics of Deprivation

Grievance-induced rebellions often result from inequities in the distribution of revenues from oil production. However, they may also result from the environmental externalities of petroleum extraction, as such activities may damage local environments and destroy the livelihood of peoples who rely upon agriculture, ranching, and fishing. The classic example of this dynamic is the Ogoni rebellion in the delta region of southern Nigeria. In this particular case, Shell Oil colluded with the corrupt and authoritarian federal government in Abuja to extract petroleum from the delta region and split the considerable revenues between the government and the corporation, repatriating very little of the wealth back to the impoverished peoples of the delta.[107] Moreover, the processes of oil extraction generated enormous damage to the region's fragile ecology. For example, the flaring of gas deposited ash laced with toxins in nearby fields, poisoning the land and greatly diminishing agricultural productivity. Consequently, many smallholder farmers were unable to make a living from meager, stunted, deformed crops. Simultaneously, frequent leakages of petroleum into the waters poisoned the local riparian ecology, resulting in vastly diminished fish populations and consequently undercutting the capacity of local fishermen to eke out a living. Wells that once provided potable drinking water are now unusable because of the exceptionally high levels of carcinogens and toxins.[108] Therefore, oil production often generates ecological externalities (costs) that increase both perceived and absolute deprivation in affected local communities. In the case of the Ogoni peoples, it was this lack of equity in revenue sharing, in combination with ecological destruction and reduced capacity to generate a decent livelihood that contributed to their calculation to mount a citizens' rebellion against the Nigerian government in 1992.[109] This example shows how insecurities may cross domains—in this case from the domain of energy to the environmental domain and then to the economic and military domains.

Ultimately, most of the effects of intra-state strife on US national security are indirect. For example, internal disruptions in Nigeria can result in international increases in the price of crude oil, which then impose greater costs on the international economy and on consumer countries such as the US. When multiple internal disruptions of producer states occur simultaneously, and such disruptions generate price spikes in global crude oil markets that are exacerbated by speculation, the economies of consumer nations may be disrupted. Should Arab Spring–type rebellions erupt throughout the Persian Gulf countries, as they may in years to come, the resulting global increase in crude-oil prices could be quite damaging to the world economy. On occasion, intra-state disruptions that inhibit oil production and restrict exports of crude oil may draw in the United States and the other great powers. NATO's intervention in Libya in 2011 is a clear example of how internal disruptions can lead to externalities (in this case the disruption of flows of crude oil to Southern Europe) that may, in turn, lead to intervention by great powers.

Terrorism

There is some preliminary evidence linking oil revenues to Islamic terrorism. Steve Yetiv contends that petrodollar flows have facilitated Islamic terrorism "by helping to fund the terrorist infrastructure," and that oil "has also offered the political issues, such as perceived American efforts to steal or control Persian Gulf oil and resentments against the Saudi royal family that have motivated al-Qaeda, that have generated the anti-Americanism from which al-Qaeda benefits, and that have helped al-Qaeda recruit followers and gain sympathy in some quarters."[110]

Terrorism doesn't occur in a vacuum, nor does it arise in some *ex nihilo* fashion, and it is important to understand the psychological roots of Islamic violence directed against the Western world and certain Arab countries. In the domain of energy there are profound historical grievances against the West that reverberate throughout the Islamic and/or Arab world, largely in reaction to the frequently illiberal behavior of Western agents and powers and their corporate allies. As I have argued above, British and US intelligence forces collaborated to depose the democratically elected Iranian prime minister Mohammed Mossadegh in Operation Ajax. This was done simply because Mossadegh wanted a better revenue-sharing agreement with the international oil companies—that is, one that would return a more equitable payment to the Iranian people. Not only did the US and Britain depose Mossadegh; they shattered the nascent democracy in Iran and imposed the rule of authoritarian strongmen in the form of the Shah Reza Pahlavi, plunging Iran into tyranny. One tyranny would eventually give way to another, as the despotic rule of the Shah gave way to the violent Islamic Revolution of 1979 and the rise of the virulently anti-Western theocracy led by Ayatollah Khomeini. As Yetiv notes, "the US role in the Persian Gulf, critical for protecting the free flow of oil at reasonable prices, has fed a not uncommon perspective of America as imperialist, power-hungry, oil-seeking, and crusading."[111] Thus, the use of force by Western powers (notably Britain and the US) to prop up tyrannies in the Persian Gulf region has fed into the anti-Western discourse that now pervades the Islamic world. That discourse has, in turn, enabled the recruitment of disaffected and dispossessed Muslims into terrorist networks that seek to strike against these despotic regimes in the Gulf, and against their historical basis of support in the countries of the West.

Complex interdependence, visible in the collapse of space wrought by processes of globalization, and discernible in the collapse of time wrought by advances in communications and travel technologies, has drawn the nations of the world in an ever tighter web of interconnectivity, one that exhibits properties both benign and malign. However, contrary to the musings of liberal optimists that such connectivity would automatically result in peace,[112] this deep connectivity has produced a backlash from peoples who resent and resist the Westernization of their cultures. This anger and resistance often takes the form of terrorist violence against Western interests and peoples and their allies in the Islamic world.

Thus, systems-level analyses that simply "black box" sovereign states, and fail to acknowledge the importance of non-state actors such as networks, are less than helpful in explaining or understanding the threat of terrorism. Yetiv argues that realists "downplay the crucial connection between oil and transnational problems, because these problems are not centrally about state actors."[113] However, he also shows an appropriate degree of pessimism toward aspects of archetypal liberal theory, particularly its assumptions about complex interdependence: "[L]iberal theorists and some empiricists argue that interdependence decreases conflict between states. They may be right, but what happens when we extend our purview to the issue area of global oil and to an arena beyond interstate relations? Here, the positive assumptions that liberal theory makes about interdependence and conflict only mislead us."[114]

The rise of the al-Qaeda network began after the Soviet Union's invasion of Afghanistan in December of 1979. Oil revenues (primarily from Saudi sources) were used to fund the development of the mujahidin forces that fought against the Soviet invaders, specifically through the funding of madrassas that infused the Afghan resistance with Wahhabist Islamic ideology.[115] Furthermore, Saudi and US funds were directed to the mujahidin through Pakistan's Inter-Services Intelligence for the purpose of providing military training and armaments. With the Afghan resistance's defeat of the Soviet Union in 1989, the mujahidin subsequently dispersed, only to coalesce again years later under the black banner of al-Qaeda.

A decisive turning point in the development of al-Qaeda occurred with the onset of the Gulf War in 1990–91. The large-scale deployment of US-led United Nations forces in northern Saudi Arabia for the purposes of protecting the Saudi oil fields from further Iraqi aggression infuriated many in the Muslim world. Osama bin Laden claimed that the presence of large forces of "infidels" so close to the Muslim Holy sites of Mecca and Medina was a grave affront to Islam, and he subsequently used this argument as an effective recruiting tool for the nascent al-Qaeda network.[116]

Oil revenues support authoritarian governments in the Persian Gulf region that Islamic terrorists view as secular, pro-Western, and profoundly corrupt. Chief among these regimes is that of Saudi Arabia, and al-Qaeda has often lambasted Saudi elites for colluding with the US and for providing the West with cheap oil while oppressing its own citizens. Osama bin Laden argued that the Saudi political elites were essentially traitors to Islam, and he subsequently encouraged strikes against targets in the Saudi kingdom.[117] Al-Qaeda began a series of strikes upon Saudi oil-production facilities in 2003, and then conducted attacks upon civilian residential compounds in May of 2004 in the Al-Hasa province of Saudi Arabia.[118] The Saudi situation is perverse, as the House of Saud uses oil revenues to buy off elements of the domestic opposition—in particular, to fund the activities of the Wahhabi clerics who then direct said funds to the madrassas. The madrassas then turn out cohorts of angry young Muslims, who often join terrorist networks, including al-Qaeda. Thus, in many ways the House of Saud indirectly contributes to proliferation of terror elements by trying to maintain its despotic grip on power within Saudi Arabia. This assessment is echoed by analysts in the US Joint Forces Command, who suspect that "a portion of OPEC's windfall might well find its way into terrorist coffers, or into the hands of movements with deeply anti-modern anti-Western goals—movements which have at their disposal increasing numbers of unemployed young men eager to attack their perceived enemies."[119]

Not surprisingly, the links between oil and terrorism remain somewhat opaque.[120] Iran has long been a sponsor of the terrorist group Hezbollah, which is known for its violent behavior throughout the Levant, particularly against Israel.[121] Indeed, Hezbollah is now seen as an extension of the power of Iran's Supreme Leader, Ayatollah Khameini, many Hezbollah personnel having being trained in Iran. This network has provided Iran with a mechanism to project power throughout the Levant and much of the Middle East. For their part, the Saudis have worked in a more indirect manner to sponsor violence by Islamic fundamentalists. Specifically, the Saudi royal family crafted an accord with Wahhabi clerics in order to maintain their hold on domestic power. Under that pact, the House of Saud directs petrodollars to support the Wahhabi strain of Islam, which is highly aggressive and advocates violence against non-Muslims. The clerics then direct these funds into the madrassa system, which recruits young men and trains them in Wahhabi ideals. Many of the young men subsequently become politically active and join violent jihadist organizations such as al-Qaeda.[122]

In this manner, the West's path dependence (specifically its addiction to Persian Gulf oil) has inadvertently generated profound externalities in the form of Islamic terrorism. President Obama has succinctly summed up the situation: "America's dependence on oil is one of the most serious threats that our nation has faced. It bankrolls dictators, pays for nuclear proliferation, and funds both sides of our struggle against terrorism."[123] Ultimately, the great powers' attempts to control the Gulf region's oil supply, particularly the long-standing alliance between the United States and Saudi Arabia, inadvertently contributed to the formation and intensification of al-Qaeda. The United States' enforcement of the Carter Doctrine, which dictated the protection of Saudi Arabia's oil fields from Iraq, played into the hands of bin Laden, who used the US presence near Mecca to cast the US as an enemy of Islam and to depict the House of Saud as corrupt pawns of the US. Yetiv concurs: "For al-Qaeda and its sympathizers, oil is seen as an Arab resource controlled by a few greedy and corrupt families across the Gulf who serve America's interests and power, power which is then used to oppress Muslims around the world."[124]

Consequences for US Security

At the international level, the pattern that has been in evidence since 1990 is one of stronger countries attacking weaker oil producers or states through which oil transits. This dynamic has been observed in many of the major wars of the post–Cold War era, including Iraq's invasion of Kuwait, Operation Desert Storm, the Iraq War, Russia's invasion of Georgia, and NATO's intervention in Libya during the civil war of 2011. Yet there have been no wars between the great powers over this period. One would expect this pattern of inter-state relations to continue for some time. Increasing domestic production of oil in should help to diminish the United States' perceptions of its energy vulnerability, and consequently reduce its propensity to intervene in producer states, at least in the near future. Conversely, one would expect that China's increasing appetite for petroleum, in combination with its limited domestic production capacity and with domestic nationalism, might result in increasingly bellicose behavior by that country. This energy-aggression hypothesis is supported by China's increasingly bellicose behavior in the South China Sea and the East China Sea, particularly in regard to the demarcation of nautical borders that would affect China's capacity to extract energy resources from the sea bed. Collectively, one might reasonably expect the pattern of great powers striking lesser powers in order to attain energy resources to continue for some time.

This doesn't mean that the dominant mode of interaction between sovereign states in the domain of energy will be violent conflict. Rather, the dominant mode of interaction between countries will continue to be trade, and the frequency of inter-state war will be low. However, the dominant mode of cooperation may be punctuated by occasional conflicts when great powers perceive their national energy interests to be at risk. In all probability, the pattern of hegemonic aggression against the weak (or manipulation of the weak) in order to secure energy resources will continue for some time, particularly in the case of authoritarian states such as China and Russia.

Much of the recent literature on energy security (scholarly and popular) has exhibited a significant degree of threat inflation. For example, both Klare and Moyo have argued that the increasing scarcity of oil would foster manifestations of aggression between the great powers.[125] Contrary to these arguments, I find it highly unlikely that there will be a profound scarcity of crude oil in the near future, particularly for the United States or Russia. This new abundance of oil results from technological advances (discussed above) that have opened up substantive new terrestrial and oceanic reserves of crude oil. Because of the current pattern of asymmetrical aggression over control of crude-oil supplies, the high probability of Yergin's plateau, and the existence of nuclear weapons, the great powers probably will not come to blows over oil scarcity.

As domestic oil production continues to surge in the United States, it should help to diminish the country's more illiberal and bellicose tendencies, at least in foreign energy policy. But even though the increased production of crude oil in the US may reduce the price of oil on global markets slightly,[126] this doesn't necessarily guarantee that China will act in a peaceful manner if it encounters a scarcity of oil. Indeed, the evidence at hand points to an increasingly belligerent China that is willing to test its rivals' claims to sovereignty throughout the East and South China Seas. A pragmatic interpretation of these dynamics suggests that the United States' propensity for inter-state conflict over energy should decline somewhat, whereas China's belligerence may continue to escalate.

Tensions will come to the fore again when the fracking boom has run its course and when oil sands and sea-bed resources are depleted. However, the depletion of unconventional sources may take several decades. Barring significant advances in technical ingenuity, the exhaustion of viable unconventional oil reserves may generate economic disruption, political disruption, intra-state conflict, and wars between consumer nations. Fortunately, such prospects of the depletion of unconventional sources of oil remain temporally distal, and are extremely unlikely in the next decade or two. Moreover, one might reasonably expect significant technological advances in that period, particularly as the price of oil rises. Thus, one must be careful to delineate the problem correctly, and to avoid unnecessary threat inflation in the domain of foreign energy policy. There is no imminent threat of war between the great powers over oil resources, at least not in any direct sense. However, the threat of great-power war against militarily weaker but energy-rich countries will persist for some time, and will be exacerbated as unconventional sources of oil begin to be depleted. The possibility remains that heightened nationalism in China and Japan may combine with competing claims to sovereignty over the Diaoyu/Senkaku islands to generate a skirmish between China and Japan. In such an event, a miscalculation by one or both parties could result in a limited military engagement between those two countries, which could draw the US into the conflict on the side of Japan.

Nader El-Hefnawy, who writes on international affairs, argues that the United States' dependence on foreign oil may undermine its hegemonic status: "[T]he United States could ultimately lose its position as a world power ... just as the UK's position declined along with the age of coal and steam that [the UK] pioneered."[127] If this logic is correct, the rapidly increasing US domestic production of petroleum, and declining oil imports, should actually *bolster* the power of the US, and diminish US perceptions of insecurity to a degree. Consequently, the political consequences of augmented production, resulting from enhanced production of oil from unconventional sources, will be to slow the decline of American hegemony predicted by Andrew Bacevich, Robert Pape, and Chalmers Johnson, though it may not reverse it. It may also reduce the probability that the US (and other major consumer powers, such as China) will engage in bellicose actions.

Over the longer term, increasing prices for crude oil may result in economic destabilization for many of those consumer nations that fail to develop alternative energy technologies. The *perception* of increasing scarcity of crude oil, particularly in East Asia, may lead to conflict through a number of plausible scenarios. First, *perceived* scarcity may lead to conflicts over disputed resources in boundary regions that span several sovereign states, or in regions (e.g., the East China Sea) where competing claims to sovereignty foster nationalism and bellicose foreign policy. Perceptions of scarcity also may contribute indirectly to conflict by destabilizing the economies of non-adaptive consumer nations, which may then destabilize the global economy, which in turn may contribute to widespread political turbulence and manifestations of bellicose behavior. In this case, perceptions of scarcity may be more important than the empirical material reality of scarcity.[128] Such dynamics of misperception would seem to have been in play for the Bush administration as it decided to invade Iraq in 2003.[129]

Policing the global supply lines of petroleum through the direct use of the US armed forces is extraordinarily expensive. According to the Department of Defense, protecting energy-supply lines costs approximately $1 billion a year; according to the Cato Institute, it costs about $70 billion a year. The economic geographer Roger Stern estimated the aggregate costs to the US of projecting military force into the Persian Gulf region to protect energy flows at approximately $6.8 trillion over the period 1976–2007.[130] Regardless of the true figure, this projecting military force is an enormous and probably unsustainable drain on the country's coffers.

Although the armoring of international oil flows[131] and the steadily increasing flows of military aid from the superpowers to their producer-state allies will probably not generate direct conflict between the major powers, the infusion of military advisors and weapons into oil-producing states is likely to exacerbate regional security dilemmas, increasing the probability of conflict. The great powers might eventually be drawn into such conflagrations, but the probability of their engaging in direct conflict with one another will remain very low for some time. This regional dimension is missing from much of the literature on the subject, and yet these regional dynamics (including Iran's desire for hegemony over the Persian Gulf region and China's hegemonic aspirations throughout East Asia) are potentially problematic over the longer term. The potential involvement of the great powers in such regional disputes may result in accidental conflicts in which "unintended escalation" may occur.[132]

5 Oil and US Grand Strategy

Historically, US grand strategy has consisted of a symbiotic alliance between the state and corporate actors (e.g., the Seven Sisters) wherein the latter served as the mechanisms of global oil resource extraction. In turn, the US has often used its diplomatic and military power to create political and economic environments conducive to the operations of the international oil companies. As in the Twin Pillars strategy in the Persian Gulf, US grand energy strategy also has employed the tactic of using regional allies to foster regional political climates favorable to the oil companies and to the US. However, such strategies often resulted in the United States' supporting despotic and illiberal regimes, and thus the desire for power and profit often triumphed over principle in the conduct of US foreign energy policy.

In view of recent technological advances and significant changes in oil demand and oil production, it is necessary to examine the shifts in both the extractive capacity and the intent of significant producer and consumer countries. I argue that United States' grand oil strategy continues to exhibit considerable continuity with past practices, even as the international energy environment is witnessing profound shifts in oil distribution and in the intent and capacity of producer and consumer states. I also argue that the historical canons of US grand oil strategy may be increasingly archaic in a world increasingly dominated by energy nationalism, so apparent in the rise of the national oil companies.

Despite the historical dominance of the Persian Gulf in US grand oil strategy, the vast majority of the United States' oil imports come from other countries in the Americas, notably Canada, Mexico, and Venezuela. Most of the oil that the US consumes is produced domestically, and the recent surge in domestic production has permitted a significant reduction in the importing of oil.

As of 2014, Canada remains the greatest single source of oil imports to the US, followed by Saudi Arabia, Mexico, and Venezuela. In view of its overwhelming direct dependence on oil from the Americas and its diminishing reliance on Persian Gulf oil, the US should reconsider its tradition of massive military deployments in the Persian Gulf region. This would permit the development of an energy grand strategy that would focus on the stabilization of oil supplies from the zone of direct dependence, the Americas.

As continuing advances in technology allow more extraction of oil from unconventional sources throughout the Americas, the US will see disincentives to continue its formidable investments in the costly deployment of military power to "protect" the Gulf. The US would do well to reallocate funds and forces away from the Persian Gulf and toward creating a regional energy structure in the Americas. This would entail the diversion of funds away from the projection of military power and toward initiatives (economic and diplomatic) that foster the stabilization of democracy in Mexico and Brazil, lead to improved relations with Venezuela, and assist in negotiating a compact between Argentina and the United Kingdom over the oil of the Falkland Islands. Further, the US should actively engage with Canada to develop Alberta's oil sands in a manner that is economically sensible for both countries, using novel carbon-capture technologies that can reduce carbon emissions and new production technologies that can minimize the destruction of the regional ecology.

Conversely, many other countries remain primarily dependent on oil exports from the Persian Gulf, with the Asian powers (China, Japan) exhibiting particularly vulnerability to disruptions in the supply of oil from that region. Despite a degree of dependence on Gulf oil, the Europeans still obtain a considerable proportion of their oil from the North Sea, and derive some imports from North and West Africa, and so they exhibit relatively less direct dependence on Persian Gulf oil than the Asian powers. Thus, in the domain of direct dependence on oil imports, the regional strategic nature of oil becomes increasingly visible. Regarding indirect dependence, all major consumers of oil exhibit varying degrees of sensitivity and vulnerability, and the regional dimension becomes a bit more difficult to discern. Nonetheless, if unconventional oil reserves begin to wane (as they may by 2040), and if technologies to reduce dependency on oil aren't widely adopted, the regional strategic dimension will become increasingly important.

Perhaps it is best to re-conceptualize US energy grand strategy based upon a pattern of concentric circles that radiate outward from the continental US, with priority given to the nations most proximate to the US. This concentric re-conceptualization of energy security, and the prioritization of continental energy flows, is a more coherent and rational strategy than the obtuse argument (still dominant in Washington) that every oil field on the planet is of strategic importance to the US. By arguing that every oil field is of crucial security interest to the US, this proliferation of interests and lack of prioritization result in limitless interests, and in the ubiquitous projection of military power. Consequently, the militaristic mindset and the desire to securitize the entire global oil infrastructure place a profound economic burden on the US and threaten to drag it into conflicts that aren't truly in the national interest.

The pragmatic and non-ideological formulation[1] of a series of concentric rings radiating outward from the continental US derives from the simple fact that the US gets the vast majority of its imported oil from countries in the Americas, particularly Canada, Mexico, and Venezuela. Let me begin my discussion of the United States' oil grand strategy with Canada, the United States' most important partner in the domain of energy security.

Canada

Strangely, many analyses of US energy security dynamics omit any substantive discussion of Canada's central role in the provision of energy (particularly oil) to the US. This probably is attributable to the United States' unfortunate historical tendency to take Canada for granted. Indeed, Canada is the primary source of petroleum imports for the US, surpassing Saudi Arabia, Mexico, Venezuela, and Nigeria. In 2010, Canada exported roughly $200 million worth of crude oil to the US per day. In 2012 the US imported 1,078,412,000 barrels of oil from Canada, and the trend line of Canadian imports has been increasing inexorably since 1985.[2] As a function of its huge unconventional oil deposits (e.g., the oil sands of Alberta), Canada possesses the second-largest total proven oil reserves in the world (about 178 billion barrels), second only to Saudi Arabia.[3] Investment in the oil sands has resulted in substantial increases in Canada's oil production. Canada produced 3.35 million bpd in 2008 and 3.597 million bpd in 2012, and the US Energy Information Administration forecasts that Canada's oil production may exceed 4.2 million bpd by 2030.[4]

Though US-Canadian relations in the domain of energy are relatively placid at present, there has been some history of tension between the two countries over the development and export of energy resources. Before the 1970s, Canadian natural resources had typically been open to foreign investment; however, this was limited in 1973 when the Liberal government of Pierre Trudeau created the Foreign Investment Review Agency (FIRA) in an attempt to determine whether foreign investment in energy resources was truly beneficial to Canadian interests. Trudeau also nationalized foreign oil assets, creating a Crown Corporation called Petro-Canada.[5] The creation of Petro-Canada was primarily a response to the economic and political destabilization that resulted from the Arab oil embargo, in an effort to shield the Canadian economy from future energy shocks. It was also, in combination with the creation of FIRA and the Canadian Development Corporation, an attempt to increase Canadian ownership of or control over the industry.

In 1980, Trudeau, who had resigned in 1979 after his party's electoral defeat, returned to power after the defeat of his successor's party and quickly established the National Energy Policy, which was seen as both socialist and nationalist by the Reagan administration. The NEP was greeted with formal diplomatic protests from both Secretary of State Alexander Haig and President Ronald Reagan.[6] According to Marc Lalonde, then Canada's Minister of Energy, the NEP would further the national interest, as it would "establish the basis for Canadians to seize control of their own energy future through security of supply and ultimate independence from the world market."[7]

In response to the energy nationalism of the Trudeau years, the United States sought permanent access to Canadian energy reserves through the mechanism of the Free Trade Agreement concluded between Canada and the US in 1987.[8] The central energy component of the FTA is Article 904, also known as the "proportional sharing clause." Article 904 stipulates that either the US or Canada may interrupt the exporting of energy resources if a shortfall is experienced in the exporting country, but only if such constraints don't diminish the quantity that was historically made available.[9] Put simply, it obligates Canada to provide continual oil exports to the US, prohibits Canada from enacting tariffs on external sources of energy, and ensures that export prices of petroleum remain consistent with domestic prices.

Similarly, a "proportional sharing rule" appears in the North American Free Trade Agreement (NAFTA) of 1994, both in Article 315 and in Article

605. The crux of that rule is that Canada is obligated to maintain both the proportional quantity and equivalent quality of energy exports to the US, even in times of scarcity. Such protocols don't apply to Mexico, which shrewdly sought exemptions.

NAFTA has the potential to act as a significant constraint on Canadian energy sovereignty by providing US multinational corporations with their own enforcement mechanisms. Specifically, chapter 11 of NAFTA provides a mechanism for international energy corporations to sue the Canadian government for alleged violations of NAFTA rules. Such suits would then be adjudicated by NAFTA tribunals, whose decisions would subsequently take precedence over the domestic laws of the member countries.[10] In April of 2001, on the advice of the cabinet-level North American Energy Working Group (in which Canada, Mexico, and the US took part), the G. W. Bush administration called for the development of a comprehensive North American energy plan.

The US Energy Policy Act of 2005[11] specifically designates the Canadian oil sands as a strategic energy reserve for the use of the US military. That designation is articulated in a section titled "Use of Fuel to Meet Department of Defense Needs."

Early in the twenty-first century, Canada's status in the global energy hierarchy was a topic of debate. In July of 2006, before attending the Group of Eight summit in St. Petersburg, Prime Minister Stephen Harper delivered an address to the Canada-UK Chamber of Commerce in London in which he remarked that Canada was now an "emerging energy superpower."[12] It is clear that the Harper government views energy as the fulcrum of Canadian economic power in the twenty-first century, much as President Vladimir Putin sees Russian economic power as derived from energy resources. However, it is not at all clear that the United States regards Canada in a similar light. Indeed, the Obama administration has been at odds with the Harper government over extension of the Keystone XL oil pipeline, which would import huge quantities of crude oil from Alberta's oil sands into the US. The Obama administration's decision to perennially deny approval of the Keystone XL project is attributable to strenuous opposition to the project by environmentalists (an important component of the Democratic Party's base) and to soaring domestic production of crude oil in the US in recent years. Should the Obama administration continue to block the Keystone project, it will incentivize the diversion of Canadian oil away from US markets and toward Asian markets. Even in the face of considerable opposition from Native (First Nations) and environmental groups in Canada, oil from Alberta probably will reach foreign markets, either by pipeline or by railroad.

In view of the increases in US domestic oil production and the Obama administration's continuing resistance to the Keystone pipeline, US demand for Canadian oil may actually stagnate or decline from 2015 to 2025. As a consequence, it is likely that Canadian oil exports will increasingly shift away from the US and toward East Asia, particularly China and Japan. Canada's energy pivot toward Asia is already reflected in the investment patterns of Chinese NOCs that are buying up significant equity stakes in the corporations of the Alberta oil sands. For example, in December of 2009 the Canadian government announced that it had granted PetroChina permission to acquire 60 percent control of the Athabaska Oil Sands Corporation for $1.7 billion.[13] Furthermore, in 2012 PetroChina signed a memorandum of understanding with Enbridge Pipelines to construct a pipeline from Edmonton to the port of Kitimat on the Pacific coast to transport oil from the Canadian sands to China.[14] Officials in Washington have expressed their concern about the magnitude of Chinese involvement in the oil sands, yet they persist in delaying approval for the Keystone project. For example, the chair of the US-China Economic and Security Review Commission, Carolyn Bartholomew, said "I think that an acquisition [of Canadian oil sands] should raise national security questions both for the government of Canada and for the government of the United States."[15] In June of 2014, as a result of mounting frustration with the Obama administration, the Harper government approved the development of the Northern Gateway pipeline, which will transport oil to the Pacific coast and thereafter to lucrative Asian markets.[16]

To the United States' chagrin, Chinese investments in Canadian oil-sands producers have increased, particularly since the finalization of the China National Offshore Oil Corporation's acquisition of Nexen Energy's oil-sands assets in 2013.[17] That deal benefits the Canadian energy sector by supplying capital for the development of oil sands, and will augment job creation in Alberta. In addition, foreign investment in the oil sands will increase the amount of crude oil flowing into international markets, lowering global oil prices, which in turn will benefit the global economy. It also means that Canada will be forced to diversify its customer base away from the US and toward China and other Asian polities, which will in turn diminish Canada's dependence on US energy markets. The growing presence of quasi-statist Chinese oil corporations in Canadian oil fields may concern US security analysts, as it suggests that Canada may become increasingly tied to China's interests and less beholden to the US. Canada's pivot toward Asia and away from the US may become problematic in light of China's penchant for bilateral energy agreements that may ultimately send oil directly to China.

The diversification of markets for Canadian oil will benefit Canada over the longer term, and it will diminish Canada's asymmetrical interdependence with the United States somewhat. Canada's pivot toward Asia may translate into increasing leverage for Canada relative to the US, particularly if Canada pits China against the US in order to see which of these powers is more accommodating of Canadian interests. In view of the United States' historical tendency to take Canada for granted, the potential for miscalculation by the US is significant. Allowing China to acquire ever greater equity positions in oil sands corporations may seem alluring in the short term, but it may generate friction in the years to come, particularly if China's strategy of equity oil results in oil's bypassing international markets and being directed straight to China. Though fracking and deep-water drilling will enhance US domestic production in the next 10–30 years, those sources will eventually be tapped out, at least to the point that increasing prices for the remaining oil will diminish oil's status as a primary fuel for most countries. Having taken Canada for granted for decades, the US cannot dismiss China's moves to acquire increasing interests in the Canadian oil sands as inconsequential.

Mexico

Historically, Mexico has been the number-two provider of petroleum imports to the United States, but that status has eroded since 2005 as a result of the long-term depletion of its conventional petroleum reserves and consequent declines in production. Mexico's aggregate oil production declined from 3.5 million barrels per day in 2004 to just 2.9 million bpd in 2013, and its oil exports to the United States have declined by a third over the same period even as Mexico continued to provide approximately 12 percent of the oil imported into the US. Mexico has proven oil reserves of 10.2 billion barrels, concentrated largely in the Campeche Basin in the southern portion of the country.[18]

All of Mexico's easily accessible fields are now past maturity and significantly depleted. The giant Cantarell field produced only 630,000 bpd in 2009, whereas in 2004 it had produced 2.12 million bpd.[19] The Chicontepec field, once forecast to produce 700,000 bpd by 2017, produced only 35,000 bpd in 2012. The Mexican NOC Pemex conceded in 2011 that Mexico's most productive field, Ku-Maloob-Zap, was expected to pass its production peak in 2013.[20] Although there probably still are considerable sub-sea petroleum reserves in the Gulf of Mexico, Pemex may lack the technology, expertise, and capital it would need to tap such deep-water reserves. Indeed, in 2012 Pemex was subject to a 99 percent tax on its total revenue, which meant that almost all of its revenue went to the Mexican state, leaving almost nothing for capital reinvestment.

This decline in oil production portends a host of problems for Mexico, and also for the United States. Diminished petroleum revenues are problematic for the country's government, approximately 40 percent of whose annual revenues come from oil exports.[21] Short-term declines in oil revenues will affect the government's capacity to maintain order and to provide basic public services, even as the demand for such increases.[22] The state's diminished capacity will exacerbate poverty and crime. Consequently, the decline in oil production may exacerbate pressures for migration to the US, and may increase the power of the drug cartels relative to a weakening state. The weakening of the state may also result in more violence near US-Mexico border. All these changes may increase pressures for Mexicans to migrate to the US.

In 2013 Mexican policy makers recognized that this system of maximum extraction of revenues from Pemex was unsustainable, and that the company was in trouble. Consequently, the Nieto administration proposed widespread liberal reforms to the Hydrocarbons Law (1938) in order to permit joint ventures between Pemex and the international oil companies. On August 12, 2013, President Enrique Peña Nieto sent a bill to the Mexican Congress to initiate wide-ranging reforms of Pemex that would permit joint ventures between the NOC and international oil companies. Pemex would maintain the right to bid on certain lots, but would share investment capital, expertise, and revenues with its international partners.

If granted to Pemex, the new operational freedoms proposed by the Nieto administration promise to significantly enhance Mexico's oil production, as large new offshore fields may be explored and developed.[23] The

Mexican legislature ratified these proposed reforms on August 11, 2014. Nieto's vision of institutional reform and liberalization of Mexico's oil industry hinges upon Pemex's partnership with both IOCs and other NOCs. On October 1, 2014, Exxon became the first major IOC to conclude a partnership with Pemex. Chevron, Noble, and BHP Billiton remain suitors.

Brazil

In 2012 Brazil produced 2.7 million barrels per day and possessed reserves of about 12.3 billion barrels (primarily in the Santos Basin and the Campos Basin, off the southeast coast). Brazil became a net exporter of petroleum in 2009, and in 2012 Brazil exported 187,000 bpd to the US.

On November 8, 2007, the Brazilian NOC Petrobras announced the discovery of an oil field in the Santos Basin that contained between 5 billion and 8 billion barrels. At the time, that field (then called Tupi, now called Lula) was the largest oil field to be discovered anywhere since 2000, when a 12-billion-barrel field was found in Kazakhstan.[24] Analysts speculated that the Tupi field would give Brazil greater economic (and hence political) power that would help to counterbalance the ambitions of Venezuela's president, Hugo Chávez.

Tapping the pre-salt-layer fields of the Santos and Campos Basins presents complex technical challenges, requiring Petrobras to drill through 7,000 feet of water and then through 17,000 feet of sand, rock, and salt to reach the oil. In mid April of 2008, a second, larger field was found in the same region of sub-sea salt formations. Haroldo Lima, Director of Brazil's National Petroleum Agency, confirmed that it might contain about 33 billion barrels of oil, five times that of the Tupi (Lula) field. Lima stated that "it could be the world's biggest discovery in the past 30 years, and the world's third-biggest currently active field."[25] In August of 2009, the Brazilian government took a step toward nationalization by limiting the role of foreign companies in the development of the oil fields.

The discovery of large deep-water oil fields renders discussions of "peak oil" problematic, as the evolution of new exploration and drilling technologies may allow us to tap enormous oil reserves in the continental shelves and in shallower portions of the seabed. The principal constraints, then, are a shortage of deep-sea rigs capable of extracting said oil and the fact that developing such resources often takes a long time. If we witness a surge in the construction of deep-sea drilling rigs, we may not face an oil crunch for some time; if we don't, and if a surge in global demand is accompanied by "hawkish" speculation on global markets, we may face a crunch. In 2013 Petrobras announced plans to invest $147.5 billion in offshore oil exploration and production.

Brazil's prescient investment in the development of biofuels (notably cellulosic ethanol) and its recent discoveries of vast new oil deposits offshore have put that country in a position to gain economic and political power in the next 20 years and to attain a degree of energy independence that will be unparalleled in the Western world.[26] There is now some concern that certain Brazilian interests may have exaggerated how much crude oil was present in the deep-sea fields, and that Brazil may not realize some of the expected petrodollar gains. Moreover, there are some concerns that revelations of extensive corruption and Petrobras's increasing debt may impair Petrobras's ability to extract the oil that has been found in the Santos Basin.[27]

Venezuela

Venezuela possesses reserves of crude oil (including the heavy crude of the Orinoco Belt) estimated at 211 billion barrels. Venezuela nationalized its oil industry in the 1970s, forming Petroleos de Venezuela S.A. PdVSA generates about a third of Venezuela's GDP and half of the state's revenue, and accounts for 80 percent of the country's export earnings. The US Energy Information Administration estimates that Venezuela produced 2.39 million bpd in 2008 and 1.7 million bpd in 2011, and aggregate production has declined by about 25 percent since 2001.[28]

For much of the twentieth century Venezuela was a major exporter of oil to the United States, accounting for 50 percent of US oil imports in 1960. That declined to 9 percent in 2008. Venezuela's oil exports are largely regional, most of the oil going to South America, the Caribbean, and the US, and some to Europe.[29] In order to develop the heavy and sour crude of the Orinoco Belt, PdVSA has recently partnered with foreign oil companies, including Petrobras of Brazil, CNPC of China, Petropars of Iran, and ONGC of India.[30]

Hugo Chávez's rise to power resulted in the increasing use of rents derived from petroleum extraction to develop a foreign policy that directly challenged US hegemony in Latin America and the Caribbean. This strategy entailed "soft power" mechanisms under the banner of the "new Bolivarian revolution," the provision of heavily discounted oil to Venezuela's regional allies,[31] and the development of "hard power" through the purchase of weapons.[32] "Between 2004 and 2006," the Council on Foreign Relations reported, "Venezuela spent roughly $4.3 billion on weapons, according to a January 2007 Defense Intelligence Agency report. As part of deals signed with Russia in 2006, Venezuela purchased 100,000 Kalashnikov rifles, 24 Sukhoi-30 fighter planes, and 53 Russian helicopters. In March 2008, it hired Belarus to build an air defense system."[33]

In November of 2001, Chávez established the Hydrocarbons Law by a presidential decree,[34] which increased royalties on companies operating in Venezuela from 16.6 percent to 30 percent for light crude, and from 1 percent to 16.6 percent for the extra-heavy crude of the Orinoco Belt. Once a major oil exporter, Venezuela has witnessed a considerable decline in production since 2002, largely because of the policies of the Chávez administration. The decline in production worsened after a prolonged strike by PDVSA workers and Chávez's subsequent move to fire much of PDVSA's management in February of 2003. With aging infrastructure, a dearth of foreign capital investment and technology, and dwindling management expertise, Venezuela will have a difficult time returning to the levels of production witnessed in 2002.

In recent years Venezuela has impeded US energy security by openly soliciting China's intervention and cooperation in exploring and developing new oil reserves. Specifically, Venezuela has asked China for assistance in the development of an oil pipeline that would run through Colombia to the port of Tumaco on the Pacific in order to provide shipments directly to Asia, bypassing the Panama Canal.

Further, the Chávez regime signed significant oil deals with Brazil, Argentina, Uruguay, and Paraguay, and also signed deals with 13 countries in the Caribbean basin (which resulted in the creation of Petrocaribe).[35] "Soft power" strategies are manifest in this mechanism, which provides about 80,000 barrels per day to the region. Venezuela provided about 59 million barrels of oil to the region under Petrocaribe in the years 2005–2008. Unfortunately for Venezuela, many of the countries that received Venezuelan oil under the Petrocaribe program have now incurred large debts to Venezuela, and so Venezuela finds itself increasingly unable to collect rents on the oil it has exported.[36]

Chávez also used petro-diplomacy to improve Venezuela's relations with Cuba, providing discounted oil exports to help sustain the Castro regime.

This began with the signing of the Convenio Integral de Cooperacion in 2000. In 2005 Chávez decided to increase the exporting of subsidized oil to Cuba. Venezuela has a separate deal to supply Cuba with 90,000 bpd of oil and refined products such as gasoline. According to the Council on Foreign Relations, "Venezuela is selling up to 100,000 barrels of oil per day to Cuba, discounted by as much as 40 percent. In exchange, thousands of Venezuelans have traveled to Cuba for medical treatment, and Cuban doctors help administer health care programs for low-income Venezuelans."[37] During 2006 Chávez offered subsidized oil to low-income families in the United States, a clear projection of Venezuelan soft power and an attempt to undercut the legitimacy of the Bush administration.

Despite the anti-US rhetoric of Chávez's administration and that of his successor, Nicolás Maduro, the high level of economic interdependence of Venezuela and the US make it extremely unlikely that the former would curtail shipments of oil to the latter. However, as Venezuela tilts toward China it may acquire the capacity to diversify its exports away from the US. The completion of an oil pipeline from Venezuela through Colombia to the Pacific probably would make the costs of transportation tolerable to China, so the prospect of intensification of the oil trade between Venezuela and China is plausible.

The Chávez regime actively sought to maximize the international price of oil, in collaboration with price hawks in Iran and Russia. Moreover, Chávez and President Mahmoud Ahmadinejad of Iran visited each other numerous times and signed a number of agreements between the two countries facilitating trade, enhancing diplomacy, and facilitating investment. And Chávez's purchases of Russian weapons systems provided Venezuela with a degree of political capital in Russia as Chávez sought Russian aid in maintaining elevated international oil prices.

Chávez died in 2013. His death was expected to usher in a new era of increased cooperation between Venezuela and the United States, but that hasn't happened yet. As of late 2014 Venezuela was beset by soaring inflation, scarcities of goods, widespread corruption, and criminal violence. Unfortunately, Chávez's successor, Maduro, has adopted a similarly confrontational stance toward the US while consolidating his grip on power in Venezuela. Indeed, the new regime seems to exhibit an even greater propensity for autocracy and ineptitude than its predecessor, and Maduro has asked the National Assembly for the power to be able to rule by decree.[38] Venezuela presents the US with two complications for its foreign energy policy. First, the Maduro regime may maintain the hawkish position of its predecessor within the context of OPEC. Second, the greater danger is the prospect of widespread economic and political chaos in Venezuela that might interrupt energy flows to Western markets and inflate international crude-oil prices. Even if domestic strife should destabilize the Maduro regime, there is no guarantee that the government that would succeed it would be competent and capable of stabilizing Venezuela or that it would seek a better relationship with the US. Declining oil revenues will impede the government's capacity to provide public goods and services, increasing the likelihood of insurrection and violence.

A conclusion that can be drawn from this section is that the United States would benefit from a new foreign energy policy that would focus on cooperating with other countries in the Western Hemisphere, working to offset the growing influence of China, and using technology transfer to open up new unconventional fields (either terrestrial or oceanic) in those countries. The United States' historically dismissive treatment of its neighbors in the Western Hemisphere has been counterproductive. Thus, the US would be wise to improve its relations with Canada, Mexico, Venezuela, and Brazil and to eschew its myopic obsession with maintaining hegemony over the energy resources of the chaotic Persian Gulf.

Russia

Few countries surpass Russia in exemplifying how oil, illiberal statism, and violence are related. Under Putin, Russia has shown itself to be both a powerhouse in the domain of energy and a resurgent great power bent on geopolitical expansion. In this section, I argue that control over energy flows was a factor in Russia's invasion of Georgia in 2008 and in its seizure of Crimea in 2014.

Russia has long been one of the world's greatest oil-producing countries, and it derives much of its economic and political power from its enormous energy reserves. There is a powerful positive association between rents derived from energy production and the economic vitality of Russia.[39] Because it is extraordinarily dependent on revenue from petroleum exports, malignant networks of clientelism, patronage, and corruption have come to dominate the Russian state since the end of the Cold War.

Russia has enormous hydrocarbon reserves (estimated at about 60 billion barrels of oil in 2012[40]). Most of its fully developed fields are located in Western Siberia, and there is now considerable energy exploration going on in Eastern Siberia. Though Russia's oil reserves aren't as great as Saudi Arabia's, its projected oil holdings comprise 42 percent of the non-OPEC reserves, giving Russia a considerable degree of clout in global energy markets.[41] Russia expects significant production from Eastern Siberian fields (particularly from those recently discovered on and near Sakhalin Island), and these lucrative energy resources will be exported southward to China, Japan, and other energy-hungry countries.[42] The development of East Siberian energy resources is also part of Russia's strategy to limit its exposure to markets in Europe (particularly in the face of EU sanctions over the Ukraine crisis) and re-orient toward the growing economies of the Pacific Rim.

The Russian penchant for seeing natural resources as a mechanism to augment the power of the state is nothing novel,[43] but Putin has argued that Russia's restoration to great-power status depends on its ability to use its energy flows as a mechanism of political power. Prospects for cooperation between Russia and the NATO countries have been undermined by Russia's penchant to use energy flows as mechanisms to project political power against weaker states (among them Ukraine, Georgia, and Belarus) that have depended on Russia for energy.[44] Putin completed his PhD work at the St. Petersburg Mining Institute in June of 1997. In his thesis he called for the Russian state to reassert its control over the nations natural resources wresting the control of such resources from oligarchs. He argued that Russia should then use its energy assets to restore its economic vitality, to exert political power over other countries, and thus to propel Russia's return to its former status as a global energy superpower.[45] Russia's energy resources have enhanced its capacity for the "strategic manipulation" of other polities.[46]

Historically, the vast majority of Russia's oil exports have flowed westward to Europe, notably to Germany, the Netherlands, and Poland. For example, in 2010 only 12 percent of Russian production was exported to East Asia (predominantly to China), and less than 6 percent of Russian oil went to the Americas (primarily the United States). However, this pattern is changing. Recent (2014) discussions between Putin and Premier Xi Jinping of China have resulted in several agreements to substantially increase Russian oil exports to China. As of 2011 China had become the number-four importer of Russian oil, and so China's asymmetrical dependence on Russian energy flows is progressively tying Russia and China together. This gradual reorientation of China's energy imports toward Russia and away from the Persian Gulf reflects China's concerns about the US Navy's capacity to interdict and or otherwise disrupt China's oil-supply lines from the Gulf. Thus, we should expect to witness increasing cooperation between Russia and China in the sphere of energy.

Russia's increasingly bellicose behavior since 2008 seems to be related in part to its energy and security interests. This is not to be so reductionist as to imply that energy interests are the sole motivation for Russia. Rather, it seems that when there is the combination of a Russian ethnic diaspora, energy resources, and/or transit mechanisms (i.e., pipelines) in a contiguous state, this confluence of ideational and material motivations has provided the impetus for Russian intervention. When such ethnic and energy factors have been combined with stark asymmetries of power, Russia has often invaded the weaker territory.

In the case of the Russian invasion of Georgia in 2008 and the subsequent "annexation" of South Ossetia and Abkhazia, energy interests played a central role in Russia's decision making. Specifically, the development of the Baku-Tbilisi-Ceyhan pipeline provided an economic threat to historical Russian dominance over transport of lucrative energy exports from the Caspian region to the West. In this case, the Russian invasion of northern Georgia clearly sent a powerful message to the pro-American government of Mikael Saakashvili. Russia masked its intent by stating that its goal was "protection" of the Russian diaspora, but arguably Russia's true interest lay in maintaining its position as regional hegemon in the domain of energy. Regrettably the international community failed to punish Russia for its naked aggression in 2008, and the Russians learned that the use of force had paid off. The US, which had promised aid to Georgia, provided no substantive aid, and lost credibility among allies throughout Eastern Europe.[47]

Russia's invasion and annexation of Crimea in 2014 was also related to Putin's desire to acquire energy assets. Admittedly, there are multiple reasons underpinning Russia's calculus of aggression—among them retention of Russian naval bases in the region, "protection" of the Russian ethnic diaspora there, and a desire to claim the lucrative energy assets in the Black Sea that lie off the coast of Crimea. The seizure of Crimea extends Russian jurisdiction over the sub-sea oil and gas reserves that lie within the 200-nautical-mile limit, reserves that Russia had unsuccessfully sought to acquire from Ukraine in 2012. The seizure of these energy reserves will enrich Russia while depriving Ukraine of the same assets and thereby entrenching Ukraine's dependence on Russia for energy.[48] Paradoxically, then, the United Nations Convention on the Law of the Sea (UNCLOS) treaty of 1982, which sought to limit conflict, is now encouraging aggression between sovereign states in their quest to lay sovereign claim to oceanic energy resources.

The invasion of Georgia and the seizure of Crimea illustrate a pattern, wherein a resurgent great power uses its asymmetries of power (primarily military force) to seize contiguous territories that either contain significant energy assets (Crimea) or represent a threat to Russian regional hegemony in the domain of energy (Georgia). In both cases the international community has largely stood by and watched as Russia's irredentist ambitions have led to seizures of territory from other sovereign states.

China

Few would have foreseen the explosive economic growth generated by the People's Republic of China in recent decades. This surge of Chinese economic development has provided a boon to the global economy, and China's economy has expanded at a rate of about 9 percent a year since 1978. In parallel with this economic boom, there has been a surge in global prices for many commodities, particularly crude oil. China possesses the world's largest population (1.4 billion, more than half of whom now live in cities[49]), and automobile ownership is increasing. There were 240 million cars in China in 2013.[50]

China was largely self-sufficient in oil until 1993; indeed, it was a net exporter. After 1993, however, it became a net importer. This shift was due primarily to the stagnation of domestic oil production, in conjunction with surging domestic demand for petroleum derivatives that resulted from its burgeoning industry and the expansion of China's middle class.[51] In 1998, China recognized its increasing dependence on foreign oil and reorganized its domestic petroleum sector, consolidating state-owned petroleum assets into three companies: the China Petrochemical Corporation (Sinopec), the China National Petroleum Corporation (CNPC), and the China National Offshore Oil Corporation (CNOOC).[52]

With rapid economic expansion, China's oil consumption rose from 4.7 million barrels per day in 2000 to 10.6 million bpd in December of 2012.

According to analysts at Deutsche Bank, China's oil consumption increased by another 4.9 percent (468,000 bpd) during 2013.[53] China is now poised to surpass the United States in total demand for imported oil. It now imports 6 million barrels per day (56.6 percent of its total daily consumption), twice as much as it imported in 2005.

China's approach to energy security is markedly different from Western countries' market-based approaches. China has employed a strategy of negotiating bilateral exploration and production accords with oil-rich countries in order to evade the vagaries of international oil markets. Specifically, China prefers to negotiate directly with oil-producing countries over the price for a given quantity of oil, and over rights to exploration and production.[54] China's behavior appears to be increasingly mercantilist, and represents a growing challenge to the US-led market-based system that has been historically dominant. China's neo-mercantilist behavior was noted in the 2006 White House report *The National Security Strategy of the United States of America*, which argued that China was "holding on to old ways of thinking and acting that exacerbate concerns throughout the region and the world." These old ways include "acting as if they can somehow 'lock up' energy supplies around the world or seek to direct markets rather than opening them up—as if they can follow a mercantilism borrowed from a discredited era."[55]

Unfortunately, even as many scholars and policy makers in the West hold on to optimistic liberal beliefs that promise increasing cooperation with China, China's behavior in the domain of energy remains fundamentally illiberal in its approach. According to the political scientists David Victor and Linda Yueh, "China's push into Africa, Central Asia, and other energy-rich regions, which usually involves special government-to-government deals, is a rejection of the reigning market-based approach to energy security. And because oil, gas, and coal are global commodities, these exclusive, opaque deals make it harder for the markets to function smoothly, thus endangering the energy security of all nations. They also complicate efforts to hold energy suppliers accountable for protecting human rights, ensuring the rule of law, and promoting democracy."[56]

The quest for material resources is a major factor in China's foreign policy, particularly its policy toward Africa.[57] Susan Shirk argues that China places little faith in global energy markets, and that the regime is concerned that supply disruptions may jeopardize the stability of the country. "From

China's perspective," she writes, "it looks like global energy markets are dominated by the Western oil companies. And the US Navy controls the vital international sea lanes on which the ships carrying China's imported oil must travel. What really worries China's leaders is that the United States and its European allies could sever China's oil supplies if there was a crisis in the Taiwan Strait or elsewhere."[58] Furthermore, Shirk writes, "Chinese mistrust of American intentions toward them—heightened by the firestorm of American opposition to the bid by ... CNOOC to acquire the American oil company UNOCAL—makes them particularly prone to thinking of energy competition as a 'great game' driven by political rivalries."[59]

China also seeks to enhance its energy security by purchasing significant equity positions in foreign oil corporations.[60] In December of 2009 Petro-China acquired a 60 percent controlling interest in Athabaska Oil Sands' Dover and McKay River projects in Canada for $1.6 billion. In aggregate, from 2009 to 2010, Chinese NOCs made $6.9 billion in oil equity acquisitions. In early 2011, the China National Petroleum Corporation admitted that it was intensifying its tactic of acquiring significant share positions in foreign oil corporations. China indicates that it plans on $60 billion in further energy acquisitions before 2020.[61]

China's keen interest in Canada's oil sands is a potential point of friction between China and the US over the longer term, particularly if China continues to pursue such tactics of purchasing majority equity positions in foreign oil corporations. China is currently cooperating with the Enbridge corporation in a project to build a pipeline (called the Northern Gateway) from Alberta's oil sands to the port of Kitimat on the Pacific coast, angering environmentalist groups and triggering some concern in the US. The proposal for the Northern Gateway, approved by the Harper government in June of 2014, is likely to be contested in the courts.

On a more optimistic note, Chinese investments in the oil sands may free up additional oil that will help to alleviate some of the East Asian pressures on international oil markets and help to moderate global increases in the price of oil somewhat.

The political scientists Darryl Press and Eugene Gholz argue that the possibility that increasing Chinese demand that will propel oil prices ever higher threatens the US economy and American interests more than Chinese ownership of oil does.[62] "The United States," they write, "should not worry that China is locking up oil supplies with prepurchase agreements or that China is investing to develop overseas oil reserves. The real energy "problem" that China poses for the United States is more quotidian: rapid Chinese economic growth increases Chinese demand for oil, and that drives up global prices."[63] Herein lies the crux of the problem for the United States. There are only two ways to contain China's soaring demand for energy. One is to slow its economy; the other is to increase its energy efficiency through technology transfer. Neither is probable. Insofar as the legitimacy of the PRC government is built on sustained economic growth, attempts by the US to slow Chinese economic growth would be regarded as a provocation, an attempt to undermine the PRC government. And technology transfer is problematic because many US firms are duly concerned about China's penchant for stealing design secrets and blatantly violating patent law.

On a strategic level, China has adopted what it calls the "string of pearls" approach, which entails a system of alliances between China and countries that possess harbors along oil trans-shipment routes from the Persian Gulf—among them Cambodia, Thailand, Burma, Bangladesh, and Pakistan.[64] A substantial buildup in naval capacity is consistent with China's desire to project power, and in particular to safeguard the transshipment of energy flows to China from the Persian Gulf. Until the pipelines from Siberia are completed, China remains primarily dependent on the Persian Gulf for its oil imports. The Strait of Malacca is a choke point, and such shipments are vulnerable to piracy, accidents, or interdiction by US naval forces.[65] Recognizing such vulnerabilities, the PRC is building up its capacity to project naval power in an effort to control the sea lanes in the South China Sea and in the Indian Ocean.[66]

In view of increasing US domestic oil production and soaring Chinese imports, China currently exhibits greater vulnerability in the domain of energy security than the US does. China's enhanced energy vulnerability remains a function of the United States' capacity to project power globally by means of its unrivaled navy. Despite China's claims that its huge investments in naval power are defensive, the US may interpret Chinese moves as bellicose, and may respond by becoming increasingly wary. Thus, energy insecurity in the context of international anarchy exacerbates the security dilemma in East Asia. The dynamics of misperception lead both parties to believe that they are acting in defensive fashion while they participate in an arms spiral that only confirms the fears of "the other." This spiral of misperception is the true danger, particularly since the lack of transparency in

China's processes of military and foreign policy decision making increases the probability of misperception by the US.[67]

In order to circumvent some of its perceived energy vulnerabilities, China has actively sought to foster energy interdependence with Russia. The development of pipelines to carry flows of crude oil and natural gas from East Siberia to the Chinese industrial heartland would limit the power of the US Navy to interdict Chinese energy flows in the event of a crisis between China and the US. Such projects are now underway. In 2010 Russia completed the extension of an oil pipeline southward to connect with the oil-production center of Daqing in northern China, striking a deal to supply China with 20 years' worth of crude oil.[68] On October 18, 2013, Prime Minister Dmitry Medvedev and several Russian companies (among them Rosneft and Novatek) signed joint production agreements and other covenants with the China National Petroleum Corporation to increasingly divert oil and liquefied natural gas away from European markets toward lucrative Chinese markets in the East.[69]

The new energy diplomacy between Russia and China serves the interests of both countries, reducing China's energy vulnerability and allowing Russia to tap and export the wealth of natural resources in its far eastern territory. Although this nascent concord between China and Russia reduces the ability of the US Navy to obstruct or interdict China's supply of energy from the Persian Gulf, the augmented flow of oil and gas from Russia to China may also help to mitigate some of the tensions between China and its neighbors over sub-sea energy resources.

In recent years the surging demand for oil (and gas) in East Asia has exacerbated historical tensions between China and Japan, particularly as nationalist elements on both sides use the energy issue to drum up support for their cause. Thus, surging demand for energy throughout the region could lead to minor skirmishes between the two Asian powers. One dispute between China and Japan has to do with the chain of islands called the Diaoyu by the Chinese and the Senkaku by the Japanese, which are projected to contain oil reserves that could last 45 years.[70] Potentially rich deposits of oil and gas also lie in the Sea of Japan. These energy-laden portions of the seabed are governed by the May 2008 accord to develop gas fields signed between Japan and China. Unfortunately, that bilateral accord has not been observed by the signatory parties, and tensions continue to rise over the contested zones.

In 2014, friction began to intensify between and China and Vietnam regarding their conflicting claims to sovereignty over sub-sea energy reserves in the South China Sea. The dispute involves an area near the Paracel Islands that is estimated to hold up to 11 billion barrels of oil. In early May, China sent a flotilla (including drilling vessels and warships) to initiate exploration and drilling in the area and thus launch a unilateral claim to that territory.[71] Although both parties are discussing the possibility of forwarding their disputed claims to the UN for adjudication under the UNCLOS (an unusual move for China), boats from both sides have periodically rammed one another, and anti-Chinese rioting has taken place in Vietnamese cities.[72]

Japan

Despite its perennial status as a resource-poor country, Japan is the third-largest oil consumer in the world (after the United States and China) and the second-largest importer of crude oil. The political scientist Raymond Vernon summarized Japan's predicament this way: "Oil, from the Japanese viewpoint, was not just another basic commodity; it was the country's historic Achilles' heel."[73] During the 1970s oil imports represented 80 percent of Japan's aggregate energy consumption, but innovations in energy efficiency saw oil decline to 45 percent of aggregate Japanese energy consumption in 2010. Moreover, domestic reserves of crude oil declined from 58 million barrels in 2007 to 44 million barrels in early 2010.

The demand for oil had been declining steadily since the promulgation of the Japanese government's National Oil Strategy in 2006. That strategy emphasized energy efficiency and conservation. However, oil imports to Japan have surged since the 2011 Fukushima disaster as Japanese public opinion has turned against nuclear power.[74] Since then Japan has sought to shift its energy mix away from nuclear power, but unfortunately this has meant an increasing reliance on the burning of imported fossil fuels (coal, natural gas, and oil) to produce electricity. Japan's increasing reliance on fossil fuels may aggravate existing sovereignty disputes over island chains in the East China Sea that are thought to straddle significant reserves of oil and gas. The main reason for the development of the Japanese navy in recent years is the fact that the vast majority of Japan's energy imports (among other materials) are transported past Taiwan. Should

China use military force to reclaim Taiwan, and remain hostile to Japan over the Diaoyu/Senkaku issue, the Chinese navy may be able to interdict Japan's energy imports.[75] Cognizant of China's growing military strength and Japan's continued vulnerability, the administration of Prime Minister Shinzō Abe has recently argued that Article 9 of the Japanese Constitution should be reinterpreted to permit the Japanese military to participate in "collective security" actions should an Allied country be attacked.[76]

Interestingly, a decision by the United States to block southward extension of the Keystone pipeline would probably divert a considerable amount of Canadian "unconventional oil" toward Asian markets, particularly China and Japan. This diversion of Canadian crude oil might help to defuse some of the regional tensions that have been exacerbated by soaring energy demand, although it would do little to combat the nationalist elements in both countries. An increase in exports of Canadian crude oil to East Asia might help to diminish Japanese fears that the PRC could employ its naval forces to sever Japan's oil supply from the Persian Gulf, as Canada's oil imports wouldn't pass through regions where the Chinese navy would be dominant.

Disputes over East Asian Islands

Except in the Persian Gulf region, resource wars between sovereign states are rather uncommon. However, there is some limited potential for intra-state conflict over energy resources in the territorial seas that border China. Specific areas that may be subject to such delimitation conflicts are the Diaoyu/Senkaku islands in the East China Sea (claimed by China and Japan) and the Spratly and Paracel Islands in the South China Sea (claimed by China, Malaysia, and the Philippines).

These islands were of little interest to China until potentially significant oil and gas reserves were discovered in the seabed around them during the late 1960s.[77] After these discoveries, South Vietnam awarded exploration and development contracts to foreign companies in the summer of 1973.[78] As a consequence of Vietnamese claims to the region, the Chinese produced hoary texts from the Han Dynasty that alluded to Chinese ownership of the islands, arguing that such scripts provided evidence that the islands had been considered Chinese for thousands of years.[79] In February of 1992 China formally declared its sovereignty over the Diaoyu, Spratly, and Paracel island chains and indicated that it would use force to defend its claims.[80]

By and large, realist scholars (e.g., John Mearsheimer and Aaron Fried-berg) share a conviction that China cannot rise to great-power status in a peaceful fashion.[81] The political scientist Ian Alastair Johnston argues that China's penchant for viewing the world through the lens of realpolitik may contribute to sporadic regional manifestations of violence as China rises to great-power status. This growing penchant for belligerence is manifest in China's increasingly frequent maritime disputes with its neighbors.[82]

However, it is dangerous to assume that Chinese decision-making pro-cesses operate in a purely monolithic and rational fashion, as structural realists might argue. In fact, the army often takes action without the prior consent of (or even without informing) the Ministry of Foreign Affairs or other elements of the civilian leadership.[83] In many of the looming dis-putes over the subsea resources of the region, domestic politics (occasion-ally manifesting in violent bouts of nationalism) may prove problematic as it foments conflicts between states. The Diaoyu/ Senkaku dispute has been exacerbated as a result of such domestic politics. In this case, Chinese and Japanese power-seekers have employed historical Sino-Japanese animus and questions of sovereignty over the islands to inflame nationalist pas-sions and irredentist debates among their populations, and have thereby prevented rational resolution of the dispute.[84]

One of the principal archetypal liberal objections to scenarios of inter-state energy resource conflict is that international law will provide an effec-tive mechanism for the peaceful resolution of disputes. Yet the historical record on this is ambivalent. Specifically, the UNCLOS treaty is often ambig-uous as to which seabed resources properly belong to whom. International law is largely a product of the asymmetries in power relations between the great powers when the particular legal regime in question was formed. Not-withstanding Hugo Grotius's initial foray into international maritime law in *Mare Liberum* (1609), much of the body of international marine law was drawn up in the nineteenth and twentieth centuries according to the dic-tates of the hegemonic powers (Great Britain, and then the United States). Thus, it is a bit naive to expect a rising hegemonic competitor (e.g., China) to observe a constellation of rules and norms that they had little or no hand in crafting; particularly if such rules run contrary to that power's interests. Even the US, the architect of much of the body of international law since

1945, found it expedient to flout international law when it wished to do so, the classic case being that of Nicaragua in 1984.[85] The great powers tend to observe the protocols of international law when it suits their interests to do so. Though international law may help to mitigate some of the rising tensions in the East China Sea, the US should not be so naive as to think that China is much concerned about its compliance with the dictates of international accords.

Would it be rational for China to engage in a conflict with Japan over claims to the Diaoyu/Senkaku islands? Of course not, for such a conflict would risk destabilizing the economy of the Pacific Rim, damaging the global economic recovery, and possibly drawing the US into the conflict on the side of Japan. Thus, a spat over a relatively insignificant and isolated chain of islands that sit astride what may be substantial energy resources has the potential to evolve into a far more dangerous affair. Though war over such resources would be irrational, the history of war is rife with misperceptions,[86] miscalculations, and decisions undertaken to slake the passions of nationalist fervor. Indeed, the history of international politics is replete with "irrational" decisions, including Hitler's decision to launch Operation Barbarossa against the Soviet Union, the United States' intervention in Vietnam, the Soviet Union's invasion of Afghanistan, and (most recently) the Iraq War.

The Persian Gulf

Despite the empirical fact that inter-state war is a perennial feature of the Persian Gulf, one the greatest challenges to the political stability of the countries of that region is not war but the spread of technology. New exploration technologies (detailed in the chapters above) have made possible new the discovery of previously unknown shale-oil deposits and deepwater deposits in the Americas. As new exploration and drilling technologies spread around the world, they promise to locate and develop vast new quantities of oil, which in turn should moderate or even reduce the international price of oil. As global oil prices plateau, oil rents derived from export will decline, and if they should decline significantly then revenues needed that prop up the authoritarian regimes of Saudi Arabia and Iran will begin to evaporate. The dissipation of petrodollar-derived income streams will result in contraction of revenues available to Saudi Arabia and Iran to prop up clientelist networks that allow the regimes in power there to maintain their grip on it. The decline of those revenue streams will limit or erode state capacity to such an extent that Saudi Arabia and Iran may have a very hard time providing public goods to their citizens, which should diminish citizens' perceptions of the legitimacy of their countries' governments.[87] Thus, the proliferation of oil extracted from unconventional sources threatens the political stability of authoritarian petro-states in the Persian Gulf region and may augur a period of intense destabilization caused by rebellion and revolt.

The Persian Gulf region exhibits properties of a "regional security complex."[88] Historically such complexes have drawn the interest of great powers. The presence of oil facilitates and exacerbates the regional security dilemma in the Persian Gulf—primarily through the mechanism of petrodollars, which make it possible to purchase expensive weapons systems and to maintain large armies. Oil rents also help to perpetuate the authoritarian modes of rule practiced by the ruling families of Saudi Arabia and Kuwait and the theocracy of Iran.

The oil-price revolution of the 1970s and the consequent surge in petrodollars to the countries of the Persian Gulf region led to the rapid militarization of Iraq and Iran. The regional arms race that ensued resulted in the devastating War of the Cities that raged between Iraq and Iran from 1980 to 1988. Thus the petrodollars of the 1970s exacerbated the regional security dilemma (primarily between Shia and Sunni powers), fomented a regional arms race that resulted in the Iran-Iraq War, and resulted in approximately a million deaths. Moreover, the War of the Cities[89] was primarily material in its origins: Iran and Iraq fought over territory, particularly the rich oil fields and refineries of the regions bordering the Shaṭṭ Al-'Arab River. Each country persistently targeted the other's oil-production infrastructure so as to weaken its opponent economically. The economic damage to both countries was enormous.

Although de-territorialization and dematerialization are very much in vogue today,[90] the logic of de-territorialization and dematerialization doesn't hold sway in the Persian Gulf region. Possession of territory in that region confers mastery over the energy resources that lie underground, and thus the logic of materiality continues to hold sway. Gause notes that "border disputes, always a potential cause of conflict, become even more salient when the territory in dispute has oil under it." "A cursory look at the wars in the Gulf, " he writes, "could lead one to see each as a fight for regional dominance and the expansion of oil control."[91]

The material presence of oil, a strategic commodity, has historically drawn the great powers into the region, notably Britain and then the United States. The United States' desire to maintain its position of regional hegemony is clearly expressed through the presence of the US Navy's Fifth Fleet in the Gulf, and by the US military bases throughout the region. What is often lost on many observers, however, is that oil's capacity to draw the great powers into the region *exacerbates* the regional security dilemma. The United States' presence in the Gulf is considered a stabilizing force by most American analysts; however, from the vantage point of Iran the presence of US forces may be perceived as a threat that exacerbates Iranian perceptions of insecurity. Insecurity and fear have been behind Iran's bid to improve its conventional weapons and to develop nuclear weapons. Nuclear weapons and improved conventional weapons will be perceived as defensive in nature by Iran, but as offensive by the United States, the Sunni countries of the Gulf, and Israel.

Iran

Iran is the third-largest producer of oil in OPEC (after Saudi Arabia and Iraq), generating about 3.6 million bpd of crude oil and having estimated reserves of 138 billion barrels. Before the Islamic fundamentalist revolution of 1979, Iran produced 5 million bpd, but the combination of international sanctions, limited investment (domestic and foreign), decline of technology, damage from warfare, and natural decline has greatly reduced its production since 1979. The US Energy Information Administration estimates that between 400,000 and 700,000 barrels of Iranian crude oil are lost per year as a result of the declining productivity of mature fields.[92] The US has enacted significant sanctions on Iran, prohibiting the importation of Iranian petroleum. The sanctions are enforced by the Office of Foreign Assets Control of the US Department of Treasury, as delineated in the Iran Transactions Regulations. Much of Iran's exported oil now is exported to Japan, China, India, South Korea, and Italy.[93]

Iran now poses several potential problems for the international community. First, it has proved itself hostile to the OECD countries by its persistently hawkish behavior in the context of OPEC, openly breaking with the dovish Saudis in recent years and seeking to keep global oil prices elevated.

Consequently, during the period 2005–2008 the OPEC hawks (Iran and Venezuela) engaged in production cuts to inflate global oil prices. Although this behavior augmented their oil-derived revenues in the short term, it also threatened to destabilize the global economy. Iran's ambition to develop nuclear weapons poses a considerable threat to the stability of the Persian Gulf region, to the security of Israel, and to the international community.

Unfortunately, the oil wealth of the Persian Gulf has facilitated Iran's nuclear weapons program through mechanisms both direct and indirect. First, oil revenues have contributed to the militarization of the region, and the desire to protect the flow of Gulf oil to the global economy has drawn the United States into the region. The militarization of the region has generated an intense regional security dilemma. Insecurity and fear (of the Sunnis, of Israel, and of the US) have led the Iranians to build up their military capabilities, which in turn may be perceived by others as offensive behavior. Consequently, such perceptions may generate further dynamics of insecurity that lead to further militarization by the other players in the region, which in turn perpetuates insecurity in a positive feedback loop. According to the political scientist Mohsen Milani, Iran's insecurity is attributable to ancient tensions between Persians and their Arab neighbors, the considerable military presence of the US in the waters of the Persian Gulf, and the significant threat of Israeli strikes.[94] Iran's nuclear weapons program is at least partially a response to this intense regional security dilemma, and the government in Tehran uses the nuclear program in its nationalist rhetoric to reinforce its domestic political position. Paradoxically, the pursuit of nuclear weapons may invite the external aggression that Iran had sought to deter.

However, the countries of the West find the prospect of a nuclear-armed Iran unacceptable, primarily because of Iran's threats against Israel and its historical support of terrorist organizations such as Hezbollah. For that reason, the United States and the European Union, beginning in 2011, led an initiative to place an international embargo on Iran's oil exports. From April 2012 to early 2013, Iranian oil exports declined by 40 percent as a result of sanctions against the regime in Tehran. Iran's revenues from oil exports declined by 45 percent over that period, and oil exports declined from 1.74 million bpd to 1.5 million bpd. Though some question the efficacy of the sanctions, the rationale behind them is that the Iranian government derives 80 percent of its revenues from oil exports.[95] Those revenues then typically translate into increased state capacity, which may be used

either to provide public goods for the people or to support the military and
the development of nuclear weapons. Thus, cutting off the flow of oil revenues to Iran should impede Iran's progress in its pursuit of weapons technologies but it will also probably inflict a degree of economic pain upon the
Iranian people, many of whom oppose the authoritarian regime in Tehran.
Nor have the sanctions generated significant change in the domestic political alignments of Iran, despite the election of Hassan Rouhani (thought to
be a reformist) as president. The country remains a largely despotic theocracy that crushes political opposition with force. Despite the increasing
economic impact of the sanctions, Iran has indicated little willingness to
curtail its development of nuclear technologies.

A military strike against Iran probably would drive the international price
of oil to exceptional heights. The Libyan conflict is instructive. Though
only 2 million bpd of Libyan light sweet crude was taken off the market
in early 2011, the global price of oil soared from about $80 per barrel to
$115 per barrel, a 43.75 percent increase in price over just two months.
This price increase occurred despite a reassurance by the Saudis that they
would match any shortfall and despite their protestations that the global
market was oversupplied. Yergin argues that the IEA possesses sufficient
stocks in the SPR systems of member countries (roughly 1.5 billion barrels)
to offset the loss of Iranian production for two years.[96] Perhaps, but Yergin's assumption is problematic, as the speculative intensity in oil (i.e., the
financialization of crude oil), would translate into soaring prices for Brent
Crude, particularly as SPR stocks were increasingly depleted. Thus, any military action against Iran would result in rampant speculation in crude-oil
futures, and probably would generate a considerable price spike. The price
spike would result in some very real economic damage to those consumer
countries that remained highly dependent on crude oil, and it might pose
a considerable threat to the fragile global economy.

Saudi Arabia

Long an ally of the United States, Saudi Arabia is yet another example of the
United States' illiberal policy of supporting despotic regimes in the name of
guaranteeing energy security to the West. The United States' provision of
global public goods (in the form of global energy flows) is dependent upon
oil derived from regimes that oppress their own peoples. These despotic
regimes are in turn protected by US military might.

The Saudis remain strategically important for the United States in a number of ways. First, they are an important ally in the Persian Gulf, assisting in the United States' projection of force throughout the region. Second, they are a dovish presence within OPEC, working to moderate the global price of oil and keep it within a range that sustains the global economy. Their capacity to operate as a "swing producer" is important in this regard, as the Saudis maintain the ability to increase or decrease aggregate oil-production capacity in order to moderate prices.

As I have argued above, Saudi Arabia may face inexorable internal political challenges resulting from declining global oil prices, as the spread of technology makes it more practicable to extract oil from unconventional sources. The deterioration of oil rents resulting from falling oil prices will make it harder for the Saudi regime to buy off domestic elements that seek significant political reforms. The potential political destabilization of Saudi Arabia could have far-reaching implications for global energy security and for the wider political destabilization of the Gulf region. Paradoxically, then, the diffusion of technology and the extraction of oil from unconventional sources may imperil the political stability of the states of the Gulf region, which would then in turn drive up global oil prices at the margin. Thus, it seems reasonable to expect that the increasing extraction of oil from unconventional sources may result in increasing political volatility for the regimes of the Persian Gulf region, even as it improves the energy security of the US.

However, such volatility is not necessarily a negative outcome, particularly if it forces autocratic petro-states such as Saudi Arabia to move toward democratic reforms.[97] Over the long term, the democratization of these states may help to ameliorate the region's security dilemma to some degree. Saudi Arabia's role in the recent decline of oil prices is grounded in a desire to undercut unconventional producers. The Saudis have a "war chest" of about $783 billion to draw upon, but it isn't likely that they will be able to avert OPEC production cuts before 2017.

The Arctic

Melting of the polar ice has begun to open the Arctic region to international trade and resource exploration. Contrary to the popular arguments of Michael Klare and Scott Borgerson, who predict looming conflict over the lucrative sub-sea resources of the region, I argue that the equation is more complex than many have assumed. First, the Arctic is vast, and the distribution of oil deposits appears to be diffuse across the region. Moreover, the region remains so environmentally daunting that most oil exploration and drilling will be occurring in the littoral areas, on the continental shelves. Second, the technology for effective exploration and drilling in the deep waters of the high Arctic (not the littoral regions) is some time away, and the costs remain exorbitant—particularly in the face of increasing production of relatively cost-effective terrestrial "unconventional oil." The increasingly global diffusion of terrestrial fracking and computer visualization technologies means that many Arctic states (including Russia) will have greater economic incentive to develop littoral and land-based unconventional reserves, as opposed to the costly and risky reserves of the high Arctic seas. The Russians will do far better to develop their terrestrial reserves in Eastern Siberia, and their newly seized littoral reserves in the Black Sea, than to engage in costly ventures in the Bering Sea that could put them at odds with the US.

Although Russia has greater capacity than other countries to develop deep-water Arctic energy resources, the probability of Russia's engaging in conflict with other countries in the region (Canada, Denmark, the United States, Norway) remains remote, particularly insofar as Russia seems bent upon developing fields in eastern Siberia for the purpose of exporting oil to China and Japan. However, Russia's recent aggression toward Georgia and Crimea is at least partially tied to its desires to protect (and extend) its regional hegemony in the domain of energy. In view of this emerging pattern of asymmetrical conflict between Russia and its weaker neighbors over energy resources, it isn't inconceivable that Russia might project its power in parts of the Arctic region in order to lay claim to more sub-sea energy reserves. Though the technology needed to claim deep-water reserves in the high Arctic ocean isn't likely to be developed for some time, the Russians may be eyeing territory closer to home. However, it is important to note that Putin's bids for expansion are contingent on Russia's possessing clear military dominance over the other nation. It is far more plausible that Russia will continue its bellicose behavior in seizing energy assets throughout central Asia than that it will engage in aggression against members of NATO.

In sum, the Arctic territories are vast and apparently replete with hydrocarbon resources, the environment of the region remains hostile to exploration and deep-sea drilling, and technologies to deal with such environmental issues (icebergs, waves, and extreme depths) are still in their infancy. Although climate change may result in warming of the region, and presumably reduce some of these hazards, it is highly improbable that we will see a scramble for high Arctic resources that results in conflict before 2025. Moreover, the development of technologies to improve terrestrial oil exploration and extraction mitigate against any scramble for energy resources in the high Arctic. Thus, the probability of energy-induced inter-state conflict in the region will remain low for some time, and the probability of cooperation (either between states or between states and corporations) to develop such lucrative resources in the region remains high.

Africa

President George W. Bush's creation of the Africa Command in 2007 was a powerful indicator of the United States' growing desire to protect its energy-supply lines in developing countries. It reflects the United States' perceptions at the time that resources in general, and oil in particular, were becoming increasingly scarce as a result of the surge in global demand for energy that arose from rapid economic growth in the so-called BRIC countries (Brazil, Russia, India, and China). In recent decades, the US has focused on the armoring of the global energy infrastructure, often with a focus on force projection to protect certain states. In Africa this meant US security guarantees to protect important oil exporters (Angola and Nigeria), and often the use of hard and soft power to prop up illiberal regimes across the continent. Unfortunately, this mindset has resulted in a legacy of militarism and illiberalism in the United States' oil foreign policy throughout Africa. In fact, it is commonplace in the US national-security community for analysts to insist that the military protection of all energy assets across the African continent is essential to US national security. This type of thinking is nonsense, as it inevitably leads to the logic that the US military and intelligence structures must engage in the deployment of force across this vast region, leading to a dynamic of hyper-militarization that imposes ever greater costs upon the republic. This false logic of militarization doesn't account for the diffusion of technology that allows for dispersed extraction from unconventional sources, as this diffuse distribution of global oil extraction makes it increasingly problematic for terrorists to disrupt global energy networks. This is not to say that terrorist strikes on energy infrastructure aren't problematic;

however, distributed networks of global oil production make it far more difficult for terrorists to achieve maximum disruption of energy flows and international markets. In fact the militarist mindset so dominant in Washington often plays into the terrorists' hands, as the desire to harden the energy infrastructure of regions of the world that aren't critical to US energy security simply results in an ever-greater loss of blood and treasure for the US. Consequently, the US should abandon the current strategy, which is based on the ubiquitous deployment of force, and should focus on protecting Nigeria and Angola while fostering their democratization.

Angola is the most important African state to US oil foreign policy, much more important than Nigeria. It is the eighth-largest exporter of oil to the US and largest exporter in African, supplying about 376,000 barrels per day in mid 2013. Thus, the disruption of oil supplies from Angola could be considered a challenge to the national energy security interests of the US. Angola joined OPEC in 2007, but doesn't always toe the institutional line. It has a wealth of offshore pre-salt-layer deposits, and so projections of its production are positive. Oil exports accounted for 98 percent of government revenue in 2011, and Angola boasted the third-largest economy in Africa, largely as a result of revenues from exports of oil.[98] It has proven oil and gas reserves of 9.5 billion barrels. Both the IOCs and the Chinese NOCs Sinopec and CNOOC are already extensively involved in Angola and working with the Angolan national oil company Sonangol in various capacities.

Nigeria is the largest producer of oil on the African continent at 2.2 million bpd, with estimated reserves of 37.5 billion barrels. Although not as important as Angola, Nigeria is also a significant supplier of oil to the United States, at roughly 77,000 barrels per day in 2013. Oil accounts for 95 percent of the country's foreign exchange earnings, and generates 80 percent of government revenue. Revenues derived from oil exports often result in side payments to placate acrimonious domestic factions, mostly Islamic, in the north.

The delta region in the south remains the locus for oil production. However, local militant groups have been staging attacks on oil-production infrastructure in the ecologically-sensitive Niger Delta since 2006.[99] Such attacks arise from a deep sense of grievance against the government and the IOCs, as oil extraction has damaged the local ecology, undermining agriculture and fishing by locals, and the state fails to return much of the oil profits to this damaged region.

Unfortunately, this connection between the ecological degradation of the Delta region, the ensuing destruction of people's livelihoods, and the ensuing people's revolt against the companies and the corrupt government has been lost on many inside the beltway. Instead, the predominant analysis within the beltway has been to brand these marginalized peoples as pirates, insurgents, and even terrorists. Doubtless, some of the rebels targeting oil-production facilities in Nigeria are in fact of dubious character, but to aggregate those Nigerian citizens agitating for a better life, and resisting the depredations of the oil companies and the corruption of the government, in with common criminals is to be myopic. Again, the United States' historical support for the government, and for the oil companies operating in the Delta region, against the impoverished and brutalized peoples of the Delta region, illustrates the very illiberal nature of US foreign energy policy. Again, the United States seems quite satisfied to support corrupt and authoritarian regimes such as Nigeria, as long as the oil flows continue to prop up the global economy. Thus, the supposedly liberal global energy order, and the provision of such public goods by a supposedly benign liberal hegemon, depend largely on the United States' support for highly illiberal and even despotic regimes that brutalize their own citizens.

The portrait I have painted of the United States' often illiberal behavior in the sphere of energy foreign policy is not flattering. It raises serious questions about archetypal liberal arguments that assume that the United States is in a fact a benign hegemon dedicated to the provision of global public goods. Moreover, I argue that the supposedly liberal international energy order is anything but liberal, that this order is built upon alliances between the countries of the West, and fundamentally illiberal and often despotic states that routinely punish and marginalize their own citizens.

Conclusion

Oil sustains our civilization, but this dependence on petroleum has come at enormous costs. Oil has generated powerful distortions in the conduct of US foreign policy; it has resulted in highly illiberal behavior by certain democracies (particularly the United States), it has contributed to maladaptation (as interest groups block societal adoption of cleaner technologies), it has contributed to dangerous externalities such as terrorism and ecological degradation, and it has provided an impetus for war between greater and lesser powers.

The Era of "Unconventional Oil"

Most political scientists wisely eschew attempts at prediction. However, to a certain degree we are capable of analyzing existing trend lines and extrapolating them into the near future. As a function of demographic momentum, we can say with some assurance that the global population will continue to grow, with estimates of about 9 billion by the middle of the century. The continuing rise of the middle class in many developing countries is also an interesting phenomenon, as even with improvements in efficiency it promises a significant increase in the worldwide demand for energy for the foreseeable future. In conjunction with the inexorable growth of the human population and the rise of the middle class in developing countries, the global demand for oil (and its derivatives) will probably continue to increase for decades.

The contention that the planet is rapidly running out of oil, which was widespread in the first decade of this century, is somewhat inaccurate. Though the era of cheap oil is certainly over, the era of "unconventional

oil" is just beginning in earnest, and this is manifest in the increasing productivity of unconventional terrestrial and oceanic reserves. This surge in
the productivity of unconventional sources stems from recent advances in
exploration technologies (e.g., computer visualization) and in extraction
technologies (deep-water and horizontal drilling techniques and fracking).

The spread of such oil exploration and extraction technologies from
the United States to other polities, largely through the mechanism of the
international integrated oil and oil service companies, will result in the
development of unconventional oil reserves around the world. This global
diffusion of advanced technologies will often manifest as a result of partnerships between international oil companies and national oil companies,
and it should result in the liberation of enormous amounts of "unconventional oil," at least in the next few decades. The reserves of national oil
companies will probably increase in the near future (10–20 years) thanks
to such technological advances, but may exhibit diminishing returns after
a period of gains.[1]

Consequently, we should see some minor increases in the global production of crude oil until 2030, which will be followed by a plateau effect.
Global oil resource availability should then begin to decline in per capita
terms. During the plateau phase, surging global population growth, in conjunction with the expansion of the global middle class and its hunger for
resources (energy, water, housing, food, etc.), will strain the ability of global
energy mechanisms (producers and markets) to deliver oil at prices that
permit the further expansion of the global economy. This effect may be
ameliorated to some degree by advances in efficiency, but it is doubtful that
efficiency alone will compensate entirely for increasing global demand. The
era of "unconventional oil" will last for some time, perhaps decades, but
eventually these reserves will be depleted. There is undoubtedly a great deal
of "unconventional oil" left on the planet, but there is no way of knowing
how long it will last, as this is conditional on future global demand, further
advances in technology, prices, and the inescapable constraints of geology
and time.

The significant increase in the domestic (US) production of "unconventional oil" will diminish (but not eradicate) the United States' dependence
on foreign oil for some time. Although the US enjoys diminished dependence on other countries for oil, it will continue to have to import oil in

order to satiate its appetite for oil and oil derivatives. Thus, proclamations of imminent "energy independence" are more propaganda than substance.

Illiberalism and the Pax Americana

The central argument of this volume is that the United States is *not* simply a benign hegemon that seeks to provide global public goods, such as the protection of the world's energy flows. In fact, the United States' quest for global hegemony in the domain of strategic energy resources (e.g., oil) has resulted in patterns of profoundly illiberal behavior, particularly outside of the context of the developed countries. This illiberal conduct is manifest in the Nixon Doctrine, in the Carter Doctrine, and in such clearly illiberal undertakings as Operation Ajax and the Iraq War. Pursuit of hegemony over energy resources, often through mechanisms of hard power (coups and wars), has contributed to the militarization of the republic and to perceptions that the US is increasingly acting in an illiberal (even imperial) fashion, and not as a benign hegemon, particularly in the domain of energy. Ultimately, its recurrent illiberal conduct in these domains may affect the perceived legitimacy of the US government by the American people and by the international community.

In this vein, the United States' perennial pursuit of hegemony over oil supplies has engendered illiberal alliances with some of the most authoritarian regimes in the world. The United States' long-standing pacts with Saudi Arabia and Kuwait undermine perceptions of American legitimacy in the Islamic world. Furthermore, the United States' destabilization of democratic Iran in the 1950s, and its subsequent support for the regime of the Shah, led many people in developing countries to loathe the United States' willingness to sacrifice principle in the name of power and avarice.

I have argued that the international political economy of oil is also quite illiberal in nature. The United States' pursuit of hegemony in the domain of energy continues to rely upon the international oil companies, which distribute their products downstream through global market mechanisms, as the primary agents of extraction. However, it is important to note the increasing dominance of the state (as in the cases of China and Russia) and thus of national oil companies in the domain of international oil production. Sovereign states now possess most of the remaining oil reserves on the planet, and are developing these reserves through their national oil companies. Often they use subsidies to deliberately adjust the prices of crude oil and its derivatives. The American market-based approach stands in contrast to the nationalist NOC-based approach of China, but these two visions of the global energy order aren't necessarily incompatible.

Since 2000 the NOC-based approach has generated considerable success, and the IOCs were largely marginalized as their estimated reserves dwindled. However, since 2010 sophisticated new exploration and extraction technologies have begun to shift the balance of power back toward the IOCs, particularly as the NOCs recognize that such technologies are essential to the development of unconventional oil reserves in their own countries. Thus, the IOCs may be slightly less marginalized in the future as they use their technological sophistication to broker collaborative projects with the statist NOCs. Nonetheless, there is an enormous amount of statism within these supposedly free markets, and China appears to be engaging in increasingly neo-mercantilist behavior in its quest to lock up international oil supplies, primarily through bilateral contracts with oil-producing countries.

Oil and Conflict

Andrew Bacevich argues that the United States has become an "empire of consumption."[2] This characterization rings true, particularly in the domain of energy, and it has affected our conduct of foreign policy in a negative manner, making us far more bellicose and interventionist than need be. Hunger for oil has driven the US to manifest an aggressive presence in regions (such as the Persian Gulf) where perpetual violence drains the coffers of the republic. Thus, our addiction to material consumption is generating immense costs to the nation, both in blood and in treasure.

Though oil has driven the United States into conflict with some other countries, it has not caused conflict between the great powers. Much of the popular writing on energy and security published in the years 2000–2014 exhibits a degree of threat inflation, with dire warnings of imminent conflict between the great powers over energy. First, to reiterate, there is no immediate empirical acute scarcity of oil that will drive the great powers to make war upon one another. Contrary to the arguments advanced by Michael Klare and Dambisa Moyo, I argue that the potential for war between the great powers over oil is low to non-existent, at least for some time. This is a function of several variables: the historical evidence that oil has not induced great-power conflict since World War II, the exorbitant costs of war between great powers owing to the existence of nuclear weapons, and steadily increasing supplies of oil from unconventional sources.

Conversely, I argue that there is a distinct pattern of asymmetrical conflict between greater and lesser powers over the control of energy resources, and this pattern of energy-based conflict is likely to continue for some time. The evidence provided above demonstrates a clear pattern of stronger states attacking weaker states in order to attain mastery over the oil resources (or transit conduits) of the weaker polity. Numerous instances of inter-state conflict since 1980 attest to the viability of this asymmetrical resource conflict model, including Iraq's invasions of Iran and Kuwait, the US-led expulsion of Iraq from Kuwait, and the Russian assaults on Georgia and Ukraine. There is growing evidence that perceptions of oil scarcity (and often misperceptions) can induce stronger powers to make war upon lesser powers that are producers or transit states.[3] I have argued that the George W. Bush administration's inaccurate perception of an imminent global shortage of oil contributed significantly to the United States' decision to invade Iraq in 2003.

As the United States' domestic production of crude oil increases in the next 20 or so years, we should expect to witness diminished bellicosity on the part of the US, at least in terms of conflicts resulting from US decision makers' *perceived* scarcity of energy resources. However, the United States' drift toward introversion and peace doesn't mean that China will be equally placid in the domain of energy security. We are now witnessing increasing friction and acrimony between China and other weaker polities in East Asia. Such tensions are already evident in the ongoing spats between China and Vietnam in the South China Sea, and between China and Japan over the Senkaku Islands and sea-bed energy resources throughout the East China Sea. The combination of historical animosity between China and many of its neighbors, and rising nationalism across the region,[4] may combine with a desire to capture energy resources to generate skirmishes between China and its neighbors. In view of the stark power asymmetry between China and Vietnam, and their recent history of animosity, the probability of conflict over energy resources in the South China Sea is moderate. Conversely, because the power asymmetries between China and Japan aren't yet significant, and because the US is a staunch military ally of

Japan, the probability of extensive conflict between China and Japan over energy reserves remains rather remote.

Perception is often more important than reality, particularly in international politics.[5] I argue that the difference between perceptions of scarcity and the empirical "reality" of scarcity may in fact play a significant role in fostering conflicts over energy resources. For example, in the early 2000s the neo-Malthusian perspective that the world was rapidly running out of crude oil was the dominant mindset in academe and in the popular literature. (For examples, see works by Matthew Simmons, Michael Klare, and Thomas Homer-Dixon.) However, that assumption was valid only to the extent that the "easy" oil (large hydrocarbon reserves close to the surface) was becoming depleted. In this sense, Malthusian arguments proved influential in altering the perceptions of political elites, generating the widespread belief that global oil supplies were in fact running out.[6] Consequently, such perceptions of energy scarcity may have contributed to increasingly confrontational and mercantilist actions by the US and China, respectively, and notably to the United States' invasion of Iraq. Such perceptions of oil scarcity, in combination with the phenomenon of "paper barrels," also contributed to the rampant speculation on global markets that resulted in the oil-price spike of 2008.

Strikes against the global energy infrastructure by terrorists may enhance the potential for international cooperation as countries recognize that they face a common enemy. Though this may challenge certain assumptions of archetypal liberal thought, it is consistent with the assumptions of shadow liberalism.

Theoretical Considerations

In this volume I have questioned the usefulness of both realism (particularly its structural variants) and archetypal liberalism to those grappling with the complex issues arising in the domain of energy. Most realists remain largely disinterested in questions of energy, ranking them as second-tier problems that have little consequence for the great powers. Moreover, many realists continue to regard non-state actors as inconsequential, something that is highly problematic in the domain of energy and international politics.

Liberal theories permit an enhanced analysis of the nexus between energy and international politics, primarily as they conceptualize a diverse range of agents that interact with the state in order to influence outcomes. Specifically, I have argued that interactions between the state and corporate entities have profoundly influenced the conduct of US foreign policy in the domain of energy. Indeed, the US government and the international energy companies have co-evolved, such that they are now largely symbiotic in their relationship, with corporate entities enjoying significant influence over the decision-making processes of political elites.

However, I have criticized archetypal liberal thought as overly optimistic, and have outlined a novel variant of liberal international theory—shadow liberalism. Shadow liberalism questions the narrative of the United States as a benign hegemon bent on the equitable provision of global public goods, particularly in the domain of energy. Shadow liberalism acknowledges that there are enormous inequities in global power structures, and that current US hegemony is built upon a historical litany of often illiberal behavior. Thus, I argue that the modern "liberal" international order contains a strain of illiberalism, particularly in the treatment of people in developing countries. The United States' complicity in the suppression of democracy in Iran, its support of highly illiberal regimes throughout the Persian Gulf, and its proclivity to engage in military action in order to protect its hegemony over oil are all indicative of this profoundly illiberal strain in US energy foreign policy.

To the limited extent that the United States has articulated a grand strategy in the domain of energy and international politics it is often ill defined, reckless, and irrational, particularly in the domain of oil. The four conceptual pillars of this grand strategy are the symbiotic relationship between the international oil companies and the US, the use of global market mechanisms to maintain the flow of oil, the problematic strategy of alliances between the US and illiberal autocratic regimes, and the militarization of the global energy infrastructure.

Moreover, the lack of prioritization of defined objectives in the United States' energy foreign policy is nonsensical and often destructive. By declaring our intent to protect all oil infrastructure around the world, and consequently militarizing this infrastructure, we prioritize nothing. Thus, the United States' interests in the domain of energy are currently limitless, resulting in the perennial overextension of US military forces, at exorbitant costs to the republic. Pardon the heresy, but every region of the world is *not* of equal importance to the US from the standpoint of energy security. There are certain primary nodes within this complex system that are more important than other secondary or tertiary nodes. Thus, it is time to think of "triage" when it comes to thinking strategically about which energy resources the US absolutely needs to protect. The global energy system is highly complex, but we cannot and should not try to securitize and consequently militarize all the nodes and pathways in this intricate system.

Instead of concentrating on the hardening and militarization of global energy infrastructure, the United States should focus on developing and/or augmenting the *resilience* of global energy infrastructures. Thus, we need to prioritize the protection of certain crucial nodes in the system while focusing on the development of resilience in the greater system. The advantage is that this focus on systemic resilience is likely to cost much less than a mass armoring of the system, and it should also allow the US to avoid being drawn into armed conflicts in regions of tangential importance to its national interest. The diffusion of fracking technologies and the development of unconventional oil will then augment the resilience of the global energy infrastructure.

Ultimately, the surge in domestic production of oil from unconventional sources bodes well for the US economy for some time, and is likely to forestall economic decline. Furthermore, this surge in US hydrocarbon resources, in conjunction with a projected scarcity of oil (in per capita terms) for China, may slow or stall a hegemonic power transition from the US to China in the near future. Hence, this turn in the energy fortunes of the US may allay American decline, and may impede the rise of China.

International Organizations

One of the greatest failings of the United States' grand energy strategy is a reliance on international energy institutions that are increasingly archaic and sclerotic. These institutions, notably the International Energy Administration, were crafted to deal with the supply shocks of the 1970s, but find themselves increasingly unable to deal with the various shocks induced by the financialization of oil (e.g., "paper barrels" and exchange-traded funds) and by rampant speculation in the early years of the twenty-first century. The international energy regime in the aggregate is weak, and is best thought of as a quasi-regime. Though there are a number of international institutions in the domain of energy (e.g., the IEA, OPEC) they are increasingly characterized by stickiness rather than efficacy. The IEA was particularly ineffective in moderating the global oil-price spike of 2008, and was only partially effective in tempering the spike that occurred during Libya's civil war of 2011. Moreover, the IEA's structure is increasingly archaic, as it limits membership to the OECD countries and excludes important consumer countries (China and India) and oil-producing countries (Brazil). This exclusion of major consumers and producers suggests that the institution is becoming increasingly ineffective, even in its very narrow capacity as a clearinghouse for data on production and consumption. Thus, at the very least, the US should prioritize a comprehensive revamping of the IEA to include China, India, and Brazil.

China

China's rise to the status of a strategic competitor presents significant challenges for the corporatist US energy model, particularly as China is engaging in a largely mercantilist approach to the acquisition of foreign oil supplies. China's foreign oil strategy is based on the use of quasi-statist NOCs as mechanisms to engage with oil-producing countries either through bilateral fixed-price contracts that avoid international markets or through the purchase of foreign firms to create "equity oil" assets that are essentially owned by the Chinese state. On one level, China's use of the NOCs may be positive insofar as it helps to satiate China's appetite for energy, and may correspondingly relieve some pressure on international oil prices. Conversely, success by the Chinese NOCs in employing neo-mercantilist bilateral contracts and equity oil strategies to lock up unconventional oil sources throughout the Americas may undermine the market mechanisms that underpin US energy security.

On a pessimistic note, a grand concert of powers, wherein the United States and China equitably share in the responsibilities of providing global energy public goods, also remains unlikely. China seems quite content to continue to free-ride on the US as the guarantor of global energy flows, offloading the costs onto the US even as China reaps the rewards. Even though the increased production of crude oil in the US has reduced the price of oil on global markets somewhat,[7] this doesn't necessarily guarantee that China will act in a peaceful manner if it encounters a scarcity of oil in years to come. Indeed, the evidence at hand points to an increasingly belligerent China that is willing to test its rivals' claims to sovereignty throughout the East and South China Seas. A pragmatic interpretation of these dynamics suggests that, whereas the United States' propensity for inter-state conflict over energy should decline somewhat, China's belligerence may continue to escalate.

The nascent energy alliance between China and Russia presents American policy makers with something of a conundrum. On the positive side, it may help to satiate China's hunger for energy resources to a degree, and help to maintain China's economic growth (which is clearly a boon to the global economy). Moreover, if China can obtain energy supplies from Russia that will reduce China's incentives to engage in aggressive behavior toward its neighbors in East Asia, at least in regard to questions of sovereignty over energy reserves. On the negative side, the burgeoning energy alliance between Russia and China will limit the US Navy's ability to circumscribe China's power by interdicting energy flows from the Persian Gulf. Further, it will bolster the power of the illiberal regimes in China and Russia—regimes that may have interests that are inimical to those of the West.

The Persian Gulf

The United States' grand energy strategy (such as it is) has relied upon the hardening of global oil infrastructure, and in particular, the militarization of the Persian Gulf region. Not only has this strategy been terribly costly to the US in blood and treasure; it is also increasingly foolhardy in view of the increasing diffusion of production of oil from unconventional sources and the increasing diffusion of pipelines.

The US government should be cognizant of the risks that it inadvertently generates to its own interests and to its national security. For example, it is a truism in Washington that the United States' involvement in the Persian Gulf region is a stabilizing force. However, any comprehensive understanding of the United States' historical pattern of involvement in the region acknowledges that the US presence can actually work to destabilize the region as well. Operation Ajax in Iran and the invasion of Iraq in 2003 were hardly stabilizing actions in any meaningful sense. Moreover, the Iraq War created a fragile and sectarian democracy in Iraq, which at the time of writing is in danger of complete collapse. The widening war between Sunni militias and Shiites, in conjunction with the intervention of Iran and Syria on the battlefield against ISIS, promises mounting chaos for the entire Middle East. How, then, have US actions, from the Bush administration's invasion in 2003 to the disintegration of the Iraqi state during the Obama administration (2014), stabilized the region? Clearly the actions (and incompetence) of both the Bush and Obama administrations have bequeathed a legacy of chaos and violence to the region.

Again, contrary to the common "wisdom" in Washington, the United States' presence in the Gulf may actually exacerbate the security dilemma in the region.[8] For example, the presence of the Fifth Fleet in the Gulf may reassure the Saudis, the Kuwaitis, and the Israelis, but it is perceived by Iran as a potential threat. Consequently Iran has sought to develop nuclear weapons, arguably as a defensive measure. The pursuit of nuclear weapons by Tehran is then interpreted as a hostile move by Saudi Arabia, Iraq, Israel, and the United States, and thus it only intensifies the militarization of the region. Thus, all parties seek greater security, and develop their military capacities in order to attain such security, but the very processes of mass militarization then amplify the perceptions of insecurity by all players in the region.

The United States should work to shore up responsive and effective democratic regimes in the region, particularly in Iraq and in Saudi Arabia, and to develop confidence-building measures among the countries of the region in order to mitigate the security dilemma. The evolving dialogue between the Obama and Rouhani administrations is a step in the right direction, as is the CIA's long-overdue admission of complicity in Operation Ajax.

In view of the surge in domestic energy production, I argue that the United States may have a defined interest in drawing down some of its military power (and thereby reducing its expenditures) in the Persian Gulf. This doesn't mean that we should stop providing aid to the tottering democracy in Iraq, and we would continue to support Saudi Arabia (although we should advise the Saudis that it would be in their self-interest to initiate democratic reforms). This would help to reduce insecurity in the region and would simultaneously save the US a considerable degree of funds that could be spent elsewhere. The US would presumably maintain bases in Qatar and in Saudi Arabia should it be necessary for US military forces to return.

A drawdown of American power in the Persian Gulf region would allow a conceptual shift in US foreign energy policy that would prioritize the protection of assets in the Americas by ensuring stable flows of oil from Canada, Mexico, and Venezuela. Furthermore, withdrawal of US forces from the Persian Gulf doesn't necessarily entail an increased presence in the region on the part of China and/or India, as neither of those countries currently possesses enough naval capacity to project power into the theater of the Persian Gulf.

The Americas

The Obama administration's decision to delay approval of the Keystone pipeline presents the United States with a conundrum. In the short term, it makes some sense, insofar as the United States' production of crude oil is booming and the decision promises to reorient Canadian oil exports toward Asia (particularly toward energy-poor China and Japan). The diversion of Canadian oil to East Asia may also help to mitigate some of the tensions between China and Japan over the sub-sea energy resources of that region, particularly around the Diaoyu/Senkaku Islands. Environmentalists argue that preventing the extension of the Keystone XL pipeline to the US may prevent an environmental catastrophe, however, if this should occur the Canadians will simply sell the oil to Asian interests, and the carbon emissions will still flow into the atmosphere. Thus, the obstruction of the Keystone XL project will simply displace carbon emissions from the US to East Asia, an externalization of externalities. The development of unconventional reserves will simply intensify greenhouse gas emissions and exacerbate the already visible effects of climate change.

The United States should actively work with Mexico to foster the liberalization of Pemex, encouraging cooperation between Pemex and the IOCs, while ensuring a decent rate of profit for the Mexican state that can be invested in public goods. An equitable arrangement that fosters cooperation between the IOCs and Pemex will allow the latter access to advanced technologies that will permit enhanced exploration and extraction of crude oil, particularly in deep-water and shale environments. Revenues generated from this arrangement will help to stabilize the Mexican state and consequently help to alleviate the United States' concerns about the fragility of governance in its southern neighbor.

Despite the obdurate and incompetent Maduro administration in Venezuela, the United States should work to develop positive relations with the Venezuelan people. For its part, Venezuela would do well to recognize that, given proper regulation and revenue-sharing agreements, IOCs might work in a productive partnership with PDVSA that would involve technology transfers to increase Venezuela's production of crude oil, particularly from unconventional sources. The US should seek to improve communications with the Maduro administration, and use flows of aid and trade to assist in the stabilization of the Venezuelan economy and the democratization of that polity. The US should emphasize principle over profits, argue for the protection of human rights, and promote a gradual shift away from authoritarian rule in Venezuela.

Throughout South America the United States should work actively to broker deals that will enhance energy extraction, but these deals must be equitable and benefit both the people of the country in question and the IOCs. The US should resist pressure from the IOCs to permit unjust deals that only favor the corporations, as these arrangements will simply drive oil-producing countries into the arms of the Chinese NOCs, and alienate those oil-producing countries from the US. Unfortunately, in view of the persistent corruption that permeates the US and the profound influence of the IOC lobbies in Washington this ideal arrangement may simply be wishful thinking.

Contrary to arguments based on scarcity and inter-state conflict, I consider it highly improbable that there will be a profound scarcity of crude oil in the next 20–30 years, particularly for the United States, Russia, or Canada. Because of the evident pattern of asymmetrical aggression over control of crude-oil supplies, the high probability of Yergin's plateau, and the existence of nuclear weapons, the great powers will probably not come to blows over oil scarcity, at least not directly. Political tensions will come to the fore again when the fracking boom has run its course, oil sands are depleted, and sea-bed resources are tapped out. However, this depletion of unconventional oil sources may take several decades, perhaps longer. Barring significant advances in technical ingenuity, the eventual exhaustion of viable unconventional oil reserves would eventually generate economic disruption, political disruption, intra-state conflict, and possibly skirmishes between consumer countries. Fortunately, the depletion of unconventional oil sources is extremely unlikely in the near term. Moreover, one might reasonably expect significant technological advances in the domain of energy over the next 20 years, particularly as the price of oil remains elevated.

Obviously, reducing the United States' dependence on oil, and particularly foreign oil, primarily through the development of clean alternative energy sources, would free us from the constrictions of such a problematic foreign policy. Reducing the influence of oil money and lobbyists in American politics is also desirable (if difficult). Mechanisms by which this might be done include comprehensive campaign finance reform, slashing federal and state subsidies for oil exploration and development, and developing a federal policy to reverse the odious and anti-democratic US 2010 Supreme Court ruling in *Citizens United vs. Federal Election Commission*.

Unfortunately, such systemic revisions will prove extremely difficult to attain, particularly insofar as political elites benefit from the status quo and will continue to block efforts at reform. Thus, it is important to consider how ingenuity, both technical and social, might be more effectively employed to divert US energy grand strategy onto a more sensible and sustainable path. In the technical domain, fossil fuels still remain cheaper than renewables for the most part. Hence, scientists should focus on increasing the efficiency of motors that utilize renewable power, and develop energy storage mechanisms for renewable systems, while simultaneously reducing costs.

In the realm of social ingenuity, we should abandon the notion that every oil field on the planet is of critical strategic interest to the US. Second, we should move toward a hemispheric model that prioritizes regional energy security. This may not have much of an effect on global pricing mechanisms, but the development of regional exchanges in conjunction with regional energy infrastructural development may cushion the US somewhat from international price and/or demand shocks in the future. Additionally, humanity needs to slow the rate of global population growth and to reduce the oil consumption of the burgeoning global middle class. The Obama administration's recent directive to increase the fuel efficiency of new cars and trucks is a positive and significant step in the right direction.[9]

Increasing energy self-sufficiency, preferably through the development of renewable energy, may help the United States to disengage from the Persian Gulf and other chaotic and perennially violent areas of the world. A prioritization of issues in US foreign energy policy would permit a degree of disengagement from regions where our engagement has proved excessively costly and/or counterproductive. The US should embark upon a more nuanced approach that is based on the prioritization of key energy assets and regions. Paradoxically, under a policy of prioritization and limited disengagement the United States' power resources (economic, diplomatic, and military) might improve over time. This would allow the US to put its own house in order[10] and to avoid additional debacles in the Persian Gulf.

Notes

Introduction

1. K. O'Neill, *The Environment and International Relations* (Cambridge University Press, 2009).

2. R. Deibert, *Black Code: Surveillance, Privacy and the Dark Side of the Internet* (Signal, 2013).

3. S. Elbe, *Security and Global Health* (Polity, 2010); C. Enemark, *Disease and Security: Natural Plagues and Biological Weapons in East Asia* (Routledge, 2007); A. Price-Smith, *Contagion and Chaos: Disease, Ecology, and National Security in the Era of Globalization* (MIT Press, 2008).

4. D. Byman, *Deadly Connections: States That Sponsor Terrorism* (Cambridge University Press, 2007).

5. This archetypal vision of liberal internationalism is evident in R. Keohane and J. Nye, *Power and Interdependence* (fourth edition: Longman, 2012), and to some degree in recent works of G. John Ikenberry, such as *Liberal Leviathan: The Origins, Crisis, and Transformation of the American World Order* (Princeton University Press, 2011).

6. The proposition that the quality of international anarchy may in fact be cooperative emanates from H. Bull, *The Anarchical Society: A Study of Order in World Politics* (Macmillan, 1977).

7. This proposition will be discussed at length below.

8. A detailed examination of shadow liberalism will be presented in the volume that is scheduled to follow this one.

9. G. Ikenberry, *Reasons of State: Oil Politics and the Capacities of American Government* (Cornell University Press, 1988).

10. Niall Ferguson refers to this modern de-territorialization of the American empire in *Colossus: The Rise and Fall of the American Empire* (Penguin, 2004).

11. Ikenberry, *Liberal Leviathan*; J. Nye, *The Future of Power* (PublicAffairs, 2011).

12. J. Mearsheimer, "Imperial by design," *The National Interest*, no. 111 (January/February 2010): *16–34*.

13. This is not a Marxist argument, although some may see certain elements of this analysis as consistent with certain assumptions of dependence theory. On the latter subject, see I. Wallerstein, *World Systems Analysis: An Introduction* (Duke University Press, 2004).

14. M. Klare, *Rising Powers, Shrinking Planet: The New Geopolitics of Energy* (Metropolitan Books, 2008); Klare, *The Race for What's Left: The Global Scramble for the World's Last Resources* (Picador, 2012).

15. D. Moyo, *Winner Take All: China's Race for Resources and What It Means for Us* (Basic Books, 2012).

16. See M. Klare, *Blood and Oil: The Dangers and Consequences of America's Growing Dependency on Imported Petroleum* (Holt, 2008).

17. S. Yetiv, *Crude Awakenings: Global Oil Security and American Foreign Policy* (Cornell University Press, 2004); Nye, *The Future of Power*.

18. In all probability, continuing advances in technology will augment the discovery and extraction of global oil resources from 2015 to 2030.

19. On the issue of misperception as a cause of war, see R. Jervis, *Perception and Misperception in International Politics* (Princeton University Press, 1976).

20. See M. Klare, *Resource Wars: The New Landscape of Global Conflict* (Holt, 2002); T. Homer-Dixon, *The Upside of Down: Catastrophe, Creativity, and the Renewal of Civilization* (Island, 2006).

21. Cantarell is the largest oil field in Mexico. Ghawar is the largest field in Saudi Arabia.

22. D. Yergin, *The Quest: Energy, Security, and the Remaking of the Modern World* (Penguin, 2011).

23. Energy deprivation may be defined as a shortage of energy at affordable prices for the middle and working classes within a polity.

24. Energy abundance refers to a supply of affordable energy for the middle and working classes within a given polity.

25. S. Krasner, *Defending the National Interest: Raw Materials Investments and US Foreign Policy* (Princeton University Press, 1978).

26. J. Nye, "Energy security strategy," in *The Strategic Imperative: New Policies for American Security*, ed. S. Huntington (Ballinger, 1982).

27. R. Vernon, *Two Hungry Giants: The United States and Japan in the Quest for Oil and Ores* (Harvard University Press, 1983).

28. G. Ikenberry, *Reasons of State: Oil Politics and the Capacities of American Government* (Cornell University Press, 1988).

29. E. Kapstein, *The Insecure Alliance: Energy Crises and Western Politics Since 1944* (Oxford University Press, 1990).

30. D. Deudney, *Renewable Energy: The Power to Choose* (Norton, 1983).

31. Henry Kissinger, quoted in C. Ebinger, *The Critical Link: Energy and National Security* (Ballinger, 1982).

32. M. Ross, *The Oil Curse: How Petroleum Wealth Shapes the Development of Nations* (Princeton University Press, 2012); J. Duffield, *Over a Barrel: The Costs of US Foreign Oil Dependence* (Stanford University Press, 2008); J. Colgan, *Petro-Aggression: When Oil Causes War* (Cambridge University Press, 2013).

33. S. Yetiv, *The Petroleum Triangle: Oil, Globalization, and Terror* (Cornell University Press, 2011); Yetiv, *Crude Awakenings*.

34. D. Stokes and S. Raphael, *Global Energy Security and American Hegemony* (Johns Hopkins University Press, 2010).

35. Also see B. Shaffer, *Energy Politics* (University of Pennsylvania Press, 2009).

36. Yetiv, *Crude Awakenings*.

37. Ikenberry, *Liberal Leviathan*.

38. K. Waltz, *Theory of International Politics* (Waveland, 2010); J. Mearsheimer, *The Tragedy of Great Power Politics* (Norton, 2002).

39. Mearsheimer, "Imperial by design."

40. Interesting attempts to bridge the intellectual schism between liberal and realist theory have been made before, although their assumptions diverge from those presented below. See, in particular, C. Kupchan and G. Ikenberry, "Liberal realism: The foundations of a democratic foreign policy," *The National Interest*, fall 2004: 38–49.

41. On the foundations of archetypal liberal theories of international relations, see Keohane and Nye, *Power and Interdependence*; G. Ikenberry, *After Victory: Institutions, Strategic Restraint, and the Rebuilding of Order After Major Wars* (Princeton University Press, 2000).

42. This term came to me in April of 2012 during a discussion with G. John Ikenberry in Colorado Springs. He encouraged me to pursue this pessimistic theoretical reformation of liberalism.

43. See A. Bacevich, *The New American Militarism: How Americans Are Seduced by War*, second edition (Oxford University Press, 2013).

44. L. Jacobs and B. Page, "Who influences US foreign policy?" *American Political Science Review* 99 (2005), no. 1: 107–123.

45. The emphasis on blood and treasure is taken from the work of Immanuel Kant, in his reference to the costs of war endured by the body politic. See, e.g., *Perpetual Peace: A Philosophical Sketch* (1795).

46. See A. Mazur, "How does population growth contribute to rising energy consumption in America?" *Population and Environment* 15 (1994), no. 5: 371–378.

47. Source: http://www.census.gov/ipc/www/idb/worldpopinfo.php

48. Source: www.census.gov/popclock

49. J. Gillis and C. Dugger, "UN sees rise for the world to 10.1 billion," *New York Times*, May 4, 2011.

50. See UN Population Division, *World Population Prospects, the 2010 Revision* (http://esa.un.org/unpd/wpp/index.htm).

51. Source: http://www.census.gov/population/www/projections/summarytables.html

52. All data here are from the US Energy Information Administration. All percentages were calculated by the author.

53. E. Caroom and D. Murtaugh, "Bakken oil weakens as North Dakota reports record production," Bloomberg News, November 15, 2013.

54. Source: www.eia.gov/dnav/pet/hist/LeafHandler.ashx?n=PET&s=MOCLEUS2&f=M

55. Highway Statistics Series, Federal Highway Administration, US Department of Transportation (http://www.fhwa.dot.gov/policyinformation/statistics.cfm).

56. Author's calculations, based on raw data from www.eia.gov/countries/index.cfm.

57. Source: www.eia.gov/todayinenergy/detail.cfm?id=10451

58. E. Morse, "Low and behold: Making the Most of Cheap Oil," *Foreign Affairs* 88 (September-October 2009), no. 5: 36–52.

59. Stokes and Raphael, *Global Energy Security and American Hegemony*, p. 47.

60. Ibid.

61. Keith Crane, Andreas Goldthau, Michael Toman, Thomas Light, Stuart Johnson, Alireza Nader, Angel Rabasa, and Harun Dogo, *Imported Oil and US National Security* (RAND, 2009), p. 9.

62. Homer-Dixon, *The Upside of Down.*

63. P. Millard and J. Brice, "Brazil oil field may hold 16 billion barrels of oil," Bloomberg News, October 28, 2010.

64. B. Swint, "The Falkland Islands brace for oil wealth," *Bloomberg Businessweek* (www.businessweek.com), April 4, 2013.

65. See B. Tissot and D. Welte, *Petroleum Formation and Occurrence: A New Approach to Oil and Gas Exploration* (Springer, 1978); J. Speight, *The Chemistry and Technology of Petroleum,* fourth edition (CRC Press, 2006); J. Stainforth, "Practical kinetic modeling of petroleum generation and expulsion," *Marine and Petroleum Geology* 26 (2009), no. 4: 552–572.

66. T. Malthus, *Essay on the Principle of Population* (1798).

67. W. Jevons, *The Coal Question: An Inquiry Concerning the Progress of the Nation, and the Probable Exhaustion of Our Coal Mines* (Macmillan, 1865).

68. P. Ehrlich, *The Population Bomb* (Macmillan, 1971).

69. T. Homer-Dixon, *The Ingenuity Gap* (Knopf, 2000).

70. See J. Simon, *The Ultimate Resource* (Princeton University Press, 1983).

71. J. Hamilton, Causes and Consequences of the Oil Shock of 2007–08, Brooking Papers on Economic Activity (conference draft, spring 2009).

72. S. Mulligan, "Energy, environment, and security: Critical links in a post-peak world," *Global Environmental Politics* 10 (2010), no. 4: 79–100.

73. Morse, "Low and behold," p. 37.

74. Ibid., p. 38.

75. Yergin, *The Quest.*

76. US Joint Forces Command, *Joint Operating Environment 2010,* p. 24.

77. Source: www.eia.gov/countries/index.cfm?view=reserves

78. M. Ross, *The Oil Curse: How Petroleum Wealth Shapes the Development of Nations* (Princeton University Press, 2012).

79. This editorial decision resulted from reviewers' comments on the original manuscript, which was deemed to be a bit too long. I intend to tackle such thorny questions in a future volume.

Chapter 1

1. V. Smil, *Energy in World History* (Westview, 1994).

2. Aristotle, *Physick*, Book 8.

3. A. Crosby, *Children of the Sun: A History of Humanity's Unappeasable Appetite for Energy* (Norton, 2006), p. 4.

4. W. Ostwald, *Energetische Grundlagen der Kulturwissenschaften* (Klinkhardt, 1909).

5. L. White, "Energy and the evolution of culture," *American Anthropologist* 45 (1943), no. 3: 335–337.

6. Smil, *Energy in World History*.

7. J. Tainter, *The Collapse of Complex Societies* (Cambridge University Press, 1988), p. 91.

8. W. McNeill, *The Rise of the West: A History of the Human Community* (University of Chicago Press, 1963).

9. Crosby, *Children of the Sun*, p. 8.

10. Ibid., pp. 64–66.

11. J. Needham, *The Development of Iron and Steel Technology in China* (Heffer, 1964).

12. H. Vogel, "The Great Well of China," *Scientific American* 268 (1993), no. 6: 116–121.

13. J. Harris, "The rise of coal technology," *Scientific American* 233 (1974), no. 2: 92–97; Smil, *Energy in World History*, p. 159.

14. Crosby, *Children of the Sun*, p. 70; Smil, *Energy in World History*, pp. 158–159.

15. Smil, *Energy in World History*, p. 167; R. Forbes, "Bitumen and petroleum in antiquity," in *Studies in Ancient Technology*, volume 1, ed. R. Forbes (Brill, 1964).

16. A. Nikiforuk, *Tar Sands: Dirty Oil and the Future of a Continent* (Greystone Books, 2008), p. 8.

17. Crosby, *Children of the Sun*, p. 91.

18. K. Beaton, "Dr. Gesner's kerosene: The start of American oil refining," *Business History Review* 29 (1955), no. 1: 28–53.

19. Ontario Ministry of Natural Resources, Oil, Gas and Salt Resources Act Reasoned Decisions (http://www.mnr.gov.on.ca/en/Business/OGSR/2ColumnSubPage/STEL02_167105.html).

20. Smil, *Energy in World History*, p. 167.

21. V. Smil, *Energy at the Crossroads* (MIT Press, 2004), p. 184.

22. The first prototype of the light bulb was developed by Humphry Davy, an English chemist, in 1806. In 1878 another Englishman, the chemist and physicist Joseph Swan, refined Davy's design

23. See Ikenberry, *Reasons of State*, p. 59.

24. Vernon, *Two Hungry Giants*, p. 58.

25. D. North, "In anticipation of the marriage of political and economic theory," in *Competition and Cooperation: Conversations with Nobelists about Economics and Political Science*, ed. J. Alt et al. (Russell Sage Foundation, 1999), p. 316.

26. P. Pierson, *Politics in Time: History, Institutions, and Social Analysis* (Princeton University Press, 2004), p. 2.

27. Ibid., p. 2.

28. "The shadow of the past" is a term used by Ikenberry on p. 194 of *Reasons of State*.

29. M. Levi, "A model, a method, and a map: Rational choice in comparative and historical analysis," in *Comparative Politics: Rationality, Culture, and Structure*, ed. M. Lichbach and A. Zuckerman (Cambridge University Press, 1997), p. 28.

30. J. Hacker, *The Divided Welfare State: The Battle over Public and Private Social Benefits in the United States* (Cambridge University Press, 2002), p. 54.

31. Pierson, *Politics in Time*, p. 10.

32. Ibid., p. 18. Also see R. Collier and D. Collier, *Shaping the Political Arena: Critical Junctures, the Labor Movement, and Regime Dynamics in Latin America* (Princeton University Press, 1991); F. Baumgartner and B. Jones, *Agendas and Instability in American Politics* (University of Chicago Press, 1993).

33. W. Williams, *Empire as a Way of Life: An Essay on the Causes and Character of America's Present Predicament along with a Few Thoughts about an Alternative* (Oxford University Press, 1980, p. ix.

34. Vernon, *Two Hungry Giants*, p. 127.

35. Kissinger, quoted on p. 16 of M. Graetz, *The End of Energy: The Unmaking of America's Environment, Security, and Independence* (MIT Press, 2011).

36. S. Page, "Path dependence," *Quarterly Journal of Political Science* 1: 87–115, p. 91.

37. Ibid., p. 88.

38. W. Freudenburg and R. Gramling, *Blowout in the Gulf: The BP Oil Spill Disaster and the Future of Energy in America* (MIT Press, 2010).

39. J. Eilpering and S. Highham, "How the Mineral Management Service's partnership with industry led to failure," *Washington Post*, August 24, 2010; C. Savage, "Sex, drug use and graft cited in Interior Department," *New York Times*, September 10, 2008; J. Eilpering and M. Lebling, "MMS' troubled past," *Washington Post*, May 30, 2010.

40. A. Giddens, *The Politics of Climate Change* (Polity Press, 2013), p. 36.

41. M. Stoff, *Oil, War, and American Security* (Yale University Press, 1980), p. 2.

42. P. Tertzakian, *A Thousand Barrels a Second: The Coming Oil Break Point and the Challenges Facing an Energy Dependent World* (McGraw-Hill, 2007), p. 37.

43. Winston Churchill, quoted on p. 156 of D. Yergin, *The Prize* (Simon and Schuster, 1991).

44. L. Turner, *Oil Companies in the International System* (Allen and Unwin, 1979), p. 25.

45. Yergin, *The Prize*, p. 112.

46. Lord Curzon, quoted in J. Duce, "The changing oil industry," *Foreign Affairs* 40 (1962), no. 4: 627–634.

47. Berenger, quoted on p. 10 of P. L'Espagnol de la Tramerye, *The World Struggle for Oil* (Knopf, 1924), p. 10.

48. Krasner, *Defending the National Interest*, pp. 106–107.

49. Ibid., p. 49.

50. Quoted on p. 48 of Ikenberry, *Reasons of State*.

51. Stoff, *Oil, War, and American Security*, p. 62.

52. D. Yergin, "Energy security and markets," in *Energy and Security: Strategies for a World in Transition*, ed. J. Kalicki and D. Goldwyn (Johns Hopkins University Press, 2013), p. 80.

53. Stoff, *Oil, War, and American Security*, p. 26.

54. Walton C. Ferris to Max W. Thornburg, "Project for Study of US Foreign Oil Policy," 24 November 1941, NA, RG 59, 811.6363/1–2142.

55. United States Air Force Historical Research Agency 506. 619A: SHAEF, Office of Assistant Chief of Staff, G2. Subject: Interrogation of Albert Speer, Former Reich Minister of Armaments and War Production. 5th Session, 10.30 to 12.30 hrs, 30 May 1945.

56. J. Hayward, "Hitler's Quest for Oil: The Impact of Economic Considerations on Military Strategy, 1941–2," *Journal of Strategic Studies* 18 (1995), no. 4: 94–135, p. 94.

57. On Operation Overlord and the Normandy invasion, see A. Beevor, *D-Day: The Battle for Normandy* (Penguin, 2010).

58. Stoff, *Oil, War, and American Security*, p. 32.

59. Ibid., p. 70.

60. Yetiv, *Explaining Foreign Policy*, p. 27. Also see W. Jensen, "The importance of energy in the First and Second World Wars," *Historical Journal* 3 (1968): 538–554.

61. Stoff, *Oil, War, and American Security*, p. 59. Also see Roosevelt to Stettinius, February 18, 1943, *Foreign Relations of the United States 4* (1943), p. 859.

62. A. Miller, *Search for Security: Saudi Arabian Oil and American Foreign Policy*, 1939–1949 (University of North Carolina Press, 1980), pp. 128–131.

63. W. Pincus, "Secret presidential pledges over years erected US shield for Saudis," *Washington Post*, February 9, 1992.

64. C. Sulzberger, *New York Times*, February 22, 1945.

65. S. Telhami and F. Hill, "America's vital stakes in Saudi Arabia," *Foreign Affairs* 81 (2002), no. 6: 167–173, p. 170.

66. See Graetz, *The End of Energy*, p. 22.

67. President's Material Policy Commission, Resources for Freedom, volume I, June 1952, *passim*.

68. Ibid., p. 3.

69. M. Byrne, "CIA Admits it was behind Iran's coup," *Foreign Policy* 20, August 2013. (Absence of page numbers indicates that the source was the online edition of the journal.)

70. M. Ruehsen, "Operation 'Ajax' revisited: Iran 1953," *Middle Eastern Studies* 29 (1993), no. 3: 467–486.

71. A. Saikal, *The Rise and Fall of the Shah* (Princeton University Press, 1980), p. 42.

72. Dwight Eisenhower to Everett Hazlett, 21 June 1951, in *Ike's Letters to a Friend 1941–1958*, ed. R. Griffith (University Press of Kansas, 1984), p. 86.

73. See CIA Clandestine Service History "Overthrow of Premier Mossadeq of Iran, November 1952–August 1953" (www.nytimes.com/library/world/mideast/iran-cia-intro.pdf).

74. Ruehsen, "Operation 'Ajax' revisited," pp. 481–482.

75. Vernon, *Two Hungry Giants*, p. 70.

76. Graetz, *The End of Energy*, p. 19.

77. See ibid., p. 29.

78. Graetz, *The End of Energy*, p. 21.

79. B. Beaubouef, *The Strategic Petroleum Reserve: US Energy Security and Oil Politics, 1975–2005* (Texas A&M University Press, 2007), pp. 22–23.

80. R. Nixon, *The Real War* (Warner Books, 1980), pp. 90–91.

81. R. Train, "The environmental record of the Nixon administration," *Presidential Studies Quarterly* 26 (1996), no. 1: 185–196.

82. "Nixon's speech on energy policy and 'Project Independence,' 1973" (www.cfr.org/energy/nixons-speech-energy-policy-project-independence-1973/p24131).

83. Yetiv, *Crude Awakenings*, p. 142.

84. Arthur Burns, quoted on p. 38 of Graetz, *The End of Energy*.

85. Duffield, *Over a Barrel*, p. 64.

86. Ibid., p. 81.

87. Beaubouef, *The Strategic Petroleum Reserve*, p. 36.

88. Duffield, *Over a Barrel*, p. 74.

89. J. Carter, State of the Union Address, January 23, 1980.

90. A. Bacevich, "The Carter Doctrine at 30" (http://www.worldaffairsjournal.org/new/blogs/bacevich/The_Carter_Doctrine_at_30).

91. Ibid.

92. Yetiv, *Explaining Foreign Policy*, second edition (2011), p. 32; *Public Papers of the Presidents of the United States: Ronald Reagan* (Government Printing Office, 1981), pp. 873, 952.

93. National Security Decision Directive 114, US Policy Toward the Iran-Iraq War, November 26, 1983.

94. J. Mundale, Presidential Use of Force in Defense of Key Shipping Chokepoints: The Suez, The Gulf, and the Future, US Coast Guard Academy, 2012 (http://64.177.72.250/pubs/Fellows_2007/Mundale.pdf).

95. B. Peniston, *No Higher Honor: Saving the USS* Samuel B. Roberts *in the Persian Gulf* (Naval Institute Press, 2006), p. 217.

96. Beaubouef, *The Strategic Petroleum Reserve*, p. 15.

97. D. Goldwyn and M. Billig, "Building strategic reserves," in *Energy and Security*, ed. Kalicki and Goldwyn, pp. 512, 524.

98. Beaubouef, *The Strategic Petroleum Reserve*, p. 6.

99. Yetiv, *Explaining Foreign Policy*, p. 174.

100. Ibid., p. 175.

101. J. Hamilton, Causes and Consequences of the Oil Shock of 2008–9, Working Paper, Brookings Institution, 2009 (http://www.brookings.edu/~/media/projects/bpea/spring%202009/2009a_bpea_hamilton.pdf).

102. S. Hargreaves, "Obama's desperate SPR oil play," CNNMoney (http://money.cnn.com), June 24, 2011.

Chapter 2

1. International Energy Agency, *World Energy Outlook 2012* (http://www.iea.org/publications/freepublications/publication/English.pdf).

2. M. Philips, "Unlocking the crude oil bottleneck at Cushing," *Bloomberg Businessweek* (www.businessweek.com), May 16, 2012; J. Mouawad and M. Fackler, "Dearth of ships delays drilling of offshore oil," *New York Times*, June 19, 2008.

3. N. Choucri, *International Politics of Energy Interdependence* (Lexington Books, 1976), p. 53.

4. I. Goldin and M. Mariathasan, *The Butterfly Defect: How Globalization Creates Systemic Risks, and What to Do about It* (Princeton University Press, 2014), pp. 19–29.

5. Joseph Schumpeter, *Capitalism, Socialism, and Democracy* (Harper, 1942).

6. Yetiv, *Crude Awakenings*, p. 6.

7. Smil, *Energy at the Crossroads*, p. 149.

8. Crane et al., *Imported Oil and US National Security*, p. 12.

9. See Yergin, *The Prize*.

10. Crane et al., *Imported Oil and US National Security*, p. 13.

11. Graetz, *The End of Energy*, pp. 17–18.

12. D. Tokic, "The 2008 oil bubble: Causes and consequences," *Energy Policy* 38 (2010), no. 10: 6009–6015.

13. M. El-Gamal and A. Jaffe, *Oil, Dollars, Debt, and Crises: The Global Curse of Black Gold* (Cambridge University Press, 2009), p. 21.

14. R. Gibbons, "Oil edges up as the greenback slumps," *Globe and Mail*, April 21, 2011.

15. Shaffer, *Energy Politics*, p. 34.

16. El-Gamal and Jaffe, *Oil, Dollars, Debt, and Crises*, p. 8.

17. Ibid., p. 9.

18. Ibid., p.9.

19. T. Grant, N. Vanderklippe, and C. Taito, "High prices crunch US oil demand," *Globe and Mail*, May 13, 2011.

20. Crane et al., *Imported Oil and US National Security*, pp. 14–15.

21. A. Goldthau and J. Witte, eds., *Global Energy Governance: The New Rules of the Game* (Brookings Institution Press and Global Public Policy Institute, 2010), p. 10.

22. Homer-Dixon, *The Upside of Down*.

23. Morse, "Low and behold," p. 43.

24. Ibid., pp. 41–42

25. Smil, *Energy at the Crossroads*, p. 189.

26. Yetiv, *Crude Awakenings*, p. 14.

27. Ibid., p. 15.

28. Ikenberry, *Reasons of State*.

29. Moyo, *Winner Take All*.

30. Vernon, *Two Hungry Giants*, p. 20.

31. Ibid., pp. 36–37.

32. El-Gamal and Jaffe, *Oil, Dollars, Debt, and Crises*, pp. 20–21.

33. Shaffer, *Energy Politics*, p. 17.

34. El-Gamal and Jaffe, *Oil, Dollars, Debt, and Crises*, p. 148.

35. C. Kruppa, AP, "Oil jumps to above $112 in Asia on signs rising fuel costs not slowing demand," *Washington Post*, April 20, 2011.

36. Nye, *Future of Power*, p. 315.

37. Ibid., p. 326.

38. Faith Birol, quoted in M. Babad, "Why high oil prices threaten the recovery," *Globe and Mail*, January 6, 2011.

39. Duffield, *Over a Barrel*, p. 52.

40. M. Delucchi and J. Murphy, "US military expenditures to protect the use of Persian Gulf oil for motor vehicles," *Energy Policy* 36 (2008), no. 6: 2253–2264.

41. M. Copulos, *America's Achilles Heel: The Hidden Costs of Imported Oil* (National Defense Council Foundation, 2003).

42. A. Dancs, M. Orisich, and S. Smith, *The Military Cost of Securing Energy*, 2008 (vcnv.org/files/NPP_energy_defense_spending_full_report.pdf).

43. US Embassy, Riyadh, Saudi Arabia, SUBJECT: IS THIS OIL MARKET BROKEN? VIEWS FROM RIYADH (cable dated 2008–06–03T15:39, reprinted in *The Guardian* February 8, 2011).

44. Fyfe, quoted in Z. Espana and C. Milhench, "IEA cuts global oil demand growth forecast," *Globe and Mail*, May 12, 2011.

45. Crane et al., *Imported Oil and US National Security*, pp.16–17.

46. Moyo, *Winner Take All*, pp. 82–84; Goldthau and Witte, *Global Energy Governance*, p. 11.

47. Nye, *The Future of Power*, p. 68.

48. Crane et al., *Imported Oil and US National Security*, p. 19.

49. Ibid., p. 20.

50. C. Eddings and A. Sherman, "OPEC recycles dollars into debt," bloomberg.com, March 19, 2012.

51. International Monetary Fund, *World Economic Outlook, April 2007: Spillovers and Cycles in the Global Economy*. See http://www.imf.org/external/pubs/ft/weo/2007/01/.

52. Kalicki and Goldwyn, *Energy and Security*, p. 9.

53. Yetiv, *Crude Awakenings*, p. 4.

54. El-Gamal and Jaffe, *Oil, Dollars, Debt, and Crises*, p. 17.

55. Ibid., p. 17.

56. Ibid., p. 147.

57. J. Hamilton, Nonlinearities and the Macroeconomic Effects of Oil Prices (revised version, November 15, 2010), Department of Economics, University of California, San Diego (http://dss.ucsd.edu/~jhamilto/oil_nonlinear_macro_dyn.pdf).

58. Graetz, *The End of Energy*, pp. 180–181.

59. A. Jaffe, Energy Policy in the Obama Administration: A Year in Review, white paper, James A. Baker III Institute for Public Policy, 2010, p. 7.

60. J. Fleming and B. Ostdiek, "The impact of energy derivatives on the crude oil market," *Energy Economics* 21 (1999), no. 2: 135–167; M. Murdock and N. Richie, "The United States Oil Fund as a hedging instrument," *Journal of Asset Management* 9 (2008), no. 5: 333–46.

61. Jaffe, Energy Policy in the Obama Administration, p. 6.

62. El-Gamal and Jaffe, *Oil, Dollars, Debt, and Crises*, p. 21.

63. M. Bildirici, E. Aykaç Alp, and T. Bakırtaş, "The Great Recession of 2008 and oil prices," *Journal of Energy and Development* 35 (2011), no. 1: 1–31, pp. 4–5.

64. S. Brush and J. Gallu, "Crude oil manipulation suit may fuel debate on speculation rules," bloomberg.com, May 24, 2011.

65. D. Sheppard, "Goldman spooks oil speculators with call to take profit," Reuters, April 11, 2011.

66. El-Gamal and Jaffe, *Oil, Dollars, Debt, and Crises*, p. 112.

67. A. Bakr and R. Shamseddine, "Oil market oversupplied: Saudis," *Globe and Mail*, April 17, 2011.

68. R. Lenzner, "ExxonMobil CEO says oil price should be $60 to $70 per barrel," http://blogs.forbes.com, May 14, 2011.

69. El-Gamal and Jaffe, *Oil, Dollars, Debt, and Crises*, p. 82.

70. Vernon, *Two Hungry Giants*, p. 31.

71. Goldthau and Witte, *Global Energy Governance*, pp. 15–16.

72. Duffield, *Over a Barrel*, p. 36.

73. Morse, "Low and behold," p. 37.

74. Prepared testimony of Mikkal Herberg, Hearing on Energy Trends in China and India: Implications for the United States, Senate Foreign Relations Committee, July 26, 2005.

75. Moyo, *Winner Take All*.

76. Quoted in B. Mullins and D. Berman, "Republicans urge White House to review CNOOC's Unocal bid," *Wall Street Journal*, June 29, 2005.

77. See S. Lohr, "Unocal bid opens up new issues of security," *New York Times*, July 13, 2005.

78. The Exon-Florio Amendment, 50 U.S.C. app 2170, was passed under the Omnibus Trade and Competitiveness Act of 1988.

79. Klare, *Rising Powers, Shrinking Planet*, p. 30; Human Rights Watch, *Sudan, Oil and Human Rights* (2003), pp. 478–486, 606–607.

80. Crane et al., *Imported Oil and US National Security*, p. 39.

81. C. Krauss, "Exxon and Russia's oil company in deal for joint projects," *New York Times*, April 16, 2012.

Chapter 3

1. Richard Perle, Testimony before US Congress, Senate, Committee on Banking, Housing and Urban Affairs, Proposed Trans-Siberian Natural Gas Pipeline: Hearings, 97th Congress, first session, 1981, pp. 113–117.

2. See, for example, *Global Energy Governance*, the archetypal liberal institutionalist work by Goldthau and Witte.

3. Stoff, *Oil, War, and American Security*, p. 5.

4. W. Stivers, "A note on the Red Line Agreement," *Diplomatic History* 7 (1983), no. 1: 23–34.

5. T. Moran, "Managing an oligopoly of would-be sovereigns: The dynamics of joint control and self-control in the international oil industry," *International Organization* 41 (1987), no. 4: 575–607.

6. J. Bamburg, *History of the British Oil Company* (Cambridge University Press, 2009), p. 19.

7. Kapstein, *The Insecure Alliance*, p. 45.

8. N. Samuels, "The European Coal Organization," *Foreign Affairs* 25 (July 1947), no. 4: 728–736.

9. Kapstein, *The Insecure Alliance*, p. 30.

10. B. Buzan, O. Waever, and J. de Wilde, *Security: A New Framework for Analysis* (Lynne Rienner, 1998), pp. 97–99.

11. The Schuman Declaration was the brainchild of French Foreign Minister Robert Schuman and the French diplomat Jean Monnet.

12. Source of quotation: W. MacDougall, "Political economy versus national sovereignty: French structures for German economic integration after Versailles," *Journal of Modern History* 51 (1979), no. 1: 4–23.

13. Expiry of the European Coal and Steel Community Treaty, European Union press release, June 19, 2002 (http://europa.eu/rapid/pressReleasesAction.do?reference=MEMO/02/145&format=HTML&aged=0&language=EN&guiLanguage=en).

14. On this functionalist vision of fostering economic interdependence to move beyond nationalism and militarism, see E. Haas, *The Uniting of Europe* (Stanford University Press, 1958).

15. M. Olson, *The Logic of Collective Action* (Harvard University Press, 1965), p. 15 (emphasis in original).

16. Public bads may also be referred to as externalities (a term derived from the economics literature). For a discussion of public bads, see J. Fearon and D. Laitin, "Neotrusteeship and the problem of weak states," *International Security* 28 (2004), no. 4: 5–23.

17. R. Geiss and A. Petrig, *Piracy and Armed Robbery at Sea* (Oxford University Press, 2011); M. Murphy, *Small Boats, Weak States, Dirty Money* (Columbia University Press, 2010).

18. Kapstein, *The Insecure Alliance*, p.15.

19. Ibid., p. 15.

20. See the arguments of Stokes and Raphael on this point, even though they view it through a realist lens.

21. See C. Le Quéré et al., "Trends in the sources and sinks of carbon dioxide," *Nature Geoscience* 2, 2009: 831–836; S. Doney et al., "Ocean acidification: The other CO_2 problem," *Annual Review of Marine Science* 1 (2009): 169–192; J. Orr et al., "Anthropogenic ocean acidification over the twenty-first century and its impact on calcifying organisms," *Nature* 437 (2005): 681–686.

22. On pandemics as public bads, see Price-Smith, *Contagion and Chaos*. For specifics on the economic costs of the SARS epidemic, see J.-W. Lee and W. McKibbin, "Globalization and disease: The case of SARS," *Asian Economic Papers* 3 (2004), no. 1: 113–131.

23. Kapstein, *The Insecure Alliance*, p. 14.

24. F. Walters, *A History of the League of Nations* (Oxford University Press, 1952), pp. 667–668.

25. M. Daoudi and M. Dajani, *Economic Sanctions: Ideals and Experience* (Routledge & Kegan Paul, 1983), p. 63.

26. C. Ristuccia, "1935 sanctions against Italy: Would coal and crude oil have made a difference?" Paper, Linacre College, University of Oxford (http://www.nuff.ox.ac.uk/economics/history/paper14/14paper.pdf).

27. Also see Crane, *Imported Oil and US National Security*, pp. 25–26.

28. S. Sagan, "The origins of the Pacific War," *Journal of Interdisciplinary History* 18 (1988), no. 4: 893–922.

29. T. Park et al., "Resource nationalism in the foreign policy behavior of oil exporting countries," *International Interactions* 2 (1976), no. 4: 247–262; Crane, *Imported Oil and US National Security*, p. 26.

30. Y. Meital, "The Khartoum Conference and Egyptian policy after the 1967 war: A reexamination," *Middle East Journal* 54 (2000), no. 1: 64–82; Crane, *Imported Oil and US National Security*, p. 27.

31. Crane, *Imported Oil and US National Security*, p. 27.

32. Hans Morgenthau, quoted on p. 1 of Ikenberry, *Reasons of State*.

33. S. Rabe, *The Road to OPEC: United States Relations with Venezuela* (University of Texas Press, 1982), p. 112.

34. Quoted on p. 160 of Rabe, *The Road to OPEC*.

35. Rabe, *The Road to OPEC*, p. 161.

36. Nye, *The Future of Power*, pp. 66–67. Also see R. Stobaugh, "The oil companies in the crisis," *Daedalus* 104 (1975), no. 4: 179–202.

37. L. Freedman and E. Karsh, *The Gulf Conflict, 1990–91: Diplomacy and War in the New World Order* (Princeton University Press, 1993), p. 181.

38. Nye, *The Future of Power*, p. 67.

39. J. Blas, "Algeria is OPEC's new über hawk," *Financial Times*, June 14, 2012.

40. On cheating incentives within OPEC, see J. Griffin and W. Xiong, "The incentive to cheat: An empirical analysis of OPEC," *Journal of Law and Economics* 40 (1997), no. 2: 289–316.

41. R. Scott, *History of the International Energy Agency*, volume I: *Origins and Structure* (International Energy Agency, 1994).

42. Source: http://www.iea.org/Textbase/nppdf/free/3-ieahistory.pdf

43. W. Kohl, "Consumer country energy cooperation: the International Energy Agency and the global energy order," in *Global Energy Governance*, ed. Goldthau and Witte, pp. 196–197.

44. The original Corporate Average Fuel Economy standards were enacted by Congress in 1975, primarily in response to the OAPEC embargo of 1973.

45. Goldthau and Witte, *Global Energy Governance*, p. 7.

46. Duffield, *Over a Barrel*, p. 87; Kapstein, *The Insecure Alliance*, p. 179.

47. Duffield, *Over a Barrel*, p. 89.

48. Kohl, "Consumer country energy cooperation," p. 197.

49. Duffield, *Over a Barrel*, pp. 86–87. Also see Scott, *History of the International Energy Agency*, volume II, pp. 68–69.

50. Beaubouef, *The Strategic Petroleum Reserve*, p. 27.

51. Goldthau and Witte, *Global Energy Governance*, p.8.

52. Ibid., p. 11.

53. Source: http://www.eia.gov/dnav/pet/hist/LeafHandler.ashx?n=PET&s=RWTC &f=D.

54. Source: www.eia.gov/dnav/pet/hist/LeafHandler.ashx?n=pet&s=rbrte&f=w.

55. S. Randall, *United States Foreign Oil Policy Since World War I: For Profits and Security* (McGill–Queens University Press, 2007), pp. 308–309.

56. North American Free Trade Agreement, Article 605(a), 1994.

57. See G. Laxer and J. Dillon, *Over a Barrel: Exiting from NAFTA's Proportionality Clause* (Canadian Center for Policy Alternatives, 2008), pp. 26–37.

58. Duffield, *Over a Barrel*, p. 88.

59. Ibid.

60. Ibid. Also see R. Keohane, *After Hegemony: Cooperation and Discord in the World Political Economy* (Princeton University Press, 1984), pp. 228–230.

61. Beaubouef, *The Strategic Petroleum Reserve*, p. 158. On the notion of price, not supply, as the primary trigger of oil shocks, see M. Adelman, "The 1990 oil shock is like the others," *The Energy Journal* 11 (1990), no. 4: 1–13; B. Okogu, "What use the IEA emergency stockpiles? A price-based model of oil stock management," *The Energy Journal* 13 (1992), no. 1: 79–96.

62. Kohl, "Consumer country energy cooperation," p. 198.

63. Vernon, *Two Hungry Giants*, p. 114.

64. S. Brooks and W. Wohlforth, "Reshaping the world order: How Washington should reform international institutions," *Foreign Affairs* 88 (2009), no. 2: 49–63; A. Arend, "International law and the pre-emptive use of military force," *Washington Quarterly* 26 (2003), no. 2: 89–103.

65. Goldthau and Witte, *Global Energy Governance*, p. 18.

66. Ibid., p. 19.

67. Source: conversation with Ethan Kapstein, University of Texas, April 20, 2011.

68. Goldthau and Witte, *Global Energy Governance*, p. 5.

69. Duffield, *Over a Barrel*, p. 86.

70. S. Krasner, ed., *International Regimes* (Cornell University Press, 1983).

71. Nye, *The Future of Power*, p. 57.

72. Ibid., p. 64.

73. Ibid., p. 65.

74. Ibid., p. 310.

75. Ibid., p. 311.

76. Kohl, "Consumer country energy cooperation," p. 199.

77. Nye, *The Future of Power*, p. 66.

78. Goldthau and Witte, *Global Energy Governance*, p. 2.

79. One of the best estimates of civilian mortality from the Iraq War is approximately 151,000. See Iraq Family Health Survey Study Group et al., "Violence-related mortality in Iraq from 2002 to 2006," *New England Journal of Medicine* 358 (2008), no. 5: 484–493.

80. Source: conversation with Ethan Kapstein, University of Texas, April 20, 2011.

81. Yergin, *The Quest*, p. 18.

Chapter 4

1. H. Morgenthau, *Politics Among Nations*, seventh edition (McGraw-Hill, 2005); J. Schlesinger, *Political Economy of National Security: A Study of the Economic Aspects of the Contemporary Power Struggle* (Praeger, 1960); N. Spykman, *America's Strategy in World Politics: The United States and the Balance of Power* (Harcourt Brace, 1942); D. Deese, "Oil, war, and grand strategy," *Orbis* 25 (1981), fall: 525–555.

2. R. Gilpin, *US Power and the Multinational Corporation: The Political Economy of Foreign Direct Investment* (Basic Books, 1975), pp. 103–104.

3. K. Waltz, "A strategy for the Rapid Deployment Force," *International Security* 5 (1981), no. 4: 49–73, p. 52.

4. G. Frankel, "US mulled seizing oil fields in '73: British memo cites notion of sending airborne to Mideast," *Washington Post*, January 1, 2004.

5. J. Nye, "Energy security strategy," in *The Strategic Imperative: New Policies for American Security*, ed. S. Huntington (Ballinger, 1982), p. 301.

6. Keohane, *After Hegemony*, p. 32.

7. J. Schlesinger, "Foreword," in *Energy and Security*, ed. Kalicki and Goldwyn, p. xiii.

8. A. Westing, "Global resources and international conflict: An overview," in *Global Resources and International Conflict*, ed. A. Westing (Oxford University Press, 1986), p. 5.

9. Ibid., p. 12.

10. D. Stokes and S. Raphael, *Global Energy Security and American Hegemony* (Johns Hopkins University Press, 2010), pp. 1–2.

11. Of course this explains why so many realist scholars were vociferous opponents of the Iraq War from the outset, holding that Iraq didn't truly present a substantive threat to US interests, let alone its hegemony, in 2002 or early 2003. In fact, many scholars (Mearsheimer, Walt, Hendrickson) wrote actively in condemnation of the Bush administration's bellicose policies.

12. For a promising new variant of Classical realist thought, see J. Kirshner, "The tragedy of offensive realism: Classical realism and the rise of China," *European Journal of International Relations* 18 (2012), no. 1: 53–75.

13. Nye, *The Future of Power*, Public Affairs, 2011.

14. My concept of shadow liberalism is based in part on concepts first elaborated by Kupchan and Ikenberry in "Liberal realism."

15. C. Tilly, *Coercion, Capital and European States*, revised edition (Wiley-Blackwell, 1992); H. Spruyt, *The Sovereign State and Its Competitors* (Princeton University Press, 1996).

16. See "Oil Shockwave: Oil Crisis Executive Simulation" (September 6, 2005) at www.securenergy.org.

17. Klare, *Rising Powers, Shrinking Planet*, p. 7.

18. G. Gause III, *The International Relations of the Persian Gulf* (Cambridge University Press, 2010), p. 9.

19. Ibid., p. 3.

20. I. Block, "Iran and Iraq remember war that cost more than a million lives," *The Guardian*, September 23, 2010.

21. C. Fettweis, "Is oil worth fighting for? Evidence from three cases," in *Beyond Resource Wars: Conflict, Cooperation, and the Environment*, ed. S. Dinar (MIT Press, 2011), p. 205.

22. S. Yetiv, *Explaining Foreign Policy: US Decision-Making and the Persian Gulf War*, second edition (Johns Hopkins University Press, 2011), p. 22.

23. W. Cleveland, *A History of the Modern Middle East*, second edition (Westview, 2004), p. 464.

24. Source: http://topics.nytimes.com/top/news/international/countriesandterritories/kuwait/index.html?scp=2&sq=oil%20saddam&st=cse.

25. Yetiv, *Explaining Foreign Policy*, p. 22. Also see Tariq Aziz, as quoted in "Saddam says he won the war," *APS Diplomat Recorder* 54, January 20, 2001.

26. US Department of State, Office of the Historian, *Milestones: 1989–1992* (http://history.state.gov/milestones/1989-1992/gulf-war).

27. Resolution 660 was adopted by the Security Council on August 2, 1990, in response to the Iraqi invasion of Kuwait. Resolution 661, adopted by the Security Council on August 6, authorized both an embargo of Iraq and military intervention to repel Iraqi forces from Kuwait.

28. Beaubouef, *The Strategic Petroleum Reserve*, pp. 151–152.

29. L. Freedman and E. Karsh, *The Gulf Conflict, 1990–91: Diplomacy and War in the New World Order* (Princeton University Press, 1993), p. 82.

30. Source: www.eia.gov/dnav/pet/hist/LeafHandler.ashx?n=pet&s=rbrte&f=w

31. L. Brown, *International Politics and the Middle East: Old Rules, Dangerous Game* (Princeton University Press, 1984), p. 258.

32. Steven Greenhouse, "Confrontation in the Gulf; oil crisis like 1973's? It's not necessarily so," *New York Times*, August 13, 1990.

33. Editorial, *New York Times*, August 13, 1990.

34. S. Nordlinger, "Higher cost for oil hurts 3rd world economies," *Baltimore Sun*, October 12, 1990; J. Fuerbringer, "Big swings of fortune from rise in oil price," *New York Times*, December 29, 1990.

35. Freedman and Karsh, *The Gulf Conflict, 1990–91*, p. 185.

36. Ibid., p. 74.

37. Ibid., p. 214.

38. President George H. W. Bush, quoted in ibid., pp. 214–215.

39. Yetiv, *Explaining Foreign Policy*, p. 35.

40. J. Writer, R. DeFraites, and J. Brundage, "Comparative mortality among US military personnel in the Persian Gulf region and worldwide during Operations Desert Shield and Desert Storm," *Journal of the American Medical Association* 275 (1996), no. 2: 118–121.

41. J. Heidenreich, "The Gulf War: How many Iraqis died? *Foreign Policy* 90 (1993), spring: 108–125, p. 109; J. Mueller "The perfect enemy: Assessing the Gulf War," *Security Studies* 5 (1995), no. 1: 77–117, p. 87.

42. "Anthony Zinni: 'Avoid a military showdown with Iraq,'" *Middle East Quarterly* 5 (1998), no. 3: 57–65.

43. BBC News (http://news.bbc.co.uk), "Flashback: The 1991 Iraqi revolt," August 21, 2007.

44. D. Von Drehle and R. Smith, "US strikes Iraq for plot to kill Bush," *Washington Post*, June 27, 1993.

45. See F. Fukuyama, "After neoconservatism," *New York Times*, February 19, 2006.

46. BBC News (http://news.bbc.co.uk), "Israelis 'misread' Iraqi threat," December 5, 2003.

47. J. Mearsheimer and S. Walt, *The Israel Lobby and US Foreign Policy* (Farrar, Strauss and Giroux, 2008).

48. Gause, *The International Relations of the Persian Gulf*, p. 245.

49. Bacevich, *Limits to Power*, p. 55.

50. Ibid., p. 62.

51. Created by President Bush via Executive Order on January 29, 2001.

52. R. Cheney et al., *Report of the National Energy Policy Development Group* (Government Printing Office, 2001).

53. US Department of Defense, *Foreign Suitors of Iraqi Oilfields*, obtained through Freedom of Information Act request by Judicial Watch.

54. O'Neill, as quoted on p. 96 of R. Suskind, *The Price of Loyalty: George W. Bush, the White House, and the Education of Paul O'Neill* (Simon and Schuster, 2004).

55. A. Juhasz, "Why the war in Iraq was fought for Big Oil," CNN Opinion (http://www.cnn.com), April 15, 2013.

56. T. Herrick, "US oil wants to work in Iraq," *Wall Street Journal*, January 17, 2003.

57. Quoted in Juhasz, "Why the war in Iraq was fought for Big Oil."

58. Yetiv, *Explaining Foreign Policy*, p. 236.

59. President George W. Bush, as quoted in N. Turse, "The military-petroleum complex," *Foreign Policy in Focus* (http://fpif.org), March 24, 2008.

60. A. Greenspan, *The Age of Turbulence: Adventures in a New World* (Penguin, 2007).

61. Juhasz, "Why the war in Iraq was fought for Big Oil."

62. Regarding these totals, see B. Jenkins, "The invasion of Iraq: A balance sheet," http://www.rand.org/blog, March 22, 2013.

63. L. Bilmes and J. Stiglitz, "The Iraq War will cost us $3 trillion, and much more," *Washington Post*, March 9, 2008.

64. H. Hafidh, "Iraq to award oil field to ExxonMobil, Shell," *Wall Street Journal*, November 4, 2009.

65. Reuters, "Schlumberger wins contract in Iraq's W. Qurna—sources," *Reuters*, November 29, 2010.

66. B. Haas, "PetroChina to buy 25% stake in Exxon's West Qurna Iraq oil field," bloomberg.com, November 28, 2013.

67. A. Rasheed, "Iraq blacklists Chevron for Kurdish oil deals," *Reuters*, July 24, 2012.

68. H. Hafidh and B. Lefebvre, "Chevron, Reliance sign Kurdistan oil deal," *Wall Street Journal*, July 19, 2012.

69. T. Macalister, "BP 'has gained a stranglehold over Iraq' after oilfield deal is rewritten," *The Guardian*, July 30, 2011.

70. A. Rasheed and P. Mackey, "Update 3—South Iraq oilfields calm; Schlumberger to return," Reuters, November 14, 2013.

71. G. Witte, "Halliburton cited for Iraq overhead," *Washington Post*, October 25, 2006.

72. A. Fifield, "Contractors reap $138 billion from war," *CNN* (http://edition.cnn.com), March 19, 2013.

73. Yetiv, *Explaining Foreign Policy*, p. 237.

74. Klare, *Blood and Oil*, p. 82.

75. S. Hargreaves, "Iraq oil production surpasses Iran," CNN Money (http://money.cnn.com), August 10, 2012.

76. Office of the Press Secretary, "Secretary of State Powell Discusses President's trip to Africa," July 10, 2003.

77. See www.nytimes.com/interactive/2014/06/12/world/middleeast/the-iraq-isis-conflict-in-maps-photos-and-video.html?_r=0.

78. H. Tomlinson, "Iran's special forces rush in to help floundering ally," *The Times*, June 12, 2014.

79. M. Landler and M. Gordon, "US to send up to 300 military advisors to Iraq," *New York Times*, June 19, 2014.

80. J. Mearsheimer, *Why Leaders Lie: The Truth about Lying in International Politics* (Oxford University Press, 2011).

81. Ibid., p. 5.

82. K. Woods and J. Lacey, *Iraqi Perspectives Project, Saddam and Terrorism: Emerging Insights from Captured Iraqi Documents*, volume 1 (redacted), Paper P-4287, US Department of Defense, Institute for Defense Analysis, Joint Advanced Warfighting Program, 2008.

83. Suskind, *The Price of Loyalty*.

84. Mearsheimer, *Why Leaders Lie*, p. 6.

85. Ibid., p. 57.

86. A. Bacevich, *The Limits of Power: The End of American Exceptionalism* (Metropolitan Books, 2008), p. 9.

87. C. Daniel, "Kissinger warns of energy conflict," *Financial Times*, June 2, 2005.

88. See Frankel, "US mulled seizing oil fields in '73"; L. Alvarez, "Britain says US planned to seize oil in '73 crisis," *New York Times*, January 2, 2004.

89. BTC stands for Baku-Tbilisi-Ceyhan, the names of cities that constitute the major nodes along the pipeline route.

90. Klare, *Blood and Oil* and *Resource Wars*.

91. See Stokes and Raphael, *Global Energy Security and American Hegemony*.

92. K. Holsti, *The State, War, and the State of War* (Cambridge University Press, 1996), p. 15.

93. Ibid., p. 16.

94. K. Waltz, *Theory of International Politics* (Waveland, 2010); Morgenthau, *Politics Among Nations*; J. Mearsheimer, *The Tragedy of Great Power Politics* (Norton, 2002).

95. Holsti, *The State, War, and the State of War*, p. 25.

96. M. Ross, *The Oil Curse* (Princeton University Press, 2012).

97. T. Karl, *The Paradox of Plenty: Oil Booms and Petro States* (University of California Press, 1997).

98. Victor Cha, "Globalization and the study of international security," *Journal of Peace Research* 37 (2000), no. 3: 391–403.

99. The text of UN Security Council Resolution 1973 is available at www.un.org/News/Press/docs/2011/sc10200.doc.htm.

100. Graetz, *The End of Energy*, p. 27.

101. G. Greenwald, "In a pure coincidence, Gaddafi impeded US oil interests before the war," *Salon*, June 11, 2011.

102. BBC News (http://www.bbc.co.uk), "Bernanke: Sustained oil price rise danger to US economy," March 1, 2011.

103. Also see C. Buckley, "Learning from Libya: Acting in Syria," *Journal of Strategic Security* 5 (2012), no. 2: 81–104.

104. M. Lynch, "The political science of Syria's war," *Foreign Policy* 19 (2013).

105. B. Philbin, "Where Syria fits in the world's oil supply system," *Wall Street Journal*, August 27, 2013.

106. Lynch, "The political science of Syria's war."

107. E. Osaghae, "The Ogoni Uprising: Oil, politics, minority agitation and the future of the Nigerian State," *African Affairs* 94 (1995): 325–344; K. Nwajiaku-Dahou, "The political economy of oil and 'rebellion' in Nigeria's Niger Delta," *Review of African Political Economy* 39 (2012), no. 132: 295–313.

108. UNEP, *Environmental Assessment of Ogoniland*, 2011; BBC News (http://www .bbc.co.uk), "Nigeria Ogoniland oil clean-up could take 30 years," August 4, 2011.

109. S. Cayford, "The Ogoni Uprising: Oil, human rights and a democratic alternative in Nigeria," *Africa Today* 43 (1996), no. 2: 183–196.

110. S. Yetiv, *The Petroleum Triangle: Oil, Globalization, and Terror* (Cornell University Press, 2011), p. 3.

111. Ibid., p. 6.

112. See R. Keohane and J. Nye, *Power and Interdependence: World Politics in Transition* (Little, Brown, 1977).

113. Yetiv, *The Petroleum Triangle*, p. 11.

114. Ibid.

115. Ibid., p. 64.

116. D. Van Natta, "Last American combat troops quit Saudi Arabia," *New York Times*, September 22, 2003.

117. M. Al-Rasheed, *Contesting the Saudi State* (Cambridge University Press, 2007), pp. 134–210.

118. J. Teitelbaum, "Terrorist challenges to Saudi Arabian internal security," *Middle East Review of International Affairs* 9 (2005): 1–11; Yetiv, The Petroleum Triangle, p. 73.

119. United States Joint Forces Command, *Joint Operating Environment 2010*, p. 27.

120. The notable exception is Yetiv's book *The Petroleum Triangle*, which explores the linkages between oil and terrorist networks in considerable depth.

121. M. Gordon and S. Myers, "Iran and Hezbollah support for Syria complicates peace talk strategy," *New York Times*, May 21, 2013; B. Gwertzman, "The Hezbollah connection in Syria and Iran," Council on Foreign Relations (www.cfr.org), February 15, 2013.

122. Yetiv, *The Petroleum Triangle*.

125. President Barack Obama, quoted in M. Klare, "Tithing at the crude altar," *The National Interest* 102 (2009), July-August: 20–29.

124. Yetiv, *The Petroleum Triangle*, p. 73.

125. Klare, *Rising Powers, Shrinking Planet*; Moyo, *Winner Take All* (Basic Books, 2012).

126. M. Levi, *The Power Surge* (Oxford University Press, 2013).

127. N. El-Hefnawy, "The impending oil shock," *Survival* 50 (2008), no. 2: 37–66.

128. See R. Jervis, *Perception and Misperception in International Politics* (Princeton University Press, 1976).

129. National Energy Policy Development Group, *Environmentally Sound Energy for America's Future*, May 16, 2001.

130. R. Stern, "United States Cost of military force projection in the Persian Gulf, 1976–2007," *Energy Policy* 38 (2010), no. 6: 2816–2825.

131. Stokes and Raphael, *Global Energy Security and American Hegemony*.

132. Michael Klare asserts that the armoring of oil extraction by the US and China will promote direct conflict between those two powers. See Klare, "There will be blood," in *Energy Security Challenges for the 21st Century*, ed. G. Luft and A. Korin (Praeger, 2009), pp. 59–60.

Chapter 5

1. In a sense, this formulation emulates James Baker III's conceptualization of security interests during the George H. W. Bush administration. See J. Baker III, *Politics of Diplomacy: Revolution, War, and Peace, 1989–1992* (Putnam, 1995).

2. http://www.eia.gov/dnav/pet/hist/LeafHandler.ashx?n=pet&s=mttimusca1&f=a

3. http://www.eia.doe.gov/cabs/Canada/Oil.html

4. http://www.eia.gov/countries/cab.cfm?fips=CA

5. Randall, *United States Foreign Oil Policy Since World War I*, p. 307.

6. Ibid., p. 308.

7. Minister of Supply and Services, *The National Energy Program*, 1980, p.2.

8. Randall, *United States Foreign Oil Policy Since World War I*, p. 308.

9. Ibid., pp. 308–309.

10. See pp. 26–37 of Laxer and Dillon, *Over a Barrel*.

11. http://www.gpo.gov/fdsys/pkg/PLAW-109publ58/pdf/PLAW-109publ58.pdf

12. A. Hester and J. Welch, "Superhero? Oil could make Stephen Harper a Superhero," *Globe and Mail*, February 2, 2008.

13. BBC News (http://news.bbc.co.uk), "China's PetroChina invests in Canada oil sands," December 30, 2009.

14. C. Cattaneo, "Petrochina bids to help build $5.5 billion Northern Gateway pipeline," http://business.financialpost.com, March 29, 2012.

15. S. McCarthy, "China's move into oil sands irks the US," *Globe and Mail*, September 1, 2009.

16. S. McCarthy et al., "Canadian government approves Enbridge's controversial Northern Gateway pipeline," *Globe and Mail*, June 17, 2014.

17. E. Rocha, "CNOOC completes contentious $15.1 billion acquisition of Nexen," *Financial Post*, February 23, 2013.

18. J. Krauss and E. Malkin, "Mexico oil politics keeps riches just out of reach," *New York Times*, March 8, 2010.

19. http://www.eia.doe.gov/emeu/cabs/Mexico/pdf.pdf

20. R. Campbell, "Mexico raises view of peak oil from Ku Maloob Zap," Reuters, January 24, 2011.

21. http://www.eia.doe.gov/emeu/cabs/Mexico/pdf.pdf

22. M. Webber and S. Kirshenbaum, "Energy and immigration," *Boston Globe*, November 26, 2010.

23. A. Williams and C. Rodriguez, "Pemex plans drilling, logistic companies as reform looms," bloomberg.com, October 22, 2013.

24. A. Barrionuevo, "Brazil discovers an oil field can be a political tool," *New York Times*, November 19, 2007.

25. "Brazil official cites giant oil-field discovery" *New York Times*, April 14, 2008.

26. *Joint Operating Environment 2010*, p. 48.

27. J. Forero, "Brazil's oil euphoria hits reality hard," *Washington Post*, January 6, 2014.

28. http://www.eia.gov/countries/cab.cfm?fips=ve

29. http://www.eia.doe.gov/cabs/Venezuela/Oil.html

30. Ibid.

31. Shaffer, *Energy Politics*, p. 32.

32. Many of these weapons were purchased from Russian sources. See BBC News (http://news.bbc.co.uk), "Chávez in $2bn Russian arms deal," September 14, 2009.

33. C. Alvarez and S. Hanson, "Venezuela's oil-based economy," Council on Foreign Relations (www.cfr.org), February 9, 2009.

34. Fact Sheet: Arbitration between Exxon Mobil and Venezuela, February 18, 2008 (http://venezuelanalysis.com/analysis/3174).

35. D. Harman, "Chávez seeks influence with oil diplomacy," *Christian Science Monitor*, August 25, 2005.

36. "Caribbean should trade Venezuelan Oil for homegrown sun," bloomberg.com, May 26, 2013.

37. Alvarez and Hanson, "Venezuela's oil-based economy."

38. "The crunch in Caracas," *The Economist*, October 19, 2013.

39. M. Goldman, *Petro-State* (Oxford University Press, 2007), p. 80.

40. US Energy Information Administration, "Russia" (http://www.eia.gov/countries/cab.cfm?fips=RS).

41. Goldman, *Petro-State*, p. 91.

42. Asahi Shimbun (http://ajw.asahi.com), "Japanese firms plan 1400 km gas pipeline from Russia's Sakhalin."

43. Goldman, *Petro-State*.

44. Yetiv, *Explaining Foreign Policy* p. 110.

45. M. Olcott, *The Energy Dimension in Russian Global Strategy* (Baker Institute for Public Policy, 2004).

46. A. Stulberg, *Well-Oiled Diplomacy: Strategic Manipulation and Russia's Energy Statecraft in Eurasia* (SUNY Press, 2007), p. 1.

47. J. Sides, "What Russia's invasion of Georgia means for Crimea," *Washington Post*, March 5, 2014.

48. W. Broad, "In taking Crimea, Putin gains a sea of fuel reserves," *New York Times*, May 17, 2014.

49. Reuters, "China faces social, financial risks in urbanization push," March 7, 2013.

50. Bloomberg News, "China vehicle registration hits 240 million as smog engulfs cities," January 31, 2013.

51. R. Ebel, *China's Energy Future: The Middle Kingdom Seeks Its Place in the Sun* (Center for Strategic and International Studies, 2005), p. 8.

52. Ibid., p. 11.

53. "China oil demand to grow 5% in 2013: Deutsche Bank," *Financial Post*, January 23, 2013.

54. Stokes and Raphael, *Global Energy Security and American Hegemony*, p. 49.

55. White House, *National Security Strategy of the United States of America*, March 2006, p. 41.

56. D. Victor and L. Yueh, "The new energy order," *Foreign Affairs* 89 (2010), no. 1: 61–73.

57. S. Shirk, *China: Fragile Superpower* (Oxford University Press, 2008), p. 134.

58. Ibid., p. 137.

59. Ibid., p. 137.

60. Ebel, *China's Energy Future*, p. 3.

61. Y. Wang and J. Duce, "PetroChina parent to 'intensify' overseas acquisitions," Bloomberg News, January 19, 2011.

62. D. Press and C. Gholz, "Cold War Two? The (il)logic of a struggle with China for resources in the developing world" (paper presented at *International Studies Association conference*, New Orleans, 2009), p. 7.

63. Ibid., p. 9.

64. See S. Ramachandran, "China's pearl in Pakistan waters," *Asia Times Online*, March 4, 2005.

65. Ebel, *China's Energy Future*, p. 3.

66. The study, titled "Energy Futures in Asia," was conducted by Booz Allen Hamilton for the US Department of Defense in 2004. See Ebel, *China's Energy Future*, p. 55.

67. See R. Jervis, *Perception and Misperception in International Politics* (Princeton University Press, 1976).

68. BBC News (www.bbc.co.uk), "Russia and China sign a series of energy agreements," September 27, 2010.

69. Reuters, "Russia grabs China oil and gas export deals," October 22, 2013.

70. A. Guo and R. Katakey, "Disputed islands with 45 years of oil split China, Japan," Bloomberg News, October 11, 2012.

71. E. Economy and M. Levi, "Rein in China in its dispute with Vietnam over energy resources," *Washington Post*, May 15, 2014.

72. "Vietnam and the South China Sea: Rigged," *The Economist*, June 14, 2014.

73. Vernon, *Two Hungry Giants*, p. 89.

74. Vlado Vivoda, Japan's Energy Security Predicament Post-Fukushima. Working paper, Griffith Asia Institute.

75. Shirk, *China: Fragile Superpower*, p. 150.

76. Y. Hayashi, "Japan leader charts path for military's rise," *Wall Street Journal*, April 24, 2013.

77. S. Harrison, "Quiet struggle in the East China Sea," *Current History* 101 (2002), no. 656: 271–277.

78. B. Catley and M. Keilat, *Spratlys: The Dispute in the South China Sea* (Ashgate, 1997).

79. L. Jinming and L. Dexia, "The dotted line on the Chinese map of the South China Sea," *Ocean Development and International Law* 34 (2003), no. 3–4: 287–295.

80. M. Salameh, "China, oil and the risk of regional conflict," *Survival* 37 (1995), no. 4: 133–146.

81. J. Mearsheimer, "Imperial by design," in *Rising Threats, Enduring Challenge: Readings in US Foreign Policy*, ed. A. Price-Smith (Oxford University Press, 2015); A. Friedberg, *A Contest for Supremacy: China, America and the Struggle for Mastery in Asia* (Norton, 2012).

82. A. Johnson, "How new and assertive is China's new assertiveness?" *International Security* 37 (2013), no. 4: 7–48.

83. Shirk, *China: Fragile Superpower*.

84. U. Suganama, *Sovereign Rights and Territorial Space in Sino-Japanese Relations* (University of Hawaii Press, 2000).

85. W. LaFeber, *Inevitable Revolutions: The United States in Central America* (Norton, 1993).

86. C. Duelfer and S. Dyson, "Chronic misperception and international conflict: The US-Iraq experience," *International Security* 36 (2011), no. 1: 73–100.

87. Arguably such dynamics will cause problems for other autocratic petro-states as well, notably for Russia and Venezuela.

88. F. G. Gause, *International Relations of the Persian Gulf* (Cambridge University Press, 2010), p. 3. Also see B. Buzan, *People, States and Fear* (Lynne Rienner, 1991).

89. Another term for the Iran-Iraq War.

90. See, for example, J. Herbst, "Let them fail," in *When States Fail: Causes and Consequences*, ed. R. Rotberg (Princeton University Press, 2003).

91. Gause, *International Relations of the Persian Gulf*, pp. 8–9.

92. http://www.eia.doe.gov/emeu/cabs/Iran/Oil.html

93. Mohsen Milani, "Tehran's take," *Foreign Affairs* 88 (2009), no. 4: 46–54.

94. Ibid.

95. Associated Press, "Report: Iran oil revenues drop 45 percent in 9 months because of sanctions on nuclear program," *Washington Post*, January 7, 2013.

96. Yergin, *The Quest*, p. 299.

97. N. Taleb and M. Blythe, "The Black Swan of Cairo: How suppressing volatility makes the world less predictable and more dangerous," *Foreign Affairs* 90 (2011), no. 3: 33–39.

98. http://www.eia.gov/countries/cab.cfm?fips=AO

99. Associated Press, "Nigerian forces raid camps of militants in delta region," *New York Times*, December 1, 2010.

Conclusion

1. This is dependent on the ability of NOCs to partner with IOCs in mutually beneficial fashion.

2. A. Bacevich, "Twilight of the republic," in *Rising Threats, Enduring Challenges*, ed. A. Price-Smith (Oxford University Press, 2015).

3. On the role of perception and misperception in contributing to conflict, see R. Jervis, *Perception and Misperception in International Politics* (Princeton University Press, 1976).

4. See Shirk, *China: Fragile Superpower*.

5. Jervis, *Perception and Misperception in International Politics*.

6. This perception of looming energy scarcity is delineated in *National Energy Policy: Report of the National Energy Policy Development Group* (2001).

7. Levi, *The Power Surge*, p. 3.

8. R. Jervis, "Cooperation under the security dilemma," *World Politics* 30 (1978), no. 2: 167–214.

9. B. Vlasic, "US sets higher fuel efficiency standards," *New York Times*, August 28, 2012.

10. R. Haass, *Foreign Policy Begins at Home* (Basic Books, 2013).

Index